The Zondervan Minister's Tax & Financial Guide

For 2008 Tax Returns

YOUR CHURCH MAGAZINE EDITOR'S CHOICE
RECOGNIZING EXCELLENCE IN HELPING CHURCHES WITH THE BUSINESS OF MINISTRY

2009
EDITION

Dan Busby, CPA

ZONDERVAN®

ZONDERVAN.com/
AUTHORTRACKER
follow your favorite authors

We want to hear from you. Please send your comments about this book to us in care of zreview@zondervan.com. Thank you.

ZONDERVAN®

Zondervan 2009 Minister's Tax & Financial Guide: For 2008 Tax Returns

Reuests for information should be addressed to:

Zondervan, *Grand Rapids, Michigan 49530*

ISBN 978-0-310-26219-0

Publisher's note: This guide is published in recognition of the need for clarification of the income tax laws for ministers. Every effort has been made to publish a timely, accurate, and authoritative guide. The publisher, author, and reviewers do not assume any legal responsibility for the accuracy of the text or any other contents.

Taxpayers are cautioned that this book is sold with the understanding that the publisher is not engaged in rendering legal, accounting, or other professional service. You should seek the professional advice of a tax accountant, lawyer, or preparer for specific tax questions.

References to IRS forms and tax rates are derived from preliminary proofs of the 2008 forms or 2007 forms and some adaptation for changes may be necessary. These materials should be used solely as a guide in filling out your 2008 tax return. To obtain the final forms, schedules, and tables for filing your return, contact the IRS or a public library.

Printed in the United States of America

09 10 11 12 13 14 15 16 17 18 19 • 26 25 24 23 22 21 20 19 18 17 16 15 14 13 12 11 10 9 8 7 6 5 4 3 2 1

Contents . . .

INTRODUCTION

The 20th edition has been thoroughly updated to even more clearly help you understand the tax laws impacting ministers. But it is much more!

The last year brought a fresh round of tax changes that are integrated throughout the text. The voluminous laws and regulations that apply to ministers are mind-boggling. Yet this book is extremely readable and understandable—defying the complexity of the topics covered.

This book includes the basic rules for ministerial income taxes, determining social security tax liability, accountable expense reimbursement plans, housing allowance issues, and much more. It also highlights issues raised in my workshops where I have been the presenter in 38 states, speaking to thousands of ministers, plus issues from hundreds of emails and telephone calls I receive from ministers and church leaders each year! It is a veritable one-stop resource for answers to the tax and finance issues most frequently asked by ministers and churches.

When I was a college student, my father was serving in a denominational leadership position. (Dad preached for 27 years—that is, 27 years after his 65th birthday. He preached until he went to be with the Lord at age 93—preaching a total of 72 years.) After taking my first income tax class in college, I realized Dad's tax return was not being correctly prepared even though he was paying someone to prepare it. This began my mission to help ministers with tax issues—providing easy-to-understand information on complex topics.

This is still my mission today—helping ministers minimize taxes while, at the same time, filing tax returns that will enable them to sleep at night.

Dan Busby

Recent Developments

There has been a continuing string of developments impacting ministers. In this 2009 edition of this guide, the key changes are integrated throughout the text, in addition to being summarized in this section. You may monitor on-going developments at www.ECFA.org.

Senator Grassley focuses on televangelists. Sen. Charles Grassley, R-Iowa, the ranking member of the Senate Finance Committee, is investigating six major church-based ministries (sometimes known as the "Grassley Six"). None of the ministries are required to file the financial disclosure Form 990 with the IRS because they are designated as churches.

On November 6, 2007, Grassley sent letters about executive compensation and amenities and other expenses to Kenneth and Gloria Copeland of Kenneth Copeland Ministries of Newark, Texas; Creflo and Taffi Dollar of World Changers Church International and Creflo Dollar Ministries of College Park, Georgia; Benny Hinn of World Healing Center Church Inc. and Benny Hinn Ministries of Grapevine, Texas; Bishop Eddie Long of New Birth Missionary Baptist Church and Bishop Eddie Long Ministries of Lithonia, Georgia; Joyce and David Meyer of Joyce Meyer Ministries of Fenton, Missouri; and Randy and Paula White of the multiracial Without Walls International Chuch and Paula White Ministries of Tampa, Florida.

At the publication date of this book, two ministries have provided all the requested information, two have partially complied, and two have not complied. Two matters remain unclear: Will the Senate Finance Committee subpoena church representatives which are not fully compliant? Will we see proposed legislation resulting from this televangelist inquiry?

Retirement plan issues. Important retirement plan related regulations have been issued by the IRS in two areas:

- **403(b)**—The IRS has published final 403(b) regulations providing updated guidance on several administrative requirements. These final regulations complete the process that began back in December 2004 with the proposed 403(b) regulations. Most 403(b) plans will need to be revised to comply with these regulations.
- **409A**—Many churches have established informal retirement arrangements for a pastor, often a founder who served the congregation for many years. These arrangements are often made when the payments to a qualified retirement plan were not substantial during the minister's service to the congregation.

Examples of informal retirement plans include:

- A church agrees to make payments for 15 years (or another specific number of years) after the pastor leaves the church.
- A church agrees to make monthly payments to a retiring minister for the minister's life (or to a surviving spouse).

The 409A regulations are effective on January 1, 2009. Plans established before October 3, 2004, are not subject to Section 409A if the plans are not materially modified after October 3, 2004.

Cell phones. Legislation has been introduced to modernize the tax treatment of business-use cell phones. The legislation would strike cell phones and other mobile communication devices from the category of "listed property" in the tax code, meaning employers would no longer be required to maintain detailed call logs to claim a deduction.

Recognizing that employees assigned mobile phones for business use could use the same devices for personal calls, the IRS designated cell phones as "listed property," meaning that employers had to be able to track and substantiate their employees' phone usage. The law currently excludes personal calls as a deductible expense.

Business, moving, and medical mileage rates increased. The IRS increased the mileage rate to 58.5 cents a mile for all business miles driven from July 1, 2008, through December 31, 2008. This is an increase of eight cents from the 50.5 cent rate in effect for the first six months of 2008. While gasoline is a significant factor in the mileage figure, other items enter into the calculation of mileage rates, such as depreciation and insurance and other fixed and variable costs.

The new six-month rate for computing deductible medical or moving expenses also increased by eight cents to 27 cents a mile, up from 19 cents for the first six months of 2008.

Charitable mileage rate. Momentum is building on Capitol Hill for legislation that would increase the charitable mileage rate.

Under federal law, volunteers who drive their cars for charitable purposes may deduct 14 cents a mile for their car costs or be reimbursed by a charity at that rate without the payment being subject to federal income tax.

Under current law, the IRS has the power to adjust the business, medical, and moving mileage rates but only Congress can adjust the charitable rate.

First-time home buyer's credit. This new credit of up to $7,500 is for those taxpayers buying a main home after April 8, 2008 and before July 1, 2009. It is refundable to the extent it exceeds the buyer's regular tax liability. Home buyers in 2009 can elect to take the credit on their 2008 income tax returns using Form 5405. The credit is recaptured ratably over 15 years, without any interest, starting two years after the year the credit is claimed.

Tax-extenders passes Congress. Congress extended a number of tax provisions that had previously expired (the 2008 tax forms do not provide for the first three deductions), in addition to the IRA rollover:

- Deduction of state and local general sales taxes. The option to deduct state and local general sales taxes is extended through 2009.
- Qualified tuition deduction. The above-the-line tax deduction for qualified higher education expenses is extended through 2009.
- Teacher expense deduction. The provision allowing teachers an above-the-line deduction for up to $250 for educational expenses is extended through 2009.
- Additional standard deduction for real property taxes. The standard deduction for real property taxes for nonitemizers is extended through 2009. Use line 39c on Form 1040.

Key Federal Tax Limits, Rates, and Other Data

	2007	2008	2009
Standard deductions, exemptions, and exclusions			
Standard deductions	Married-Joint Return $10,700 Head of Household 7,850 Single 5,350 Married-Separate Returns 5,350	Married-Joint Return $10,900 Head of Household 8,000 Single 5,450 Married-Separate Returns 5,450	Married-Joint Return $11,400 Head of Household 8,350 Single 5,700 Married-Separate Returns 5,700
Personal & dependent exemption amount	$3,400	$3,500	$3,650
Foreign earned income exclusion	$85,700	$87,600	
Social security:			
SECA (OASDI & Medicare) rate	15.3%	15.3%	15.3%
FICA (OASDI & Medicare) rate	7.65%	7.65%	7.65%
OASDI maximum compensation base	$97,500	$102,000	$106,800
Social security cost-of-living benefit increase	3.3%	2.3%	5.8%
Social security Full Retirement Age (FRA)	65 years and 10 months	66 years	66 years
Medicare Part B premiums – Basic	$93.50	$96.40	$96.40(1)
Earnings ceiling for social security (applies to employment before FRA; special formula in FRA year)	Below FRA: $12,960 Over FRA: None	Below FRA: $13,560 Over FRA: None	Below FRA: $14,160 Over FRA: None
Earnings limit in year FRA attained	$34,440	$36,120	$37,680
Benefits and contributions:			
Maximum annual contribution to defined contribution plan	$45,000	$46,000	$49,000
Maximum salary deduction for 401(k)/403(b)	$15,500	$15,500	$16,500
401(k) & 403(b) over 50 "catch up" limit	$5,000	$5,000	$5,500
Maximum income exclusion for nonqualified plans in 501(c)(3) organizations (IRC 457)	$15,500	$15,500	$16,500
IRA contribution limit – age 49 and below – age 50 and above	$4,000 $1,000	$5,000 $1,000	$5,000 $1,000
Highly compensated employee limit	$100,000	$105,000	$110,000

(1) Premium for single taxpayers making $85,000 or less and couples making $170,000 or less.

	2007	2008	2009
Health savings accounts			
Contribution limit			
Individual	$2,850	$2,900	$3,000
Family	$5,650	$5,800	$5,950
Maximum annual out-of-pocket expense:			
Individual	$5,500	$5,600	$5,800
Family	$11,000	$11,200	$11,600
Minimum deductible:			
Individual	$1,100	$1,100	$1,150
Family	$2,200	$2,200	$2,300
Increase in annual contribution limit - 55 and older	$800	$900	$1,000
Earned income credit			
Taxable and nontaxable earned income of less than (to qualify for the earned income credit):			
No qualifying child	$14,590	$15,880	$16,560
One qualifying child	$35,241	$36,995	$38,583
Two or more qualifying children	$39,783	$41,646	$43,415
Long-term care insurance:			
Premiums deductible as medical expense based on the insured's age before close of tax year:			
40 or less	$290	$310	$320
41 to 50	$550	$580	$600
51 to 60	$1,110	$1,150	$1,190
61 to 70	$2,950	$3,080	$3,180
More than 70	$3,680	$3,850	$3,980
Per diem and mileage rates and other transportation:			
Standard per diem: Lowest rates in continental USA	Lodging $60 Meals & Incidentals $39	Lodging $70 Meals & Incidentals $39	Lodging $70 Meals & Incidentals $39
IRS high/low substitute per diem system (Effective October 1 each year)	High $246 Low $148	High $237 Low $152	High $256 Low $158
Business auto mileage rate	48.5 cents per mile	50.5 cents per mile (Jan 1-Jun 30) 58.5 cents per mile (Jul 1-Dec 31)	
Moving & medical auto mileage rate	20 cents per mile	19 cents per mile (Jan 1-Jun 30) 27 cents per mile (Jan 1-Jun 30)	
Charitable auto mileage rate	14 cents per mile	14 cents per mile	
Motorcycle mileage rate [1]	30.5 cents per mile		
Airplane mileage rate [1]	$1.07 per mile	$1.26 per mile	
Maximum value of reimbursement of business expenses (other than lodging) without receipt	$75	$75	$75
Luxury automobile value (limit on use of cents-per-mile valuation of company automobile)	$15,100	$15,000	
Monthly limit on free parking	$215	$220	$230
Transit passes/token – monthly tax-free limit	$110	$115	$120
Other:			
Sec. 179 expensing limit	$125,000	$128,000	$133,000
Gift tax annual exclusion	$12,000	$12,000	$13,000
Unified estate and gift tax exception	$2,000,000	$2,000,000	$2,000,000

(1) Privately owned vehicle mileage rates set by the U.S. General Services Administration.
Note: In some instances, the rate for a particular year may apply to a tax return filed in a subsequent year.

Line by Line

Form 1040

There are two short forms, the 48-line 1040A and the super-short, 13-line 1040EZ. Generally, ministers should use the 77-line Form 1040 instead. It accommodates every minister, and there's no penalty for leaving some of the lines blank. Besides, going down the 1040 line by line may jog your memory about money you received or spent in 2008. (Line numbers noted refer to the Form 1040 and related schedules.)

- **Filing status (lines 1 to 5). Line 2:** If your spouse died in 2008, you can still file jointly and take advantage of tax rates that would be lower than if you file as a single person or as a head of household.

  Line 3: If you're married and live in a separate-property state, compute your tax two ways—jointly and separately. Then, file the return resulting in the lower tax.

  Line 4: If you're single, you may qualify as head of household if you provided a home for someone else—like your parent. Filing as head of household rather than as a single person can save you a bundle on taxes.

  Line 5: If your spouse died in 2006 or 2007 and you have a dependent child, you can also benefit from joint-return rates as a qualifying widow(er).

- **Exemptions (lines 6a to 6d).** Remember to include a social security number for any dependent who was at least one year old on December 31, 2008. If your child does not have one, obtain Form SS-5, Application for a Social Security Number, at http://www.ssa.gov/online/ssa-5.html. If you are unable to secure the social security number before the filing deadline, file for an extension of time to file.

- **Income (lines 7 to 22). Line 7:** If your employer considered you an employee for income tax purposes, you should receive

Filing Tip

Form 1040, Line 7. All compensation from Forms W-2 is reported on line 7. Be sure your church has not included a formally and prospectively designated housing allowance in Box 1 of Form W-2. If so, deduct the housing allowance included in Box 1 and attach a schedule to explain the adjustment.

Form W-2 from the employer. The total amount of your taxable wages is shown in Box 1 of Form W-2; attach Copy B of your W-2 to your Form 1040. Include the data from other W-2s you or your spouse received on this line. If the employer erroneously included your housing allowance in Box 1, Form W-2, deduct the designated housing allowance, show the net amount on line 7, and attach an explanatory schedule.

> **Remember**
>
> Most ministers do not have to file a separate schedule if interest or dividend income is $1,500 or less; only the totals need to be reported on Form 1040.

Line 8a: Include as taxable-interest income the total amount of what you earned on savings accounts, certificates of deposit, credit union accounts, corporate bonds and corporate bond mutual funds, U.S. treasuries and U.S. government mutual funds, and interest paid to you for a belated federal or state tax refund (whether or not you have received a Form 1099-INT). If you haven't yet received any of the statements due you, call the issuer to get them. If you received more than $1,500 of taxable interest income in 2008, you must also complete Schedule B.

Line 8b: Here's where you note any tax-exempt interest from municipal bonds or municipal bond funds. Don't worry—that income is not taxable. But social security recipients must count all their tax-exempt interest when computing how much of their social security benefits will be taxable.

Line 9a: Enter as dividend income only ordinary dividends, not capital-gains dividends paid by mutual funds, which are reported on Schedule D. Your Form 1099-DIV statements show the amount and type of ordinary dividends you received during 2008. If you received more than $1,500 in dividend income in 2008, you must also complete Schedule B. Remember: Earnings from a money-market mutual fund are considered dividend income, not interest income.

Line 10: If you received a refund of a state or local tax in 2008 that you deducted on Schedule A in a prior year, include the refund here.

> **Filing Tip**
>
> **Form 1040, Line 12.** The only ministerial income that should be reported on line 12 is: fees from weddings, funerals, speaking engagements, and similar income. Unreimbursed expenses related to this income should be deducted on Schedule C or Schedule C-EZ.

Line 12: Even when you file as an employee for income tax purposes, you will probably have some honoraria or fee income from speaking engagements, weddings, funerals, and so on. This income, less related expenses (see page 16), should be reported on Schedule C or C-EZ and entered on this line.

Line 13: Enter capital-gains dividends here if you had no other capital gains or losses in 2008.

Line 15a: Report as IRA distributions even amounts you rolled over tax-free in 2008 from one IRA into another. On line 15b, you will report as taxable the amount of any IRA distributions that you did not roll over minus any return of nondeductible contributions.

Line 16a: It's likely that only a portion of the total pensions and annuities you received is taxable. Your Form 1099-R will show the taxable amount, which you enter on line 16b. If you received pensions and annuities from a denominationally sponsored plan, you may be eligible to exclude a portion or all of these payments as a housing allowance.

Line 20a: No more than 85% of your social security benefits can be taxed for 2008 and none at all if your provisional income is below $32,000 on a joint return, $25,000 for singles. If your income doesn't exceed the threshold, leave this line blank. If it does, use the worksheet on Form 1099-SSA to compute taxes on your benefits.

Line 21: If your cash housing allowance designated and paid by the employer exceeds the lowest of (1) reasonable compensation, (2) the amount used to provide a home from current ministerial income, (3) the amount properly designated by the employer, or (4) the fair rental value of the home including utilities and furnishings, enter the difference on line 21.

Filing Tip

Form 1040, Line 21. If the housing allowance designated by the employer exceeds the housing allowance exclusion to which you are entitled, you must include the difference on line 21 with a description "Excess housing allowance." Your exclusion should be limited by the lower of the fair rental value of a minister-provided home or your actual housing expenses.

- **Adjustments to income (lines 23 to 37).**

Line 25: Health savings account deduction. Contributions made by a taxpayer to a health savings account (HSA) up to $2,900 for an individual plan and $5,800 for a family plan are deductible on this line. Individuals who have reached age 55 by the end of the tax year are allowed to increase their annual contribution for years after 2008.

Line 26: If your employer paid directly or reimbursed you for your qualified moving costs incurred in 2008, these amounts would not be included as compensation on your Form W-2. Therefore, you would have no moving expenses to deduct on line 26. However, if part or all of your moving costs were not paid directly or reimbursed, deduct these expenses here.

Line 27: One-half of your social security tax that is deductible for income tax purposes is reflected on this line.

Line 33: Interest paid on a qualifying student loan may be deducted on this line.

Line 36: If you are employed as a chaplain or any other minister-employee of a nonreligious organization, use this line for your deduction of 403(b) contributions that you sent directly to the plan. On the dotted line next to line 36, enter the amount of your deduction and identify it as indicated.

- **Tax computation (lines 38 to 56). Line 39c:** This is a new line on Form 1040 for the property tax write-off for filers who do not itemize. This tax break is on top of the standard deduction and is capped at $1,000 for married couples and $500 for single filers. Nonitemizers will have to check a box on this line if they are taking the property break. There is a new worksheet in the instructions to help with the computation.

  Line 40: Claim the standard deduction only if the amount exceeds what you could write off in itemizing expenses on Schedule A. For 2008, the standard deduction is $10,900 joint, $8,000 head of household, and $5,450 single (that's up from $10,700, $7,850, and $5,350 last year). The amounts are higher if you or your spouse is 65 or older or legally blind.

  Line 52: Taxpayers with adjusted gross income of $50,000 or less may claim a credit on this line equal to a certain percentage of the employee contributions made to a retirement account or IRA.

> **Filing Tip**
>
> **Form 1040, Line 53.** If you made contributions to a 403(b) or 401(k) plan, and your adjusted gross income was $50,000 or less, you may be eligible for this credit. The credit is also available for contributions to either a traditional or a Roth IRA. The excluded portion of minister's housing does not reduce this credit.

- **Other taxes (lines 57 to 62). Line 58:** If you are a qualified minister (see pages 22-30) and have not opted out of social security, you are self-employed for social security tax purposes. Your social security is not withheld by your church but is calculated on Schedule SE if you had net earnings of $400 or more and paid with Form 1040. The tax is 15.3% of the first $102,000 of 2008 self-employment income and 2.95% of income above $102,000. If your total wages and self-employment earnings were less than $102,000, you can probably save time and headaches by filing the Short Schedule SE on the front of the SE form.

  Line 59: You will owe the tax on qualified plans plus the 10% penalty on the amount you withdrew from your IRA or another retirement plan if you were under 59½, unless you meet certain exceptions.

- **Payments (lines 63 to 72). Line 63:** Did you have a voluntary withholding arrangement whereby your employing church withheld federal income tax from your compensation? Then show the amount of federal income tax the church withheld (from your W-2) along with other federal income tax withholding from other employment of you or your spouse here. Also include tax withheld on your W-2G and other Forms 1099. The amount withheld should be shown in Box 2 of Form W-2G, in Box 6 of Form 1099-SSA, and Box 4 of other Forms 1099.

  Line 64: Don't get confused: Even though you made your fourth-quarter 2007 estimated tax payment in January 2008, it's counted on your 2007 return.

  Line 65a: Enter your earned income tax credit here or let the IRS calculate it for you. If you have a qualifying child, you must complete Schedule EIC.

- **Refund or amount you owe (lines 73 to 77). Line 77:** The IRS assumes you must pay the estimated tax penalty if you owe $1,000 or more beyond what you've paid through withholding or estimated tax and the amount due is more than 10% of your 2007 tax bill. You may qualify for one of several exceptions, however. Use Form 2210 to prove your case.

Schedule A (Itemized Deductions)

If you live in church-provided housing, you often cannot itemize. But run down Schedule A just to see whether you might have more write-offs than the standard deduction will permit.

- **Medical and dental expenses (lines 1 to 4)**. Don't overlook the cost of getting to and from the doctor or druggist. Write off 19 cents per mile for the first half and 27 cent per mile for the second half of 2008, plus the cost of parking. If you didn't drive, deduct your bus, train, or taxi fares. The cost of trips to see out-of-town specialists and as much as $50 a day for the cost of lodging when you're out of town to get medical care count toward the 7.5%. Include all your health insurance premiums, such as the $96.40 a month Medicare Part B premiums for 2008.

- **Taxes you paid (lines 5 to 9).** Even though your real estate taxes are a housing expense excludable under the housing allowance, you may still deduct them (even for multiple properties if not deducted elsewhere on the return) on line 6 as an itemized deduction—one of the few "double deductions" allowed in the tax law.

- **Interest you paid (lines 10 to 15). Line 10:** If you bought a house during 2008, review your escrow or settlement papers for any mortgage interest you paid that was not shown on your lender's year-end statement. If you paid interest on a second mortgage or line of credit secured by your home, include the interest expense here.

> **Filing Tip**
>
> **Schedule A, Lines 6, 10-12.** These lines relate to the most significant tax break available to ministers who own their own homes. Even though real estate taxes, mortgage interest, and points are excludable under the housing allowance, subject to certain limits, the same amounts are deductible as itemized deductions.

As with real estate taxes, it is possible to deduct mortgage interest as an itemized deduction even if the interest is included in housing expenses subject to a housing allowance. Interest paid on a secured mortgage is deductible on Schedule A regardless of how the proceeds of the loan are used. However, the only mortgage interest properly includible as housing expense under a housing allowance is when the loan proceeds were used to provide housing. For example, interest on a second mortgage used to finance your child's college education is deductible on Schedule A but does not qualify as a housing expense for housing allowance purposes.

Don't overlook points you paid to get the mortgage. All of the points are generally deductible as interest here. Points paid for a refinancing must be amortized over the life of the loan. But you can deduct on your 2008 return the portion of all points paid that correspond with the percentage of your refinancing used for home improvements.

- **Gifts to charity (lines 16 to 19). Line 16:** For gifts you made in 2008, you must have written acknowledgments from the charity of any single gifts of $250 or more and for all gifts of cash.

  Line 17: Deduct your charitable mileage for any volunteer work at the rate of 14 cents a mile.

- **Job expenses and other miscellaneous deductions (lines 21 to 27).** Don't assume you can't surmount the 2% AGI floor on these miscellaneous deductions. A wealth of employee business, investment, and tax-related expenses— from job-hunting costs to tax preparation fees—are deductible here. And if you bought business equipment required by your employer and you were not reimbursed, you can write off its entire cost in 2008, as much as $128,000. (However, see the allocation of expense rules, pages 112-13.)

Filing Tip

Schedule A, Line 21. Since the deduction for meal and entertainment expense is limited on Form 2106, expenses claimed on lines 21 to 23 are reduced by 2% of your adjusted gross income, and the standard deduction may be advantageous for you, using an accountable expense reimbursement plan to reduce or eliminate unreimbursed expenses is generally a wise move.

Schedule C (C-EZ)

Nearly every minister should file Schedule C or Schedule C-EZ. While a minister should receive Form W-2 for employment compensation and report the amount in Box 1 of Form W-2 on Form 1040, line 7, most ministers have some income from honoraria or fees related to weddings or funerals. Additionally, a minister may have speaking fees unrelated to the employer, product royalties, and other self-employment income reportable on Schedule C (C-EZ).

Only expenses related to the income reported on Schedule C (C-EZ) may be deducted on the form. For example, if a minister received honoraria of $500 for speaking at a church other than where employed, the $500 is reported on Schedule C (C-EZ) and the travel and other expenses related to the speaking engagement are deductible on the form. Expenses related to a minister's primary employment (compensation that was reported on Form W-2) must be deducted on Form 2106 and carried forward to Schedule A.

- **Gross receipts. Line 1:** Include income from honoraria, fees, product royalties, and other income earned as an independent contractor.

- **Total expenses. Line 2:** Only include business expenses related to the income on line 1.

Filing Tip

Schedule C-EZ, Line 2. Only business expenses related to the income reported on line 1 may be reported on line 2. A minister's housing expenses are not deducted on this form (or generally any other form). Expenses related to employee compensation must be reported on Form 2106.

Form 2106-EZ

While the goal of every minister should be to minimize unreimbursed business expenses, usually there are some unreimbursed expenses to file on Form 2106 or 2106-EZ. You may use Form 2106-EZ only if all of the following apply:

- □ You are an employee deducting expenses attributable to your job.
- □ You do not get reimbursed by your employer for any expenses. (Amounts your employer included in Box 1 of your Form W-2 are not considered reimbursement.)
- □ If you are claiming vehicle expense, you are using the standard mileage rate for 2008.

- **Vehicle expense. Line 1:** Multiply your business miles by the 2008 standard business mileage rate of 50.5 cents per mile for the first half of the year and 58.5 cents per mile for the second half. Commuting miles to and from work are excluded, regardless of how many trips per day.
- **Parking fees, tolls, and transportation. Line 2:** Enter business-related parking fees, tolls, and transportation that did not involve overnight travel or commuting to and from work.
- **Travel expense while away from home overnight. Line 3:** Enter lodging and transportation expenses connected with overnight travel away from your tax home. You cannot deduct expenses for travel away from your tax home for any period of temporary employment of more than one year.
- **Business expenses not included on lines 1 through 3. Line 4:** Enter other job-related expenses not listed on any other line of this form. Include expenses for business gifts, education (tuition and books), trade publications, etc. If you are deducting depreciation or claiming a Section 179 deduction on a cellular telephone or other similar telecommunications equipment, a home computer, etc., use Form 4562 to figure the depreciation and Section 179 deduction to enter on line 4.
- **Meals and entertainment expenses. Line 5:** Generally, you may deduct only 50% of your business meal and entertainment expenses, including meals incurred while away from home on business. Instead of actual cost, you may be able to claim the standard meal allowance (see pages 96-97) for your daily meals and incidental expenses.

> **Tax Tip**
>
> You may be able to take a credit for your educational expenses instead of a deduction on line 4. See Form 8863 Educational Credits for details.

Form 2441

If you paid someone to care for your child or other qualifying person so you (and your spouse if filing a joint return) could work or look for work in 2008, you may be able to take the credit for child and dependent care expenses.

- **Qualifying person (Line 2[a]).** A qualifying person is any child under age 13 whom you can claim as a dependent. If the child turned 13 during the year, the child is a qualifying person for the part of the year he or she was under age 13.
- **Qualified expenses (Line 2[c]).** These include amounts paid for household services and care of the qualifying person while you worked or looked for work. Child support payments are not qualified expenses. Household services include the services of a cook, maid, babysitter, housekeeper, or cleaning person if the services were partly for the care of the qualifying person.

Form 8863

You may be able to take education credits if you, your spouse, or a dependent you claim on your return was a student enrolled at or attending an eligible educational institution.

- **Hope scholarship credit (Part I).** You may be able to take a credit of up to $1,800 for qualified expenses paid in 2008 for each student who qualifies for the Hope credit (see instructions for Form 8863).
- **Lifetime learning credit (Part II).** The maximum lifetime learning credit for 2008 is $2,000, regardless of the number of students. You cannot take the lifetime learning credit for any student for whom you are taking the Hope credit.
- **Qualified expenses (Line 1[c] or Line 4[c]).** Generally, qualified expenses are amounts paid in 2008 for tuition and fees required for the student's enrollment or attendance at an eligible educational institution. Qualified expenses do not include amounts paid for room and board, insurance, medical expenses, transportation, or course-related books, supplies, and equipment.

Tip

It does not matter whether the education expenses were paid in cash, by check, by credit card, or with borrowed funds.

Form 8889

You may be required to file Form 8889 if you participated in a health savings account (HSA) in 2008.

- **HSA distributions (Line 12a).** Amounts you withdrew from your HSA in 2008 are reflected on this line. There is generally no tax impact of HSA withdrawals unless they exceed unreimbursed medical expenses.
- **Unreimbursed medical expenses (Line 13).** Medical expenses that were not reimbursed by your medical insurance may generally be included on this line.

Tip

There is no requirement to file Form 8889 if HSA withdrawals for the year do not exceed unreimbursed medical expenses.

The 1040 Challenge

Completing Form 1040 can be very challenging and take hours to complete. Although it may not seem entirely logical, the 1040 and its accompanying schedules will lead you through the process of figuring your income and deductions and computing your tax.

Form **1040** Department of the Treasury—Internal Revenue Service **U.S. Individual Income Tax Return 2008** (99) IRS Use Only—Do not write or staple in this space

For the year Jan. 1–Dec. 31, 2008, or other tax year beginning , 2008, ending , 20 OMB No. 1545-0074

Label (See instructions on page 12.) **Use the IRS label.** Otherwise, please print or type. LABEL HERE

Your first name and initial | Last name | **Your social security number**

If a joint return, spouse's first name and initial | Last name | **Spouse's social security number**

Home address (number and street). If you have a P.O. box, see page 12. | Apt. no. | ▲ You **must** enter your SSN(s) above. ▲

City, town or post office, state, and ZIP code. If you have a foreign address, see page 12. | Checking a box below will not change your tax or refund.

Presidential Election Campaign ▶ Check here if you, or your spouse if filing jointly, want $3 to go to this fund (see page 12) ▶ ☐ **You** ☐ **Spouse**

Filing Status

Check only one box.

1 ☐ Single
2 ☐ Married filing jointly (even if only one had income)
3 ☐ Married filing separately. Enter spouse's SSN above and full name here. ▶
4 ☐ Head of household (with qualifying person). (See page 13.) If the qualifying person is a child but not your dependent, enter this child's name here. ▶
5 ☐ Qualifying widow(er) with dependent child (see page 14)

Exemptions

6a ☐ **Yourself.** If someone can claim you as a dependent, **do not** check box 6a
b ☐ **Spouse**
c **Dependents:**

(1) First name Last name	(2) Dependent's social security number	(3) Dependent's relationship to you	(4) ✓ if qualifying child for child tax credit (see page 15)
			☐
			☐
			☐
			☐

If more than four dependents, see page 15.

d Total number of exemptions claimed

Boxes checked on 6a and 6b
No. of children on 6c who:
• lived with you
• did not live with you due to divorce or separation (see page 16)
Dependents on 6c not entered above
Add numbers on lines above ▶

Income

Attach Form(s) W-2 here. Also attach Forms W-2G and 1099-R if tax was withheld.

If you did not get a W-2, see page 19.

Enclose, but do not attach, any payment. Also, please use **Form 1040-V.**

7 Wages, salaries, tips, etc. Attach Form(s) W-2 — 7
8a **Taxable** interest. Attach Schedule B if required — 8a
b **Tax-exempt** interest. **Do not** include on line 8a — 8b
9a Ordinary dividends. Attach Schedule B if required — 9a
b Qualified dividends (see page 19) — 9b
10 Taxable refunds, credits, or offsets of state and local income taxes (see page 20) — 10
11 Alimony received — 11
12 Business income or (loss). Attach Schedule C or C-EZ — 12
13 Capital gain or (loss). Attach Schedule D if required. If not required, check here ▶ ☐ — 13
14 Other gains or (losses). Attach Form 4797 — 14
15a IRA distributions 15a — b Taxable amount (see page 21) — 15b
16a Pensions and annuities 16a — b Taxable amount (see page 22) — 16b
17 Rental real estate, royalties, partnerships, S corporations, trusts, etc. Attach Schedule E — 17
18 Farm income or (loss). Attach Schedule F — 18
19 Unemployment compensation — 19
20a Social security benefits 20a — b Taxable amount (see page 24) — 20b
21 Other income. List type and amount (see page 24) — 21
22 Add the amounts in the far right column for lines 7 through 21. This is your **total income** ▶ — 22

Adjusted Gross Income

23 Archer MSA deduction. Attach Form 8853 — 23
24 Certain business expenses of reservists, performing artists, and fee-basis government officials. Attach Form 2106 or 2106-EZ — 24
25 Health savings account deduction. Attach Form 8889 — 25
26 Moving expenses. Attach Form 3903 — 26
27 One-half of self-employment tax. Attach Schedule SE — 27
28 Self-employed SEP, SIMPLE, and qualified plans — 28
29 Self-employed health insurance deduction (see page 26) — 29
30 Penalty on early withdrawal of savings — 30
31a Alimony paid b Recipient's SSN ▶ — 31a
32 IRA deduction (see page 27) — 32
33 Student loan interest deduction (see page 30) — 33
34 Jury duty pay you gave to your employer — 34
35 Domestic production activities deduction. Attach Form 8903 — 35
36 Add lines 23 through 31a and 32 through 35 — 36
37 Subtract line 36 from line 22. This is your **adjusted gross income** ▶ — 37

Minus

Equals

For Disclosure, Privacy Act, and Paperwork Reduction Act Notice, see page 83. Cat. No. 11320B Form **1040** (2008)

Exemptions reduce your income by letting you subtract a fixed amount of money for yourself, your spouse, and each of your dependents.

Total Income includes:

Compensation from the church paid to you as a minister-employee for income tax purposes shown on Form W-2.

Net earnings from Schedule C (C-EZ) for income from speaking engagements, marriages, and funerals. (Schedule C will include all ministerial income and expenses if you are reporting as self-employed for income tax purposes.)

Adjustments

Adjusted Gross Income (AGI)

The 1040 Challenge

Form 1040 (2008) Page **2**

Tax and Credits

38 Amount from line 37 (adjusted gross income) 38

39a Check if: { ☐ **You** were born before January 2, 1944, ☐ Blind. / ☐ **Spouse** was born before January 2, 1944, ☐ Blind. } **Total boxes checked ▶ 39a**

b If your spouse itemizes on a separate return or you were a dual-status alien, see page 31 and check here ▶ **39b** ☐

c If you claim the standard deduction and are deducting real estate taxes, check here (see page 31) ▶ **39c** ☐

Standard Deduction for—
- People who checked any box on line 39a, 39b, or 39c or who can be claimed as a dependent, see page 31.
- All others:

Single or Married filing separately, $5,450

Married filing jointly or Qualifying widow(er), $10,900

Head of household, $8,000

40 **Itemized deductions** (from Schedule A) **or** your **standard deduction** (see left margin) . 40 — **Minus** — **Itemized or Standard Deductions**

41 Subtract line 40 from line 38 41

42 If line 38 is $119,975 or less, multiply $3,500 by the total number of exemptions claimed on line 6d. If line 38 is over $119,975, see the worksheet on page 33 . . . 42 — **Equals** — **Exemptions**

43 **Taxable income.** Subtract line 42 from line 41. If line 42 is more than line 41, enter -0- . 43 — **Taxable Income**

44 Tax (see page 33). Check if any tax is from: a ☐ Form(s) 8814 b ☐ Form 4972 . . . 44 — **Gross Income Tax**

45 **Alternative minimum tax** (see page 36). Attach Form 6251 . . . 45

46 Add lines 44 and 45 . . . . ▶ 46

47 Credit for child and dependent care expenses. Attach Form 2441 47

48 Credit for the elderly or the disabled. Attach Schedule R . 48

49 Education credits. Attach Form 8863 . . . 49

50 Foreign tax credit. Attach Form 1116 if required . . . 50

51 Child tax credit (see page 39). Attach Form 8901 if required 51 — **Minus** — **Credits**

52 Retirement savings contributions credit. Attach Form 8880 . 52

53 Credits from Form: a ☐ 8396 b ☐ 5695 c ☐ 8839 53

54 Other credits from Form: a ☐ 3800 b ☐ 8801 c ☐ ____ 54

55 Add lines 47 through 54. These are your **total credits** 55

56 Subtract line 55 from line 46. If line 55 is more than line 46, enter -0- . . . ▶ 56

Other Taxes

57 Self-employment tax. Attach Schedule SE 57

58 Unreported social security and Medicare tax from Form: a ☐ 4137 b ☐ 8919 . . . 58 — **Plus** — **Other Taxes.** All ministers must show their social security tax due on line 57.

59 Additional tax on IRAs, other qualified retirement plans, etc. Attach Form 5329 if required . 59

60 Additional taxes: a ☐ AEIC payments b ☐ Household employment taxes. Attach Schedule H 60

61 Add lines 56 through 60. This is your **total tax** . . . . ▶ 61

Payments

62 Federal income tax withheld from Forms W-2 and 1099 . . 62

63 2008 estimated tax payments and amount applied from 2007 return 63

If you have a qualifying child, attach Schedule EIC.

64a **Earned income credit (EIC)** 64a

b Nontaxable combat pay election . 64b

65 Excess social security and tier 1 RRTA tax withheld (see page 59) 65

66 Additional child tax credit. Attach Form 8812 66

67 Amount paid with request for extension to file (see page 59) 67 — **Tax Already Paid**

68 Credits from Form: a ☐ 2439 b ☐ 4136 c ☐ 8801 d ☐ 8885 68 — **Minus**

69 First-time homebuyer credit. Attach Form 5405 69

70 Recovery rebate credit (see worksheet on page xx) 70

71 Add lines 62 through 70. These are your **total payments** . . . . ▶ 71

Refund

Direct deposit? See page 59 and fill in 73b, 73c, and 73d, or Form 8888.

72 If line 71 is more than line 61, subtract line 61 from line 71. This is the amount you **overpaid** 72

73a Amount of line 72 you want **refunded to you.** If Form 8888 is attached, check here ▶ ☐ 73a — **Equals** — **Refund or Tax Payment Due**

▶ b Routing number ▶ c Type: ☐ Checking ☐ Savings

▶ d Account number

74 Amount of line 72 you want **applied to your 2009 estimated tax** ▶ 74

Amount You Owe

75 **Amount you owe.** Subtract line 71 from line 61. For details on how to pay, see page 60 ▶ 75

76 Estimated tax penalty (see page 61) 76

Third Party Designee

Do you want to allow another person to discuss this return with the IRS (see page 61)? ☐ **Yes.** Complete the following. ☐ **No**

Designee's name ▶ Phone no. ▶ ( ) Personal identification number (PIN) ▶

Sign Here

Joint return? See page 13. Keep a copy for your records.

Under penalties of perjury, I declare that I have examined this return and accompanying schedules and statements, and to the best of my knowledge and belief, they are true, correct, and complete. Declaration of preparer (other than taxpayer) is based on all information of which preparer has any knowledge.

Your signature | Date | Your occupation | Daytime phone number ( )

Spouse's signature. If a joint return, **both** must sign. | Date | Spouse's occupation

Paid Preparer's Use Only

Preparer's signature | Date | Check if self-employed ☐ | Preparer's SSN or PTIN

Firm's name (or yours if self-employed), address, and ZIP code | EIN | Phone no. ( )

Form **1040** (2008)

The 1040 Challenge

Schedule A

SCHEDULES A&B (Form 1040)

Department of the Treasury Internal Revenue Service (99)

Schedule A—Itemized Deductions

(Schedule B is on back)

► Attach to Form 1040. ► See Instructions for Schedules A&B (Form 1040).

OMB No. 1545-0074

2008

Attachment Sequence No. **07**

Name(s) shown on Form 1040 | **Your social security number**

Section	Line	Description	Box	Total
Medical and Dental Expenses		**Caution.** Do not include expenses reimbursed or paid by others.		
	1	Medical and dental expenses (see page A-1)	1	
	2	Enter amount from Form 1040, line 38 [2]		
	3	Multiply line 2 by 7.5% (.075)	3	
	4	Subtract line 3 from line 1. If line 3 is more than line 1, enter -0-		4
Taxes You Paid (See page A-2.)	5	State and local income taxes	5	
	6	Real estate taxes (see page A-5)	6	
	7	Personal property taxes	7	
	8	Other taxes. List type and amount ►	8	
	9	Add lines 5 through 8		9
Interest You Paid (See page A-5.)	10	Home mortgage interest and points reported to you on Form 1098	10	
	11	Home mortgage interest not reported to you on Form 1098. If paid to the person from whom you bought the home, see page A-6 and show that person's name, identifying no., and address ►	11	
Note. Personal interest is not deductible.	12	Points not reported to you on Form 1098. See page A-6 for special rules	12	
	13	Qualified mortgage insurance premiums (See page A-7)	13	
	14	Investment interest. Attach Form 4952 if required. (See page A-7.)	14	
	15	Add lines 10 through 14		15
Gifts to Charity	16	Gifts by cash or check. If you made any gift of $250 or more, see page A-8	16	
If you made a gift and got a benefit for it, see page A-8.	17	Other than by cash or check. If any gift of $250 or more, see page A-8. You **must** attach Form 8283 if over $500	17	
	18	Carryover from prior year	18	
	19	Add lines 16 through 18		19
Casualty and Theft Losses	20	Casualty or theft loss(es). Attach Form 4684. (See page A-9.)		20
Job Expenses and Certain Miscellaneous Deductions (See page A-9.)	21	Unreimbursed employee expenses—job travel, union dues, job education, etc. Attach Form 2106 or 2106-EZ if required. (See page A-9.) ►	21	
	22	Tax preparation fees	22	
	23	Other expenses—investment, safe deposit box, etc. List type and amount ►	23	
	24	Add lines 21 through 23	24	
	25	Enter amount from Form 1040, line 38 [25]		
	26	Multiply line 25 by 2% (.02)	26	
	27	Subtract line 26 from line 24. If line 26 is more than line 24, enter -0-		27
Other Miscellaneous Deductions	28	Other—from list on page A-10. List type and amount ►		28
Total Itemized Deductions	29	Is Form 1040, line 38, over $159,950 (over $79,975 if married filing separately)? ☐ **No.** Your deduction is not limited. Add the amounts in the far right column for lines 4 through 28. Also, enter this amount on Form 1040, line 40. ☐ **Yes.** Your deduction may be limited. See page A-10 for the amount to enter. ►		29
	30	If you elect to itemize deductions even though they are less than your standard deduction, check here ► ☐		

For Paperwork Reduction Act Notice, see Form 1040 instructions. Cat. No. 11330X **Schedule A (Form 1040) 2008**

Medical. Taxes will be minimized if the employer pays for health insurance. Minimize medical expenses using a health reimbursement arrangement.

Taxes. Real estate taxes may be deducted here even if excluded from income under a housing allowance.

Interest. Mortgage interest may be deducted here even if excluded from income under a housing allowance.

Contributions. Be sure to include gifts-in-kind on line 16.

Unreimbursed Business Expenses. It is generally wise to minimize unreimbursed business expenses by using an accountable expense reimbursement plan.

The 1040 Challenge

Schedule C-EZ

SCHEDULE C-EZ (Form 1040)

Department of the Treasury Internal Revenue Service (99)

Net Profit From Business

(Sole Proprietorship)

► Partnerships, joint ventures, etc., generally must file Form 1065 or 1065-B.

► Attach to Form 1040, 1040NR, or 1041. ► See instructions on back.

OMB No. 1545-0074

2008

Attachment Sequence No. **09A**

Name of proprietor | **Social security number (SSN)**

Part I **General Information**

You May Use Schedule C-EZ Instead of Schedule C Only If You:

- Had business expenses of $5,000 or less.
- Use the cash method of accounting.
- Did not have an inventory at any time during the year.
- Did not have a net loss from your business.
- Had only one business as either a sole proprietor, qualified joint venture, or statutory employee.

And You:

- Had no employees during the year.
- Are not required to file **Form 4562,** Depreciation and Amortization, for this business. See the instructions for Schedule C, line 13, on page C-4 to find out if you must file.
- Do not deduct expenses for business use of your home.
- Do not have prior year unallowed passive activity losses from this business.

A Principal business or profession, including product or service | **B** Enter code from pages C-8, 9, & 10 ►

C Business name. If no separate business name, leave blank. | **D** Employer ID number (EIN), if any

E Business address (including suite or room no.). Address not required if same as on page 1 of your tax return.

City, town or post office, state, and ZIP code

Part II **Figure Your Net Profit**

1 **Gross receipts. Caution.** See the instructions for Schedule C, line 1, on page C-3 and check the box if:
- This income was reported to you on Form W-2 and the "Statutory employee" box on that form was checked, or
- You are a member of a qualified joint venture reporting only rental real estate income not subject to self-employment tax . . . . ► ☐ **1**

2 **Total expenses** (see instructions on page 2). If more than $5,000, you **must** use Schedule C **2**

3 **Net profit.** Subtract line 2 from line 1. If less than zero, you **must** use Schedule C. Enter on both **Form 1040, line 12,** and **Schedule SE, line 2,** or on **Form 1040NR, line 13.** (If you checked the box on line 1, **do not** report the amount from line 3 on Schedule SE, line 2.) Estates and trusts, enter on **Form 1041, line 3** **3**

Income. Include honoraria and fee income.

Expenses. Only include expenses related to income on line 1.

Net Profit. Include in income on page 1 and on Schedule SE.

Part III **Information on Your Vehicle.** Complete this part **only** if you are claiming car or truck expenses on line 2.

4 When did you place your vehicle in service for business purposes? (month, day, year) ► ...../...../.....

5 Of the total number of miles you drove your vehicle during 2008, enter the number of miles you used your vehicle for:

a Business .... **b** Commuting (see instructions) .... **c** Other ....

6 Was your vehicle available for personal use during off-duty hours? . . . . ☐ **Yes** ☐ **No**

7 Do you (or your spouse) have another vehicle available for personal use? . . . . ☐ **Yes** ☐ **No**

8a Do you have evidence to support your deduction? . . . . ☐ **Yes** ☐ **No**

b If "Yes," is the evidence written? . . . . ☐ **Yes** ☐ **No**

For Paperwork Reduction Act Notice, see page 2. Cat. No. 14374D **Schedule C-EZ (Form 1040) 2008**

The 1040 Challenge

Form 2106-EZ

Form **2106-EZ** | **Unreimbursed Employee Business Expenses** | OMB No. 1545-0074 **2008**

Department of the Treasury Internal Revenue Service (99) | ► Attach to Form 1040 or Form 1040NR. | Attachment Sequence No. **54A**

Your name	Occupation in which you incurred expenses	Social security number

You May Use This Form Only if All of the Following Apply.

- You are an employee deducting ordinary and necessary expenses attributable to your job. An ordinary expense is one that is common and accepted in your field of trade, business, or profession. A necessary expense is one that is helpful and appropriate for your business. An expense does not have to be required to be considered necessary.
- You **do not** get reimbursed by your employer for any expenses (amounts your employer included in box 1 of your Form W-2 are not considered reimbursements for this purpose).
- If you are claiming vehicle expense, you are using the standard mileage rate for 2008.

Caution: *You can use the standard mileage rate for 2008* ***only if:*** *(a) you owned the vehicle and used the standard mileage rate for the first year you placed the vehicle in service,* ***or*** *(b) you leased the vehicle and used the standard mileage rate for the portion of the lease period after 1997.*

Part I **Figure Your Expenses**

1 Vehicle expense using the standard mileage rate. Complete Part II and then go to line 1a below.

a Multiply business miles driven **before** July 1, 2008, by 50.5¢ (.505) . **1a**

b Multiply business miles driven **after** June 30, 2008, by 58.5¢ (.585) . **1b**

c Add lines 1a and 1b **1c**

2 Parking fees, tolls, and transportation, including train, bus, etc., that **did not** involve overnight travel or commuting to and from work **2**

3 Travel expense while away from home overnight, including lodging, airplane, car rental, etc. **Do not** include meals and entertainment **3**

4 Business expenses not included on lines 1c through 3. **Do not** include meals and entertainment **4**

5 Meals and entertainment expenses: $________ × 50% (.50). (Employees subject to Department of Transportation (DOT) hours of service limits: Multiply meal expenses incurred while away from home on business by 80% (.80) instead of 50%. For details, see instructions.) **5**

6 **Total expenses.** Add lines 1c through 5. Enter here and on **Schedule A (Form 1040), line 21** (or on **Schedule A (Form 1040NR, line 9)**). (Armed Forces reservists, fee-basis state or local government officials, qualified performing artists, and individuals with disabilities: See the instructions for special rules on where to enter this amount.) **6**

Part II **Information on Your Vehicle.** Complete this part **only** if you are claiming vehicle expense on line 1.

7 When did you place your vehicle in service for business use? (month, day, year) ► .... / .... / ....

8 Of the total number of miles you drove your vehicle during 2008, enter the number of miles you used your vehicle for:

a Business .... **b** Commuting (see instructions) .... **c** Other ....

9 Was your vehicle available for personal use during off-duty hours? . . . . . ☐ **Yes** ☐ **No**

10 Do you (or your spouse) have another vehicle available for personal use? . . . . . ☐ **Yes** ☐ **No**

11a Do you have evidence to support your deduction?. . . . . ☐ **Yes** ☐ **No**

b If "Yes," is the evidence written? . . . . . ☐ **Yes** ☐ **No**

For Paperwork Reduction Act Notice, see page 4. Cat. No. 20604Q Form **2106-EZ** (2008)

Mileage. Deduct unreimbursed business mileage on line 1. It is almost always advantageous to reimburse business miles under an accountable expense reimbursement plan.

Meals and entertainment. Although deductible on this line at 50%, meals and entertainment are 100% reimbursable under an accountable expense reimbursement plan.

The 1040 Challenge

Form 2441

Form **2441**

Department of the Treasury
Internal Revenue Service (99)

Child and Dependent Care Expenses

► **Attach to Form 1040 or Form 1040NR.**

► **See separate instructions.**

OMB No. 1545-0074

2008

Attachment Sequence No. **21**

Name(s) shown on return | **Your social security number**

Part I **Persons or Organizations Who Provided the Care**—You **must** complete this part. (If you have more than two care providers, see the instructions.)

1	(a) Care provider's name	(b) Address (number, street, apt. no., city, state, and ZIP code)	(c) Identifying number (SSN or EIN)	(d) Amount paid (see instructions)

Did you receive **dependent care benefits?**
No ——► Complete only Part II below.
Yes ——► Complete Part III on the back next.

Caution. If the care was provided in your home, you may owe employment taxes. See the instructions for Form 1040, line 60, or Form 1040NR, line 56.

Part II **Credit for Child and Dependent Care Expenses**

2 Information about your **qualifying person(s).** If you have more than two qualifying persons, see the instructions.

(a) Qualifying person's name — First	Last	(b) Qualifying person's social security number	(c) **Qualified expenses** you incurred and paid in 2008 for the person listed in column (a)

3 Add the amounts in column (c) of line 2. **Do not** enter more than $3,000 for one qualifying person or $6,000 for two or more persons. If you completed Part III, enter the amount from line 35 3

4 Enter your **earned income.** See instructions 4

5 If married filing jointly, enter your spouse's earned income (if your spouse was a student or was disabled, see the instructions); **all others,** enter the amount from line 4 . . . 5

6 Enter the **smallest** of line 3, 4, or 5 6

7 Enter the amount from Form 1040, line 38, or Form 1040NR, line 36 7

8 Enter on line 8 the decimal amount shown below that applies to the amount on line 7

If line 7 is: Over — But not over	Decimal amount is	If line 7 is: Over — But not over	Decimal amount is
$0—15,000	.35	$29,000—31,000	.27
15,000—17,000	.34	31,000—33,000	.26
17,000—19,000	.33	33,000—35,000	.25
19,000—21,000	.32	35,000—37,000	.24
21,000—23,000	.31	37,000—39,000	.23
23,000—25,000	.30	39,000—41,000	.22
25,000—27,000	.29	41,000—43,000	.21
27,000—29,000	.28	43,000—No limit	.20

8 X.

9 Multiply line 6 by the decimal amount on line 8. If you paid 2007 expenses in 2008, see the instructions 9

10 Enter the amount from Form 1040, line 44, or Form 1040NR, line 41 10

11 Enter the amount from Form 6251, line 31 11

12 Subtract line 11 from line 10. If zero or less, **stop.** You cannot take the credit 12

13 **Credit for child and dependent care expenses.** Enter the **smaller** of line 9 or line 12 here and on Form 1040, line 47, or Form 1040NR, line 44 13

For Paperwork Reduction Act Notice, see page 4 of the instructions. Cat. No. 11862M Form **2441** (2008)

Care provider. If the care provider is an individual, the social security number must be provided. Otherwise, insert the employer identification number.

Qualifying persons. Only children under age 13, disabled spouse, or disabled dependents may be listed here.

The 1040 Challenge

Form 8863

Form **8863**

Department of the Treasury
Internal Revenue Service (99)

Education Credits
(Hope and Lifetime Learning Credits)
▶ See instructions to find out if you are eligible to take the credits.
▶ Attach to Form 1040 or Form 1040A.

OMB No. 1545-0074
2008
Attachment Sequence No. **50**

Name(s) shown on return | **Your social security number**

Caution: • *You cannot take the Hope credit and the lifetime learning credit for the same student in the same year.*

Part I **Hope Credit. Caution:** *You **cannot** take the Hope credit for more than **2** tax years for the **same student**.*

1	**(a)** Student's name (as shown on page 1 of your tax return) First name / Last name	**(b)** Student's social security number (as shown on page 1 of your tax return)	**(c)** Qualified expenses (see instructions). **Do not** enter more than $2,400 for each student.	**(d)** Enter the **smaller** of the amount in column (c) or $1,200	**(e)** Add column (c) and column (d)	**(f)** Enter one-half of the amount in column (e)

2 **Tentative Hope credit.** Add the amounts on line 1, column (f). If you are taking the lifetime learning credit for another student, go to Part II; otherwise, go to Part III . . . ▶ 2

Part II **Lifetime Learning Credit**

3	**(a)** Student's name (as shown on page 1 of your tax return) First name / Last name	**(b)** Student's social security number (as shown on page 1 of your tax return)	**(c)** Qualified expenses (see instructions)

4 Add the amounts on line 3, column (c), and enter the total . . . 4
5 Enter the **smaller** of line 4 or $10,000 . . . 5
6 **Tentative lifetime learning credit.** Multiply line 5 by 20% (.20) and go to Part III . . . 6

Part III **Allowable Education Credits**

7 Tentative education credits. Add lines 2 and 6 . . . 7
8 Enter: $116,000 if married filing jointly; $58,000 if single, head of household, or qualifying widow(er) . . . 8
9 Enter the amount from Form 1040, line 38,* or Form 1040A, line 22 . 9
10 Subtract line 9 from line 8. If zero or less, **stop;** you cannot take any education credits . . . 10
11 Enter: $20,000 if married filing jointly; $10,000 if single, head of household, or qualifying widow(er) . . . 11
12 If line 10 is equal to or more than line 11, enter the amount from line 7 on line 13 and go to line 14. If line 10 is less than line 11, divide line 10 by line 11. Enter the result as a decimal (rounded to at least three places) . . . 12 × .
13 Multiply line 7 by line 12 . . . ▶ 13
14 Enter the amount from Form 1040, line 44, or Form 1040A, line 28 (minus any alternative minimum tax included on Form 1040A, line 28) . . . 14
15 Enter the total, if any, of your credits from Form 1040, lines 47 and 48, or Form 1040A, lines 29 and 30 . . . 15
16 1040 filers: Enter the amount from Form 6251, line 31 (see instructions) 1040A filers: Enter the amount, if any, from the Alternative Minimum Tax Worksheet, line 20 (see instructions) . . . 16
17 Add lines 15 and 16 . . . 17
18 Subtract line 17 from line 14. If zero or less, **stop.** You cannot take any education credits . ▶ 18
19 **Education credits.** Enter the smaller of line 13 or line 18 here and on Form 1040, line 49, or Form 1040A, line 31 . . . ▶ 19

* If you are filing Form 2555, 2555-EZ, or 4563, or you are excluding income from Puerto Rico, see Pub. 970 for the amount to enter.

For Paperwork Reduction Act Notice, see page 3. Cat. No. 25379M Form **8863** (2008)

Qualified expenses. Only tuition and fees required for enrollment or attendance at an eligible educational institution are includible here.

Eligible educational institution. An eligible institution is generally any accredited public, nonprofit, or private college, university, vocational school, or other post-secondary institution.

The 1040 Challenge

Form 8880

Form **8880** Department of the Treasury Internal Revenue Service

Credit for Qualified Retirement Savings Contributions

▶ Attach to Form 1040, Form 1040A, or Form 1040NR.

▶ See instructions on back.

OMB No. 1545-0074 **2008** Attachment Sequence No. **55**

Name(s) shown on return | **Your social security number**

CAUTION: You **cannot** take this credit if **either** of the following applies.

- The amount on Form 1040, line 38; Form 1040A, line 22; or Form 1040NR, line 36 is more than $26,500 ($39,750 if head of household; $53,000 if married filing jointly).
- The person(s) who made the qualified contribution or elective deferral **(a)** was born after January 1, 1991, **(b)** is claimed as a dependent on someone else's 2008 tax return, or **(c)** was a **student** (see instructions).

		(a) You	(b) Your spouse
1 Traditional and Roth IRA contributions for 2008. **Do not** include rollover contributions	1		
2 Elective deferrals to a 401(k) or other qualified employer plan, voluntary employee contributions, and 501(c)(18)(D) plan contributions for 2008 (see instructions)	2		
3 Add lines 1 and 2	3		
4 Certain distributions received **after** 2005 and **before** the due date (including extensions) of your 2008 tax return (see instructions). If married filing jointly, include **both** spouses' amounts in **both** columns. See instructions for an exception	4		
5 Subtract line 4 from line 3. If zero or less, enter -0-	5		
6 In each column, enter the **smaller** of line 5 or $2,000	6		

7 Add the amounts on line 6. If zero, **stop**; you cannot take this credit . . . **7**

8 Enter the amount from Form 1040, line 38*; Form 1040A, line 22; or Form 1040NR, line 36 . . . **8**

9 Enter the applicable decimal amount shown below: . . . **9** X.

If line 8 is—		And your filing status is—		
Over—	But not over—	Married filing jointly	Head of household	Single, Married filing separately, or Qualifying widow(er)
		Enter on line 9—		
---	$16,000	.5	.5	.5
$16,000	$17,250	.5	.5	.2
$17,250	$24,000	.5	.5	.1
$24,000	$25,875	.5	.2	.1
$25,875	$26,500	.5	.1	.1
$26,500	$32,000	.5	.1	.0
$32,000	$34,500	.2	.1	.0
$34,500	$39,750	.1	.1	.0
$39,750	$53,000	.1	.0	.0
$53,000	---	.0	.0	.0

Note: *If line 9 is zero,* ***stop****; you cannot take this credit.*

10 Multiply line 7 by line 9 . . . **10**

11 Enter the amount from Form 1040, line 46; Form 1040A, line 28; or Form 1040NR, line 43 . . . **11**

12 **1040 filers:** Enter the total of your credits from lines 47 through 50, line 12 of the Line 11 Worksheet in Pub. 972 (see instructions), plus the amounts, if any, from line 13 of Form 8396, line 20 of Form 5695, and line 7 of Form 8859.
1040A filers: Enter the total of your credits from lines 29 through 32.
1040NR filers: Enter the total of your credits from lines 44 and 45, line 12 of the Line 11 Worksheet in Pub. 972 (see instructions), plus the amounts, if any, from line 13 of Form 8396, line 20 of Form 5695, and line 7 of Form 8859. . . . **12**

13 Subtract line 12 from line 11. If zero, **stop**; you cannot take this credit . . . **13**

14 **Credit for qualified retirement savings contributions.** Enter the **smaller** of line 10 or line 13 here and on Form 1040, line 52; Form 1040A, line 33; or Form 1040NR, line 47 . . . **14**

*See Pub. 590 for the amount to enter if you are filing Form 2555, 2555-EZ, or 4563 or you are excluding income from Puerto Rico.

For Paperwork Reduction Act Notice, see back of form. Cat. No. 33394D Form **8880** (2008)

Taxes for Ministers

In This Chapter

- Ministers serving local churches
- Evangelists and missionaries
- Members of religious orders
- Ministers in denominational service, on church assignment, and other service
- Ministers ordained, licensed, or commissioned by a local church
- Individuals not qualifying for ministerial tax treatment
- Social security tax status of ministers
- Income tax status of ministers
- Importance of the employee vs. self-employed decision
- Recommended filing status

Understanding how the various parts of the tax law fit together and apply to ministers is your primary challenge. With the big picture in mind, you can plan your tax liability instead of just letting it happen.

The key to understanding the federal tax system for ministers is to focus on tax rules that primarily benefit ministers (such as the housing allowance) and other provisions that are available to most individual taxpayers (like tax-free or tax-deferred fringe benefits).

Remember

There is some flexibility in applying certain ministerial tax provisions. For example, a minister is exempt from mandatory income tax withholding but can enter into a voluntary income tax withholding arrangement. However, if a minister qualifies for the housing allowance, he or she is subject to self-employment social security tax (using Schedule SE), not FICA—this is not optional.

There are several special tax provisions for ministers:

- Exclusion of the housing allowance for income tax purposes and the fair rental value of a church-owned parsonage provided rent-free to clergy;
- For social security tax purposes, treatment of all clergy as self-employed as it relates to income from ministerial services;
- Exemption of clergy from self-employment social security tax under very limited

circumstances;

- Exemption of clergy compensation from mandatory income tax withholding;
- Eligibility for a voluntary income tax withholding arrangement between the minister-employee and the church;
- Potential "double deduction" of mortgage interest and real estate taxes as itemized deductions and as excludable housing expenses for housing allowance purposes for ministers living in minister-provided housing.

The six special tax provisions listed above apply only to individuals who

- qualify as ministers of the gospel under federal tax rules, and
- are performing services that qualify in the exercise of ministry under federal tax rules.

Ministers Serving Local Churches

You may believe you are a minister, your employer may consider you a minister, your denomination may classify you as a minister, your parachurch employer may consider you a minister, but what does the IRS consider you? For tax purposes, the opinion of the IRS is the one that counts. But even the IRS does not consistently apply the same rules in determining who is a minister in a local church setting.

Determining whether you are a minister for tax purposes is very important. It determines how you prepare your tax return for income and social security tax purposes. A qualified minister is eligible for the housing allowance. This alone can exclude thousands of dollars from income taxation. Ministers calculate self-employment social security tax on Schedule SE and pay the tax with Form 1040. Nonministers have one-half of their social security (FICA) tax withheld from salary payments, and the employer pays the other half.

How can a church determine whether to consider me a minister for tax purposes?

If you are employed by a local church, and you are an ordained, commissioned, or licensed minister, four tests are generally applied by the IRS to determine whether you are a minister in the eyes of the IRS. You

- administer sacraments (such as performing marriage and funeral services, dedicating infants, baptizing, and serving communion),
- are considered to be a religious leader by your church or parent denomination,

Warning

Individuals serving local churches must meet certain tests to qualify as a minister in the eyes of the IRS. The individual must always be ordained, licensed, or commissioned.

- conduct religious worship, and
- have management responsibility in the control, conduct, or maintenance of your local church or parent denomination.

The IRS and the courts generally use a balancing approach to the four tests; *e.g.*, some, but not necessarily all, of the four tests must be met in determining ministerial status. This flexible approach is beneficial to many ministers because some ministers of music, education, youth, or administration will not meet all four tests.

Some individuals who are ordained, licensed, or commissioned still may not qualify for ministerial tax status. The duties performed by the individual are also important to the determination whether he or she is a duly ordained, commissioned, or licensed minister. Because religious disciplines vary in their formal procedures for these designations, whether an individual is duly ordained, licensed, or commissioned depends on a number of factors.

There is no requirement that you must be qualified to perform and actually perform every sacrament or rite of your religion. If you are qualified to perform certain sacraments and actually perform or could perform some of the sacraments on occasion, you will generally meet this test. A similar test applies to conducting religious worship and providing management services. If you currently conduct religious worship and provide management services, have done it in the past, or could do it in the future, the test will generally be met.

> **Caution**
>
> Determination of ministerial status is far from a precise matter. There has been considerable inconsistency in the position of the IRS and Tax Court on this issue across the years. Only a review of all the pertinent facts and circumstances for a particular minister will assist in determining whether an individual will qualify for ministerial tax status.

Job titles have little significance for tax purposes. A licensed, commissioned, or ordained minister may have a job title that implies a ministry function. However, the actual responsibilities of the position will determine if the four-factor test is met. Ministers performing services of a routine nature, such as those performed by secretaries, clerks, and janitors, generally do not qualify as ministers for tax purposes.

If your local church or parachurch organization ordains, licenses, or commissions ministers, it is very important that certain guidelines are followed. These issues are addressed in the 2009 edition of *The Zondervan Church and Nonprofit Tax & Financial Guide.*

What about licensed or commissioned ministers?

Some religious groups ordain, license, and commission ministers. Other groups only ordain, only commission, or only license and ordain ministers or provide some other combination of the three types of special recognition of ministers.

Will you be treated as a minister by the IRS if you are only licensed or commissioned? Perhaps. Your status with the IRS will depend on all the facts and circumstances; *e.g.*, the validity of the licensing or commissioning process, and the extent to which you administer the sacraments, are considered to be a religious leader by your church, conduct worship services, and have management responsibility in the control, conduct, and maintenance of your church.

Example: Rev. Smith is an ordained minister who serves as a minister of counseling at his church. He does not preach or conduct worship services and never administers sacraments. He has management responsibility for the operation of a counseling center in the local church. He occasionally makes hospital visits. While he qualifies under the "control, conduct, and maintenance of the church" test, he does not administer sacraments or conduct worship services. With professional advice, the church must decide whether he qualifies as a minister for tax purposes.

Evangelists and Missionaries

The qualifications for itinerant evangelists for the special ministerial tax provisions are generally the same as for ministers serving local churches.

Most evangelists are self-employed both for income tax and self-employment social security tax purposes. An exception is an evangelist who has formed a corporation and is an employee of the corporation. In this instance, the evangelist is an employee for income tax purposes but remains self-employed for social security tax purposes.

Missionaries are also subject to the same rules to qualify for ministerial status for tax purposes (see pages 26-29). Qualifying for benefits such as a housing allowance is often not so important for a minister-missionary because of the foreign-earned income exclusion. However, the issue of ministerial tax status is vitally important to determine if the minister is subject to social security as an employee or as a self-employed person.

A missionary may qualify for the foreign-earned income exclusion (Form 2555) whether or not the missionary qualifies for ministerial tax treatment. The foreign-earned income exclusion affects income tax but not social security tax.

Members of Religious Orders

Members of religious orders qualify for certain tax provisions afforded to ministers. The IRS has developed stringent characteristics to determine whether an organization is a religious order. They are as follows:

- The organization is described in section 501(c)(3) of the Internal Revenue Code.
- The members of the organization, after successful completion of the organization's training program and probationary period, make a long-term commitment to the organization (normally more than two years).
- The organization is, directly or indirectly, under the control and supervision of a church or convention or association of churches or is significantly funded by such an entity.

Special Tax Provisions	Application to Religious Order Members
• Exemption of members from self-employment social security tax in very limited circumstances.	• The rules apply to religious order members and to clergy.
• Treatment of members (who do not elect social security exemption) as self-employed for social security tax purposes for income from the religious order.	• The rules apply to religious order members and to clergy.
• Exemption of member compensation from mandatory income tax withholding.	• The rules apply to religious order members and to clergy.
• Eligibility for a voluntary income tax withholding arrangement between the member-employee and the religious order.	• The rules apply to religious order members and to clergy.
• Exclusion for income tax purposes of the housing allowance and the fair rental value of religious-order-owned housing provided rent-free to a member.	• If a member is required to live on the immediate premises of the order "for the convenience of the employer," the rental value of the housing is generally tax-free for income tax purposes. If a member does not live on the immediate premises of the order, the following guidelines generally apply: **Lay members.** The rental value of religious-order-provided housing or a housing allowance is generally subject to income tax. **Ordained, licensed, or commissioned members.** If the religious order is a church or an integral agency of a church or a church denomination, the rental value of religious-order-provided housing or a housing allowance is generally tax-free for income tax purposes. If the religious order is not a church, an integral agency of a church, or a church denomination, the rental value of religious-order-provided housing or a housing allowance is generally tax-free for income tax purposes only if the work performed by the member includes sacerdotal functions.

- The members of the organization normally live together as part of a community and are held to a significantly stricter level of moral and spiritual discipline than that required of church lay members.
- The members of the organization work or serve full-time on behalf of the religious, educational, or charitable goals of the organization.
- The members of the organization participate regularly in activities such as public or private prayer, religious study, teaching, care of the aging, missionary work, or church reform or renewal.

Housing for members of religious orders generally falls into the following categories:

- Housing is provided by the religious order on its premises, and the member is required to live in the housing.
- Member does not live on the immediate premises of the religious order.
  - □ For lay members, the rental value of religious-order-provided housing or a housing allowance is generally subject to income tax.
  - □ For members who are ordained, licensed, or commissioned, the taxability of religious-order-provided housing or a housing allowance generally depends on whether the religious order is a church or an integral agency of a church or a church denomination.

Warning

There are two types of members of religious orders:

1. members who are ordained, licensed, or commissioned by a church that is separate from the religious order, or by the religious order, if authorized by its organizing documents; and
2. lay members who are not ordained, licensed, or commissioned.

Ministers in Denominational Service, on Church Assignment, and Other Service

Ordained, commissioned, or licensed ministers not serving local churches may qualify as "ministers" for federal tax purposes in the following situations:

Denominational service

This category encompasses the administration of religious denominations and their integral agencies, including teaching or administration in parochial schools, colleges, or universities that are under the authority of a church or denomination.

The IRS uses the following criteria to determine if an institution is an integral agency of a church:

- Did the church incorporate the institution?
- Does the corporate name of the institution suggest a church relationship?
- Does the church continuously control, manage, and maintain the institution?
- If dissolved, will the assets be turned over to the church?
- Are the trustees or directors of the institution appointed by, or must they be approved by, the church and may they be removed by the church?
- Does the church require annual reports of finances and general operations?
- Does the church contribute to the support of the institution?

Assigned by a church

Services performed by a minister for a parachurch organization based upon a substantive assignment or designation by a church may provide the basis for ministerial tax treatment. The housing allowance should be designated by the employing organization, not the assigning church.

The following characteristics must be present for an effective assignment:

- A sufficient relationship must exist between the minister and the assigning church to justify the assignment of the minister.
- An adequate relationship must exist between the assigning church and the parachurch organization to which the minister is assigned to justify the assignment.

> **Caution**
>
> Too often, a denomination lists a minister as being assigned to a parachurch ministry, for example, in an annual directory, and the minister believes he or she has been assigned for tax purposes. But effective assignments are rare because of the substantive relationship and ongoing documentation of the assignment that are needed.

To substantiate the relationship between the minister and the church, the church must determine "if there is sufficient authority, power, or legitimacy for the church to assign this particular minister." Such matters as being the ordaining church, providing ongoing supervision, denominational affiliation, contributing significant financial support, or being the long-term "home church" would all appear to support this relationship.

In addressing the relationship between the church and the parachurch organization, the church must answer the question "why the church should assign a minister to this particular ministry." Essentially, the assignment of the minister must accomplish the ministry purposes of the church.

In considering an assignment, it is important to distinguish between the process of assigning and the documentation of the assignment. The process of assigning expresses the church's theology, philosophy, and policy of operation: its way of doing ministry. The documentation of the assignment provides evidence that the church is providing ministry through the particular individual assigned. The keys to a proper assignment are:

- A written policy describing the specific requirements for the relationship of the church both to the minister being assigned and to the parachurch organization to which the minister is assigned. This would include the church's theological and policy goals for the assignment.
- A formal review to confirm the qualifications of the minister and the proposed ministry with a parachurch organization.
- A written assignment coupled with guidelines explaining how the church should supervise the minister and how the parachurch organization should report to the church.
- A periodic (at least annual) formal review of the minister's activities to confirm that the assignment continues to comply with the policy.

A sample assignment letter is included in the 2009 edition of *The Zondervan Church and Nonprofit Tax & Financial Guide.*

Other service

If you are not engaged in service performed in the exercise of the ministry of a local church or are not an integral agency of a church or a church does not assign your services, the definition of a qualifying minister becomes much narrower. Tax law and regulations provide little guidance for ministers in this category. However, Tax Court cases and IRS rulings suggest that an individual will qualify for the special tax treatments of a minister only if the individual's services for the employer substantially involve conducting religious worship or performing sacerdotal functions. This definition might include preaching, conducting Bible studies, spiritual and pastoral counseling, conducting crusades, producing religious television and radio broadcasts, and publishing religious literature.

> **Caution**
>
> Many ministers are serving organizations other than local churches or integral agencies of churches and do not have an effective assignment by a church. The employer may be a rescue mission, a youth ministry, Christian radio or TV station, or a missionary-sending organization. Qualifying for ministerial status is based on the degree to which the individual is performing sacerdotal functions or conducting religious worship.

In one important case, the Tax Court ruled that a minister fulfilled his ministry through his parachurch organization by producing missions tapes for local congregations. Testimony in this case indicated an ordained minister who "seeks to proclaim the gospel in any fashion to any person or groups of persons, or who provides church-related services to congregations" is functioning as a minister.

How much time constitutes substantial involvement in conducting worship or administering the sacraments? This is difficult to say. However, in two IRS letter rulings, the IRS determined that 5% of the minister's working hours were not sufficient to qualify for tax treatment as a minister.

What if you are a minister employed by an organization that is not a church, integral agency of a church, or other religious organization? If you are an ordained, licensed, or commissioned minister conducting religious worship or performing sacerdotal functions to a substantial extent for your employer, you may qualify as a minister for tax purposes.

Based on IRS rulings, it is clear that ministers serving as chaplains in government-owned-and-operated hospitals or in state prisons fall in a special category. They are employees for social security (FICA) purposes but qualify for the housing allowance. If they have opted out of social security by filing Form 4361, the exemption does not apply to this employment.

Ministers Ordained, Licensed, or Commissioned by a Local Church

Ordination, licensing, and commissioning by parachurch organizations are generally not recognized by the IRS. While the IRS has not directly addressed the ordination, licensing, and commissioning by a local church, the following steps are recommended.

- **Appropriate bylaw provisions.** The church's bylaws should provide specific authority to license, ordain, or commission individuals as ministers of the gospel. This is essential to develop the proper chain of authority for ordination, licensure, or commissioning. The bylaw provision could be a general or summary description of ordination or licensure such as the following:

  > *An individual may be ordained, licensed, or commissioned as a minister of the gospel by ABC church after the candidate has met the qualifications for ordination, licensure, or commissioning. These qualifications may include, but are not limited to, education, experience, and training. The qualifications will be determined by the governing board of the church.*

  The bylaw language should not reference the tax benefits or provisions afforded to those who qualify for ordination, licensure, or commissioning. That could be an indication to the IRS that the church is only ordaining, licensing, or commissioning individuals for the tax benefits.

- **Development of ordination, licensure, or commissioning guidelines and procedures.** If the church wishes to ordain, license, or commission individuals as ministers of the gospel, the church governing board should adopt written guidelines and procedures for ordination, licensure, or commissioning.

- **Revocation of ordination, licensure, or commissioning status.** Ordination, licensure, or commissioning guidelines should give authority to the governing board to revoke the status, absent termination of employment; *e.g.*, in a "revocation for cause" provision. Otherwise, lifetime ordination, licensure, or commissioning status might be implied.

- **Privileges granted by ordination, licensure, or commissioning.** The procedures and guidelines should stipulate what privileges are conveyed to an individual upon ordination, licensure, or commissioning (*e.g.*, duties that changed after the individual is ordained, licensed, or commissioned, such as conducting weddings and funerals). Additional duties and responsibilities generally come with ordination, licensure, or commissioning. Additionally, detailed job descriptions could supplement the general description of the additional privileges granted.

Individuals Not Qualifying for Ministerial Tax Treatment

You do not qualify as a "minister" for federal income tax purposes if you are:

- a theological student who does not otherwise qualify as a minister,
- an unordained, uncommissioned, or unlicensed individual,
- an ordained, commissioned, or licensed minister working as an administrator or on the faculty of a nonchurch-related college or seminary,
- an ordained, commissioned, or licensed minister working as an executive of a nonreligious, nonchurch-related organization,
- a civilian chaplain at a Veteran's Administration hospital (the tax treatment of ministers who are chaplains in the armed forces is the same as for other members of the armed forces), and
- an ordained, licensed, or commissioned minister employed by a parachurch organization but who does not meet the sacerdotal function or conducting religious worship tests.

Caution

Social security is one of the most confusing issues for many ministers. FICA-type social security never applies to an individual who qualifies as a minister for tax purposes. Stated another way, if a housing allowance has been designated for you, FICA tax should not be deducted from your pay—you are responsible to determine your social security tax by completing Schedule SE each year.

Social Security Tax Status of Ministers

Ministers engaged in the exercise of ministry are always treated as self-employed for social security tax purposes. Self-employed individuals pay social security tax under the Self-Employment Contributions Act (SECA) instead of under the Federal Insurance Contributions Act (FICA).

The application of the correct method of contributing social security tax for ministers is often confusing. An employer should never deduct FICA-type social security tax from the pay of a qualified minister. If the individual is a qualifying minister, SECA coverage is then applied. The type of social security coverage is not a matter for a minister to choose. It is the responsibility of the employer to determine the appropriate type of social security based on whether the individual qualifies as a minister in the eyes of the IRS.

If an employer withholds and matches FICA-type social security tax for a qualified minister, the minister is incorrectly being treated as a lay employee. The FICA matched by the employer is improperly treated as tax-free when it is taxable for both income and social security purposes.

It is possible for a minister to be exempt from SECA in only a few situations. To claim a SECA exemption, a minister must be conscientiously opposed to receiving public insurance (including an opposition to receiving social security benefits) because of the minister's religious beliefs or because of the position of the minister's religious denomination regarding social security(see pages 127-30).

Your earnings that are not from the exercise of ministry are generally subject to social security tax under FICA (nonministerial employment) or SECA (nonministerial independent contractor earnings).

Income Tax Status of Ministers

Are ministers employees or self-employed (independent contractors) for income tax purposes? The IRS considers virtually all ministers to be employees for income tax purposes. The income tax filing status has many ramifications for what and how a church and the minister report to the IRS.

Employees report compensation on Form 1040, line 7, not on Schedule C or C-EZ (used by self-employed individuals). Employees receive Form W-2 each year from the church, while Form 1099-MISC is used to report compensation received by a self-employed individual. (Also see pages 34-35 for the employee vs. self-employed impact on the taxability of certain fringe benefits.)

Employees deduct unreimbursed business expenses, and expenses reimbursed under a nonaccountable plan, on Form 2106 (2106-EZ) with the amount carried forward to Schedule A as itemized deductions. The expenses are subject to a 2% of adjusted gross income limitation, and only 50% of business meals and entertainment expenses are deductible.

Key Issue

The defining court case on the topic of income tax status for ministers was a case in which a Methodist minister (Weber) took the position he was self-employed for income tax purposes. The Tax Court held that he was an employee for income tax purposes. The decision was elevated when a federal appeals court upheld the decision.

Self-employed individuals deduct expenses on Schedule C or C-EZ whether or not they are eligible to itemize deductions. Expenses are not subject to the 2% of adjusted gross income limitation, but the 50% of business meals and entertainment limit still applies. Whether expenses are deducted on Schedule A, Schedule C or C-EZ, they are subject to the allocation rules explained on pages 112-13.

The IRS generally applies a common-law test to ministers (and nonministers) to determine whether they are employees or self-employed for income tax purposes. Ministers are generally considered employees for income tax purposes if they

- must follow the church's work instructions;
- receive on-the-job training;
- provide services that must be rendered personally;
- provide services that are integral to the church;
- hire, supervise, and pay assistants for the church;
- have an ongoing work relationship with the church;
- must follow set hours of work;
- work full-time for the church;
- work on the church's premises;
- must do their work in a church-determined sequence;
- receive business expense reimbursements;
- receive routine payments of regular amounts;
- need the church to furnish tools and materials;
- don't have a major investment in job facilities;
- cannot suffer a loss from their services;
- work for one church at a time;
- do not offer their services to the general public;
- can be fired by the church;
- may quit work at any time without penalty.

> **Caution**
>
> With rare exceptions, ministers should receive Form W-2 from their church or other employer. Few ministers qualify as an independent contractor for income tax purposes (even though considered self-employed for social security tax purposes). A church or other employer generally has sufficient control over the minister to qualify for W-2 treatment.

Some of the above factors are often given greater weight than others. Generally a minister is an employee if the church has the legal right to control both what and how work is done, even if the minister has considerable discretion and freedom of action. The threshold level of control necessary to find employee status is generally lower when applied to professional services than when applied to nonprofessional services.

One recent Tax Court case adopted the following seven-factor test to determine if you are an employee or self-employed for income tax purposes:

- How much control does the church exercise over your work?
  - ☐ Do you have the authority to establish your own church?
  - ☐ Are you required to give an account of your pastoral ministries to an annual convention or conference at a district, state, or regional level?
  - ☐ Are you amenable to a local church board?
- Does the church or the minister invest in the facilities used in the work?
  - ☐ Who provides the church facilities?
  - ☐ Who provides an office, equipment, library, and so on?
- Does the minister have the opportunity for profit or loss?
  - ☐ Is the minister paid a fixed salary?
- Does the church have the right to discharge the minister?
  - ☐ Can the minister be removed if the church believes the minister is unacceptable?
- Is the work performed by the minister a part of the regular business of the church?
  - ☐ Is the work of the minister an integral part of the work of the church?
- How permanent is the relationship between the church and the minister?
  - ☐ Does the minister offer his or her services to the general public as would an independent contractor?
  - ☐ Does the church provide retirement benefits (such as contributions to a pension plan) for the minister?
- What relationship do the church and the minister believe they have created?
  - ☐ Does the church withhold federal income tax from the minister's salary and provide Form W-2?
  - ☐ Does the church provide the minister with a home or a cash housing allowance to provide his or her own home?

Another recent Tax Court case referenced a 12-factor test used by the U.S. Supreme Court:

1. Does the hiring party have the right to control the manner and means by which the product is accomplished?
2. Is skill required?

3. What is the source of the instrumentalities and tools?
4. Where is the location of the work?
5. What is the duration of the relationship between the parties?
6. Does the hiring party have the right to assign additional projects to the hired party?
7. How much discretion does the worker have over when and how long to work?
8. What is the method of payment?
9. What is the worker's role in hiring and paying assistants?
10. Is the work part of the regular business of the hiring party?
11. Does the hiring party provide services or products to the public?
12. Are benefits provided to the worker?

Based on the seven- and 12-factor tests, most ministers serving local congregations will be determined by the IRS to be employees for income tax purposes.

Key Issue

It is vital for churches and other employers to treat ministers as employees (Form W-2) for income tax purposes in nearly every instance. If the minister is not considered an employee for income tax purposes, it jeopardizes the tax-free treatment of many fringe benefits.

Importance of the Employee vs. Self-Employed Decision

Documenting a minister's employee status for income tax purposes is important both for the church and the minister. This issue has a direct impact on several tax-related issues:

- Minister-employees must be given Form W-2 and report their compensation on page 1 of Form 1040. They are eligible to claim unreimbursed business expenses and expenses reimbursed under a nonaccountable plan on Schedule A (nonaccountable plan reimbursements must be included in compensation on Form W-2). If you itemize deductions, business and professional expenses are deductible only to the extent that such expenses exceed 2% of adjusted gross income (AGI). Deductible business meals and entertainment expenses are limited to 50%.
- Health, accident, and long-term care insurance premiums paid directly by an employer or reimbursed by an employer, after the minister provides substantiation, are not reportable as income to the minister-employee but must be reported as taxable income to the self-employed minister.

Caution

When a church directly pays or reimburses health insurance premiums for a minister considered to be self-employed for income tax purposes, the payments are fully taxable.

Minister-employees may deduct health, accident, and long-term care insurance premiums paid personally, and not reimbursed by the church, on Schedule A as a medical and dental expense, subject to a 7.5% limitation of adjusted gross income.

The impact of a minister being considered self-employed for income tax purposes is generally very significant even if only health insurance is considered. With health insurance premiums often running $10,000 to $15,000 per year, reporting these premiums as taxable (minister-employee) versus tax-free (self-employed minister for income purposes) can impact the minister's tax bill by thousands of dollars. If health insurance premiums are included in taxable income, a low-income minister might also have his or her earned income tax credit reduced or eliminated.

Example: A church pays health insurance premiums of $12,000 for the minister (and his or her dependents). The minister has his or her own health insurance policy and the reimbursements of the premiums by the church are based on the written substantiation by the minister to the church. Since the church considers the minister as an employee for income tax purposes, the reimbursement of the health insurance premiums are tax-free for income and social security tax purposes and are not reported on Form W-2. The minister's marginal federal and state income tax rates are 25% and 5%, respectively. For social security tax purposes, the minister's rate is 15.3% (all ministers are self-employed for social security tax purposes). Therefore, the tax-free reimbursement of the health insurance premiums saves the minister over 40%, or about $5,000 (43.5% x $12,000). Conversely, if a church pays the health insurance premiums for a minister who is self-employed for income tax purposes, the total amount is taxable for income and social security tax purposes.

- Health savings accounts, health reimbursement arrangements, or flexible spending arrangements (see pages 56-57 and 59-60) are only available to minister-employees (employees for income tax purposes).
- Group-term life insurance, provided by an employer, of $50,000 or less is tax-free to employees but represents taxable income for the self-employed.
- A voluntary arrangement to withhold income tax may be used by a minister-employee but may not be used by the self-employed.

Recommended Filing Status

Nearly every local church minister qualifies as an employee for income tax purposes and should receive Form W-2. Few ministers can adequately substantiate filing as self-employed for income tax purposes.

Even though the minister might take an exception to the reporting of the church, the

INTEGRITY*Points*

- **Ministers who do not qualify for tax treatment as a minister in a local church.** While most ordained ministers employed by a local congregation qualify for ministerial tax treatment, there are many ministers who do not qualify for this special treatment. While a congregation may be able to "get away" with designating a housing allowance for an individual who does not qualify for ministerial tax treatment, the law and integrity requires more.

- **Assignment of ministers to a parachurch organization.** Many ministers request an assignment from a local congregation in relation to their employment with a parachurch organization. Why are these requests made by ministers? It's very simple! If a minister has an effective assignment, he or she has a much lower threshold to meet to qualify as a minister for tax purposes with the parachurch organization.

  What should a local congregation do when a request for assignment is received? It should determine if an assignment of the minister can be done with integrity. An effective assignment is more than the congregation simply sending a letter of assignment to the parachurch organization. For example, does the church have a written policy which outlines the criteria for assignment of ministers? Does the assignment accomplish the ministry purposes of the congregation?

- **Ministers employed by a parachurch organization.** Unless a minister has a valid assignment (see discussion above) from a church to a parachurch organization (other than a denomination or one of its agencies), qualifying for ministerial tax status with the parachurch organization is much more difficult than with a local church.

  In the non-assignment, non-denominational setting, a minister is left to rely on performing significant sacerdotal functions with respect to his or her employment with the parachurch organization.

Compensation Planning

In This Chapter

- Determine the current compensation
- Plan the compensation package
- Use fringe benefits wisely
- Use accountable expense reimbursements

Most church members in the U.S. do not know what the true compensation of their pastor really is. Even when a church financial report is presented, the data is mangled to such a degree that there typically is no clear communication of salary as contrasted with fringe benefits and expense reimbursements. Too often, all of these expense elements are added together so the appearance is that the pastor is making much more than he or she really is.

Key Issue

If a church does not increase the pastor's pay each year, it has reduced the pay. Inflation is in single digits, but it is still there, even at about three or four percent. It does cost more each year to live. And just as laypersons expect their employer to provide them with a cost-of-living pay increase each year, a pastor should expect the same.

It is often helpful to review compensation data for other ministers who serve a church of a similar size, in the same geographic area, and in the same denomination or based on no denominational affiliation. While precise data based on all of these factors is difficult to determine, the most detailed annual survey of church staff compensation available is the National Church Staff Compensation Survey published annually by the National Association of Church Business Administration (800-898-8085, www.nacba.net). This survey includes data for various ministerial levels, church business administrators, and many other staff positions.

Determine the Current Compensation

Ask a pastor how much he or she is paid and the response will often be: "My check from the church is $500 a week." But that tells us very little. Let's look at a few examples:

Example 1: Pastor A receives cash salary of $45,000 but the church does not directly pay or reimburse his health insurance premiums of $10,000. Pastor B receives cash salary of $35,000 but the church directly pays his $10,000 health insurance premiums. Which pastor has the better compensation plan based on just these factors?

Pastor B has the best plan in nearly every instance. Why? Health insurance premiums paid by a pastor have absolutely no tax value to a minister who uses the standard deduction, as does nearly every pastor who lives in church-provided housing. And even ministers who do itemize their deductions on Schedule A only receive tax benefits from the premiums when their medical expenses, including health insurance, are greater than 7.5% of their adjusted gross income.

Key Issue

In trying to determine which pastor has the best pay plan, one pastor often compares notes with another pastor by asking: "How much does your church pay you per week?" But this data doesn't begin to tell which pay plan is better. Determining what a minister is really paid is a challenging task but worth the effort.

Example 2: Is it better stewardship for a church to pay its pastor cash salary of $40,000 and provide a professional expense allowance (nonaccountable plan) of $8,000 or pay its pastor cash salary of $40,000 and reimburse up to $8,000 of professional expenses under an accountable plan?

The church is going to spend the same amount of money either way: $48,000. But the pastor will almost always have less money in his or her pocket at the end of the year with the nonaccountable plan. Why? Because the $8,000 of professional expense allowance under a nonaccountable plan must be added to the pastor's Form W-2 as taxable compensation (see chapter 5 for more information on accountable and nonaccountable plans). Then, the pastor must deduct the expenses not reimbursed under an accountable plan. If the pastor could not itemize his deductions before considering this $8,000 of unreimbursed expenses, there will be deductions lost just to get up to the itemized deduction level. And even if the minister was already beyond the itemizing threshold for the year, only 50% of meals and entertainment are deductible (versus 100% eligible for reimbursement), and the first 2% times adjusted gross income of miscellaneous expenses are not deductible.

Idea

Start by documenting the minister's pay. Use the worksheet on page 40. This exercise will reveal how well your employer has provided for fringe benefits and expense reimbursements. And it will show the gross pay (including housing allowance or parsonage value) that can be evaluated for adequacy.

Reporting Ministerial Compensation to the Church

Common reporting practice to avoid

	Church-Provided Housing	Minister-Provided Housing
Pastor's cash salary	$ 20,000	$ 30,000
Parsonage utilities	3,000	
Pension	1,000	1,000
Social security reimbursement	4,000	4,000
Health, disability, and group life insurance	8,000	8,000
Professional expense reimbursements	5,000	5,000
	$ 41,000	$ 48,000

Better reporting approach

	Church-Provided Housing	Minister-Provided Housing
Salary and equivalent compensation		
Cash salary	$ 20,000	$ 30,000
Fair rental value of parsonage provided	9,000	
Social security reimbursement (in excess of 50% of total social security)	2,000	2,000
	$ 31,000	$ 32,000
Fringe benefits		
Pension	1,000	1,000
Social security reimbursement (up to 50% of total social security)	2,000	2,000
Health, disability, and group life insurance	8,000	8,000
	$ 11,000	$ 11,000
Professional expense reimbursements	$ 5,000	$ 5,000

Confusion over how much the pastor is paid all starts with the church's financial reporting approach. In reporting to the congregation, many churches include the pastor's expense reimbursements and fringe benefits in the same section of the report with cash salary. In these examples, the common reporting practice makes it appear the pastor is being paid $41,000 or $48,000, depending on church-provided or minister-provided housing. Actually, the compensation is only $31,000 or $32,000 respectively. Use the worksheet on page 40 to determine what and how you are paid.

Minister's Compensation Worksheet

		This Year	Next Year
Salary and Equivalent Compensation:			
A.	Cash salary, less designated housing/furnishings allowance	$______	$______
B.	If parsonage owned by church, fair rental value including utilities and any housing/furnishings allowance	______	______
C.	If parsonage not owned by church, cash housing allowance provided (plus utilities, maintenance, or any other housing expenses paid directly by church)	______	______
D.	Tax-deferred payments (TSA/403[b], 401[k], IRA)	______	______
E.	Cash bonus	______	______
F.	Social security reimbursement (in excess of 50% of SECA)	______	______
G.	Other	______	______
	Total Salary	$______	$______
Fringe Benefits:			
A.	Denominational pension fund	$______	$______
B.	Social security reimbursement (up to 50% of SECA)	______	______
C.	Health reimbursement arrangement	______	______
D.	Insurance premiums paid or reimbursed by church		
	1. Health	______	______
	2. Disability	______	______
	3. Long-term care	______	______
	4. Group-term life	______	______
	5. Dental/vision	______	______
	6. Professional liability	______	______
	7. Malpractice	______	______
E.	Other	______	______
	Total Fringe Benefits	$______	$______
Professional Expense Reimbursements:			
	(limited to ordinary, necessary, and actual expenses)		
A.	Auto/travel	$______	$______
B.	Books/subscriptions/tapes	______	______
C.	Continuing education	______	______
D.	Conventions/conferences	______	______
E.	Professional dues	______	______
F.	Church-related entertainment	______	______
G.	Child care	______	______
H.	Other	______	______
	Total Professional Expense Reimbursements	$______	$______

Tax-deferred payments are shown under the salary category on this form. This presentation seems to be appropriate because it is often an option of the minister to receive the funds as salary or have them paid into a deferred plan.

Plan the Compensation Package

The participation of the pastor with an individual or a small group for compensation discussions is crucial. The entire congregation may ultimately approve the annual budget that includes pastoral pay, benefits, and reimbursements. But the pay package needs to be carefully developed before it reaches the congregational approval stage. Even the entire church board is too large a forum for the initial compensation discussions.

An annual review of a pastor's pay is vital. The pastor should know exactly what to expect from the congregation during the coming year. It is inexcusable to wait until the new church year begins or later to decide the new pay plan for the pastor.

Late in 2008 is a good time for the committee responsible for recommending compensation matters to get busy to put a plan together for the new church year that might begin in early to mid-2009. A representative or a small committee from the church board should meet with the pastor, talk about pay expectations, review past pay patterns, discuss the tax consequences of compensation components, then make recommendations to the appropriate body.

The church board should act on the recommendations by March for a fiscal year beginning in mid-2009. Then the compensation package may be included in the congregational

Pastoral Compensation Is Four-Part Harmony

An adequate expense reimbursement plan is the first compensation element to consider. An accountable plan should be formally adopted by the church.

A portion of the salary should be designated as a housing allowance for virtually every qualified minister—even those living in church-provided parsonages.

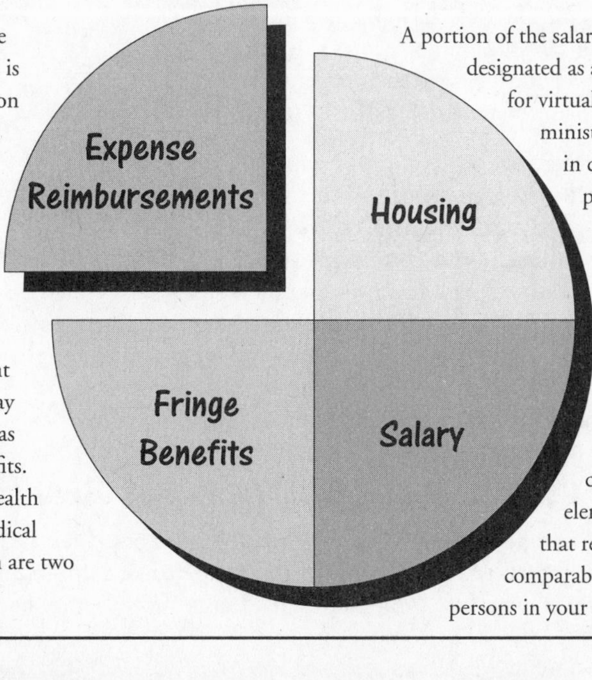

A significant amount of compensation may be legally sheltered as tax-free fringe benefits. Church-provided health insurance and a medical reimbursement plan are two key elements.

Gross salary, the portion of it designated as a housing allowance, and voluntary TSA contributions are the elements of the pay plan that represent compensation comparable to that of most laypersons in your church.

budget for the next year. The detail elements of the pay plan, while fully disclosed to the church board, are often summarized for presentation to the congregation.

Remember

All of the elements of a minister's compensation plan should be annually evaluated. A thorough evaluation is much more than just tacking on an inflationary increase to gross pay. If the gross pay was inadequate before the increase, it is still too low after the inflationary increase.

Consider goals and objectives

Does your church have goals and objectives for the church? Perhaps the goals include a percentage increase of Sunday school and worship attendance, growth in giving to missions, paying down or off the mortgage, or raising money for a building expansion.

Have you stated the specific objectives of your pastoral compensation policy? Here are a few examples:

- **Attraction.** Our goal is to attract a pastor who has a record of leading spiritually and numerically growing churches.
- **Retention.** Our goal is to increase the average time a pastor stays at our church to more than ten years.
- **Motivation and reward.** Our goal is to motivate our pastor to do what is necessary to cause our church to meet its objectives as a congregation.

Remember

Ministers who live in church-provided housing are penalized when residential real estate values are increasing. Even if real estate is modestly increasing, it is important for a church to provide an equity allowance. This annual payment in lieu of home ownership permits the pastor to invest the amount that might have been received through growth in the real estate market.

Taking your overall church goals and objectives and your pastoral compensation objectives into account, it may be helpful to establish a written compensation policy for the pastor or pastoral staff.

Example: Based on our goals to develop three satellite congregations in the next five years and expand our international missions outreach, our compensation policy will attract, retain, reward, and motivate a pastor in a fair and equitable manner, when considering the compensation of other pastors in our denomination but particularly pastors in our local community, the compensation of citizens of our community, and the members of this congregation.

Compare the job description to benchmarks of other jobs

The pastor's job description should be compared to other jobs based on the following requirements: knowledge base, problem-solving ability, and the personal accountability for results. How much are other well-educated professionals paid in the community or the area? Surely a pastor should be paid as much as an elementary school principal, middle school principal, or high school principal in your area. This data is public information and can be readily obtained.

Recognize the motivational factors and job description

It is important to recognize factors that commonly motivate pastors. These include extrinsic factors (God's call to preach the Word), intrinsic factors (the pastoral role, relationships with church attendees and those in the community), and external factors (salary and benefits).

But it is the job description for most pastors that is astounding! Typically, the job includes preaching the Word; equipping the saints for the work of ministry; administering the sacraments; visiting the sick and the needy; comforting those who mourn; correcting, rebuking, and encouraging; caring for the departments of the church; giving leadership to evangelism and education programs of the church; supervising the preparation of statistical reports; and so much more.

Key Issue

Compensation paid to the minister should be fair and a reasonable indication of the congregation's evaluation of the minister's worth. Above all, compensation should reflect the congregation's assessment of how well the minister handles a multitude of challenges and effectively serves a diverse congregation. Pay should relate to the responsibilities, the size of the congregation, the economic level of the locale, and the experience of the pastor.

Elements of the package to review

In too many congregations, the church leadership may say, "We can pay you $40,000. How do you want the money divided among salary, housing allowance, fringe benefits, and expense reimbursements?" Your salary may be considered as $40,000 when it is really considerably less. Salary is just one component of compensation. And, this approach lacks good stewardship as it almost always results in the minister paying more taxes than is necessary.

In another church, the church leadership may set your salary at $30,000, professional reimbursements at $4,000, and pension contributions at $2,000. Thus, your salary may be viewed as $36,000, not what it really is: $30,000.

Some congregations may choose to boost your salary 4% this year, leaving other elements of the pay package as they are. This practice presumes that your base salary for the previous year was adequate. This may or may not have been true.

Churches should consider salary ranges rather than fixed amounts. Show the pastor that based on experience, longevity, and education, he or she will start

Key Issue

Few churches in America compensate ministers adequately. First, consider the minister's job description. Then, compare the job description to benchmarks of other jobs in the community based on the knowledge base, problem-solving ability, and personal accountability required for the minister.

at a higher rate and receive better periodic increases.

An accountable expense reimbursement plan should be provided to every minister. An ideal policy provides for full reimbursement for all professional expenses. Alternately, the plan should provide for reimbursements up to a specified annual limit. It is generally counterproductive to set expense plan limits by segments of expense like automobile, meals and entertainment, dues, and so on. If an expense limit is set, use one limit for all business and professional expenses. (See chapter 5.)

After the reimbursement policy and the fringe benefit items are decided, housing and salary should be reviewed. Housing and salary are the true "compensation" items of the pay plan. Reimbursements are not a part of salary. Reimbursements are simply a form of church operating expenses. Fringe benefits are not salary even if they are taxable. They are simply benefits.

Just as laypersons do not include the payments made by their employers to pension or health plans as part of their salary, a congregation should not add those costs as part of the pastor's salary. True, they are a real cost for having a pastor, but they are benefits, not salary. Housing, salary, church-funded IRA payments, and voluntary tax-sheltered annuity (403[b]) contributions are generally the only elements that represent compensation comparable to most laypersons in your church.

Use Fringe Benefits Wisely

Fringe benefit plans should be established by a church separately from housing allowance resolutions, accountable expense reimbursement arrangements, and compensation resolutions. There are different tax rules that apply to gross pay, the housing allowance, and the various fringe benefits. Too often, churches try to wrap too many plans into one resolution. This can result in improperly establishing important elements in the compensation plan.

There are several key fringe benefits that many churches consider for ministers:

- **Tax-deferred accounts.** Contribute as much as you can (see chapter 3 for limitations) to tax-deferred accounts such as tax-sheltered annuities (TSAs) or 401(k) plans. Also, encourage your church to pay in the maximum to a denominational pension plan if one is available to you. Caution: Do not exceed retirement plan limits (see page 4).
- **Health insurance.** This benefit is tax-free to a minister-employee if the church pays the premiums directly to the insurance carrier. And a reimbursement to a minister-employee for health insurance premiums is tax-free if based on substantiation.

Idea

A sound fringe benefit package almost always starts with the church or other employer paying for the minister's health insurance. This is vital because the health insurance payments are tax-free. If the minister has to pay the health insurance premiums, they can be claimed on Schedule A but rarely produce a tax benefit.

Example: Is it better stewardship for a church to pay a salary of $45,000 and let the minister pay his or her own health insurance premiums of $10,000 or pay $35,000 and reimburse the minister's health insurance premiums? Pay $35,000 and reimburse the premiums. If the minister must pay the premiums, the only possible deduction is on Schedule A and then only if the minister itemizes. Even so, most of the $10,000 deduction will usually be lost because of the 7.5% times adjusted gross income limitation on medical expenses.

- **Life insurance.** When a church provides group life insurance coverage for a minister, this is an excellent fringe benefit. The first $50,000 of coverage under a nondiscriminatory plan is tax-free for the minister. Coverage over $50,000 is taxable to the minister.

- **Disability insurance.** A church can provide disability insurance coverage as a part of the minister's taxable compensation, and disability insurance benefits are tax-free. Or, the church could pay the premiums as a tax-free fringe benefit. If the premiums are tax-free to the minister, disability insurance benefits are taxable.

- **Social security reimbursement.** All ministers pay self-employment social security tax of 15.3% on the first $102,000 of income in 2008. The Medicaid tax of 2.9% is due for all income above this limit. The only exception for a qualified minister from paying self-employment social security tax is for the few ministers who qualify, file, and are approved for social security exemption.

Caution

An allowance to cover the minister's self-employment social security tax provides absolutely no tax benefit since the amount is fully taxable. However, paying at least one-half of the minister's social security tax is important, so this amount can be properly shown as a fringe benefit for compensation analysis purposes.

Churches often provide a reimbursement or allowance to assist the pastor in paying a portion or all of the social security tax. The payments are taxable for income and social security tax purposes whether paid directly to the minister or the IRS.

Use Accountable Expense Reimbursements

Since all ministers incur travel expenses while conducting the ministry of the local church, an adequate accountable reimbursement plan is vital. Auto expenses are generally a minister's most significant ministry-related expense. If payments to the

Remember

Expense allowances have no tax value to a minister—they simply represent fully taxable compensation, and the minister must try to deduct as many church-related expenses as possible. It is only through an accountable expense reimbursement plan that the reimbursement of expenses can be tax-free.

minister with respect to these and other ministry expenses are not made subject to the accountable plan rules, the payments simply represent additional taxable compensation.

Ministers also incur other business expenses such as entertainment, professional books and magazines, membership dues, and supplies. Some churches reimburse their ministers in full for these expenses. Other churches reimburse the minister for these expenses up to certain limits.

All churches should establish a fair and equitable reimbursement plan, comparable to most business situations. The reimbursement plan should meet the rules for accountable plans explained in chapter 5. Full reimbursement of reasonable professional expenses should be the goal. If the church does not reimburse you for 100% of professional expenses, the unreimbursed expenses probably will not be fully deductible for tax purposes and perhaps not deductible at all. Anything less than 100% reimbursement of church-related expenses is poor stewardship of the money entrusted to a church.

In addition to the adoption of an accountable reimbursement plan by the church, you must keep proper records and provide substantiation to the church for the expenditure of funds. The failure to account adequately for the expenses may be very expensive to you in terms of income taxes.

Avoid recharacterization of income

Some churches use a salary reduction arrangement for business expense reimbursements, falsely believing this creates a tax benefit for the minister. Under this illegal method, the church determines the combined cash salary and the reimbursable-expense dollar limit. Then substantiated expenses are subtracted from compensation.

Example: The church provides a combined cash salary and reimbursable-expense limit of $30,000. The minister substantiates $8,000 of church-related business expenses. The church reduces the $30,000 combined total by the $8,000 of expenses and provides the minister with a Form W-2 reflecting $22,000 of compensation. This is generally improper reporting since specific salary and expense plan amounts were not separately stated by the church when the compensation plan was drawn; Form W-2 must show compensation of $30,000. The minister may deduct the $8,000 of expenses on Form 2106/Schedule A or Schedule C (C-EZ), subject to limitations.

Reimbursements through salary reduction are generally not an effective method to reduce gross compensation. The valid approaches for funding expense reimbursements are as follows:

- The church may reimburse substantiated business expenses without limitation under the "accountable plan" rules discussed in chapter 5.

Example: The church agrees to provide the minister-employee with a salary of $30,000 per year plus an unlimited reimbursement of business expenses. Following the "accountable reimbursement rules," the minister substanti-

Income Tax Reporting and Expense Reimbursements

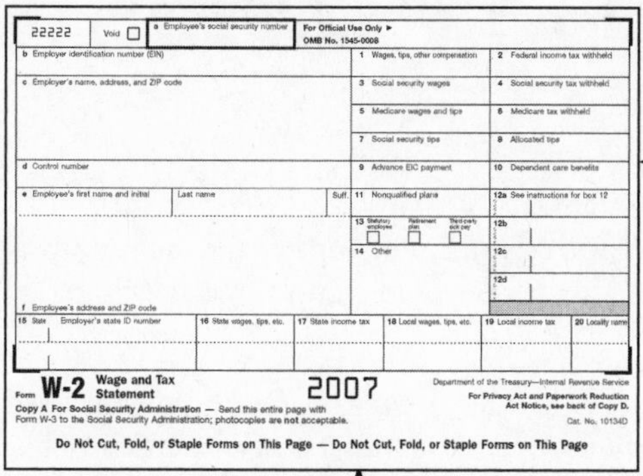
22222 Void
a Employee's social security number
For Official Use Only ►
OMB No. 1545-0008
b Employer identification number (EIN)
1 Wages, tips, other compensation
2 Federal income tax withheld
c Employer's name, address, and ZIP code
3 Social security wages
4 Social security tax withheld
5 Medicare wages and tips
6 Medicare tax withheld
7 Social security tips
8 Allocated tips
d Control number
9 Advance EIC payment
10 Dependent care benefits
e Employee's first name and initial
Last name
Suff.
11 Nonqualified plans
12a See instructions for box 12
13 Statutory employee
Retirement plan
Third-party sick pay
12b
14 Other
12c
12d
f Employee's address and ZIP code
15 State Employer's state ID number
16 State wages, tips, etc.
17 State income tax
18 Local wages, tips, etc.
19 Local income tax
20 Locality name
Form W-2 Wage and Tax Statement
2007
Department of the Treasury—Internal Revenue Service
For Privacy Act and Paperwork Reduction Act Notice, see back of Copy D.
Copy A For Social Security Administration — Send this entire page with Form W-3 to the Social Security Administration; photocopies are not acceptable.
Cat. No. 10134D
Do Not Cut, Fold, or Staple Forms on This Page — Do Not Cut, Fold, or Staple Forms on This Page

The IRS treats most ministers as employees for income tax purposes. Churches must issue Form W-2 to minister-employees.

Every church should adopt an accountable expense reimbursement plan. Expenses paid under an accountable plan are not includible on the minister's Form W-2. The expenses are not reported in any manner on the minister's Form 1040. Therefore, the expenses are not subject to any of the expense deduction limitations for Form 1040 or subject to IRS audit.

Minister-employees without accountable reimbursement plans will generally pay too much in income taxes.

ates expenses of $8,473 during the year. The church gives the minister a Form W-2 reflecting compensation of $30,000. The expenses of $8,473 are not reported by the church or the minister to the IRS.

➤ The church may reimburse substantiated business expenses up to certain limits under the "accountable plan" rules discussed in chapter 5.

Example: The church agrees to provide the minister-employee with a salary of $30,000 per year and reimburse business expenses up to $8,500 per year. Following the "accountable reimbursement rules," the minister substantiates $8,500 of expenses during the year. Additionally, the minister incurs $385 of business expenses beyond the $8,500 plan limit. The $385 of expenses are not reimbursed. The church gives the minister a Form W-2 showing compensation of $30,000. The $8,500 of reimbursed expenses are not reported by the church or the minister to the IRS. The $385 of unreimbursed business expenses may be claimed by the minister on Form 2106 (2106-EZ) and carried forward to Schedule A, miscellaneous deductions.

INTEGRITY*Points*

- **The compensation approval basics.** Although compensation approval is the responsibility of the congregation, the minister should assist the congregation in observing these three fundamental practices:

  - **Independent compensation approval.** While the congregation may consult with a minister concerning financial needs, the formal approval of a minister's compensation should be done independently of the minister. In other words, a minister should be recused from the meeting in which his or her compensation is approved.

  - **Documenting the compensation package.** A minister's compensation package should be formally documented in the minutes of the approving body. While the details of the package could be placed in a document separate from the meeting minutes, gross pay and fringe benefits should be recorded (see the 2009 edition of *The Zondervan Church and Nonprofit Tax & Financial Guide* for a sample form to record compensation).

  - **Obtaining competitive compensation data.** Congregations should annually obtain competitive data before approving a minister's compensation package. Rarely is the competitive data necessary to avoid paying excessive compensation data to a minister. The competitive data is more often important to demonstrate how much a minister's pay is below pay for a similar position in a similar church in the same geographic region.

- **Working with the congregation to optimize the stewardship opportunities.** Stewardship is generally maximized for the congregation and minister by initially focusing on fringe benefits and accountable expense reimbursements, then the housing allowance and finally cash compensation.

The Pay Package

In This Chapter

- Delaying a portion of your pay
- Which fringe benefits must be offered to all employees?
- Tax treatment of compensation elements
- Reporting compensation, fringe benefits, and reimbursements

Ask most ministers about their compensation and they will tell you the amount of their weekly check, including a cash housing allowance, but there is more to it than that. Not only is your salary subject to tax, but so are many fringe benefits that you may receive.

What are fringe benefits? A fringe benefit is any cash, property, or service that an employee receives from an employer in addition to salary. The term "fringe benefits" is really a misnomer because employees have come to depend on them as a part of the total compensation package. All fringe benefits are taxable income to employees unless specifically exempted by the Internal Revenue Code.

Many fringe benefits can be provided by a church to a minister without any dollar limitation (health insurance is an example), while other fringe benefits are subject to annual limits (dependent care is an example). The annual limits by fringe benefit type are reflected in this chapter.

Delaying a Portion of Your Pay

Following conventional advice, a minister should generally defer as much income as possible. Deferring income postpones reckoning with taxes until a future year.

You should come out ahead if you invest 100% of your money, pay no current taxes on earnings, and then pay taxes on both the principal and earnings a number of years later. Your option is to pay the taxes on all your income, including earnings, as you go.

But the principle of deferring income and taxes relies on one key assumption: The playing field remains level over the time period the income is deferred. If tax rates stay the same or go down, deferring income is generally wise. However, if tax rates go up, you could actually lose money by using this technique. If the foreign earned income exclusion is available to you, it may be unwise to defer income. Any significant change in the favorable tax rules available to ministers today would also impact the benefit of deferring income.

Many ministers have an extra potential benefit over nonministers by deferring certain types of income. If a minister has funds placed in a denominationally sponsored pension, tax-sheltered annuity, or 401(k) plan, the benefits received at retirement are eligible for exclusion under the housing allowance rules and are not subject to social security tax.

Which Fringe Benefits Must Be Offered to All Emloyees?

To qualify for exclusion from income, many fringe benefits must be nondiscriminatory. In other words, the benefits must be offered to all employees or all employees in certain classes. A fringe benefit subject to the nondiscrimination rules that is offered by a church only to the senior pastor, when other individuals are employed by the church, could trigger the nondiscrimination rules. This is particularly true for some benefits for certain key employees.

Failure to comply with the nondiscrimination rules does not disqualify a fringe benefit plan entirely. Only the highly-compensated employees lose the tax-free benefit. Other employees will still receive the benefit tax-free.

> **Tip**
>
> Churches can discriminate between employees for many fringe benefits. For example, a church can offer health insurance tax-free to one employee and not offer the coverage to another. It may be inequitable and could be inadvisable, but it's legal. There are only a handful of fringe benefits that are covered under the nondiscrimination rules.

The nondiscrimination rules apply to several types of fringe benefit plans including

- qualified tuition and fee discounts (see page 68),
- eating facilities on or near the employer's premises (see page 61-62),
- educational assistance benefits (see page 55),
- dependent care assistance plans (see pages 53-54),
- tax-sheltered annuities (TSAs), 401(k) plans, and other deferred compensation plans (see pages 64-66),
- group-term life insurance benefits (see pages 60-61),
- self-insured medical plans,
- health reimbursement arrangements (see pages 58-59),
- health savings accounts (see pages 59-60), and

- cafeteria plans (see pages 56-57), including a flexible spending account dependent care plan (see pages 53-54), and a healthcare flexible spending account.

A "highly-compensated employee" for 2008 is

- paid more than $105,000 for the previous year, or
- if the employer elects, in the top 20% of employees by compensation for the previous year.

Tax Treatment of Compensation Elements

- **Awards.** Ministers rarely receive awards based on performance. But such awards are generally taxable income unless the value is insignificant. If an award is made to the minister in goods or services, such as a vacation trip (see page 95 for trips to the Holy Land), the fair market value of the goods or services is includible in income.
- **Bonuses.** A bonus received by a minister is taxable income.
- **Books.** A church may reimburse a minister for ministry-related books with a short life (a current best-selling book) as a tax-free benefit under an accountable plan. Tax law does not provide for reimbursements of books with a long life span (a biblical commentary) under an accountable expense reimbursement plan.

  However, if an employee substantiates the cost and business purpose of books (or other property), other than those with a short life, and is reimbursed, the books generally become the property of the church.

> **Idea**
>
> To avoid confusion, it is wise for churches to have a policy covering who owns the books (and other property with a useful life longer than one year) paid for by the church. Books funded by the church budget or reimbursed under an accountable expense reimbursement plan belong to the church.

- **Business and professional expense payments without adequate accounting.** Many churches pay periodic allowances or reimbursements to the minister for business expenses with no requirement to account adequately for the expenses. These payments do not meet the requirements of an accountable expense reimbursement plan.

  Allowances or reimbursements under a nonaccountable plan must be included in the taxable income of the minister. For an employee, the expenses related to a nonaccountable reimbursement plan are deductible only if the minister itemizes expenses on Schedule A.

> **Idea**
>
> The goal of every minister should generally be to have all or most employment-related expenses reimbursed by the employer. If your expenses are not fully reimbursed, instead of getting a pay increase, you will come out ahead if you get the additional money in your accountable expense reimbursement plan.

Even then, the business expenses, combined with other miscellaneous deductions, must exceed 2% of adjusted gross income.

A portion of unreimbursed expenses are subject to disallowance when they relate to a housing allowance according to the IRS (see pages 112-13).

➤ **Business and professional expenses reimbursed with adequate accounting.** If the church reimburses the minister under an *accountable* plan for employment-related professional or business expenses (for example, auto, other travel, subscriptions, entertainment, and so on), the reimbursement is not taxable compensation and is not reported to the IRS by the church or the minister (see pages 90-92). Per diem allowances up to IRS-approved limits also qualify as excludable reimbursements (see pages 96-97).

➤ **Clothing.** Ordinary clothing worn in the exercise of your duties for the church is a personal expense and not deductible as business expense or reimbursable by the church under an accountable plan.

If you wear clothing for your ministry that is not adaptable to general use, such as vestments, it is deductible or reimbursable as a business expense.

➤ **Club dues and memberships.** Club dues are generally not deductible or reimbursable. This includes any club organized for business, pleasure, recreation, or other social purposes. The disallowance provision for club dues does not extend to professional organizations (such as a ministerial association) or public service organizations (such as Kiwanis, Rotary, and Lions clubs). If the church pays the health, fitness, or athletic facility dues for a minister, the amounts paid are generally fully includible in the minister's income as additional compensation.

➤ **Computers.** The value of the business use of a church-provided computer for home use may be excludable from your gross income as a "working condition" fringe benefit (see pages 110-11; a discussion of personally owned computers is also on these pages). In order for the exclusion to apply, your business use of the computer must

- ☐ relate to the work of the church,
- ☐ entitle you to a business deduction if you purchased the computer personally, and
- ☐ be more than 50% of your total use.

You must include the value of the benefit of a church-provided computer in income if

- ☐ your use is nonbusiness,
- ☐ your use does not qualify as a working condition fringe benefit (see the three requirements shown above), or
- ☐ you do not keep records to substantiate business use.

Even if your church-provided computer use qualifies as a "working condition" fringe benefit, you must allocate the value of your personal use of the computer and add it to your income.

Tax law does not provide for reimbursements of property, other than property with a short life (such as books), under an accountable expense reimbursement plan, when an employee substantiates the cost and business purpose. However, if an employee substantiates the cost and business purpose of property such as a laptop computer and is reimbursed, the laptop generally becomes the property of the church.

➤ **Conventions.** Expenses incurred when you attend a ministry-related convention or seminar are generally deductible. (See chapter 5 for rules for the expenses of your spouse and children.)

If the convention is held outside North America, expenses are deductible only if attendance is ministry related and it is as reasonable for the convention to be held outside North America as within it.

When a minister travels away from home to attend a convention and combines personal activities with ministry activities, the deduction for convention expenses may be subject to certain limitations. When a minister attends a convention on a cruise ship, expenses incurred in connection with the convention are deductible only if the convention is ministry related, the cruise ship is registered in the United States, and the ship does not stop at a port outside the United States or one of its possessions. Additionally, there is a $2,000 limit on expenses that may be deducted for a convention of this type.

➤ **Deferred compensation.** A church may maintain a retirement or other deferred compensation plan for employees that is not qualified under the Internal Revenue Code and is not a 403(b) tax-sheltered annuity (see pages 64-65) or a "rabbi trust" (see page 63). If the plan is unfunded (the church makes a promise, not represented by a note, to pay at some time in the future), contributions to the plan are generally not taxable currently.

Tip

Under the current 403(b) plan contribution limits, relatively few ministers will need to look for other retirement plan options. If the church funds an unqualified plan (such as purchasing an annuity contract) that is not a tax-sheltered annuity or a rabbi trust, the contributions are generally taxable currently.

Funds placed in an investment account (other than in a tax-sheltered annuity or "rabbi trust") under the church's control to provide retirement funds for the minister have no tax consequence to the minister until the funds are paid or available to the minister.

Nonqualified deferred compensation plans generally limit deferrals of compensation to amounts deferred before they are earned and to the lesser of $15,500 (2008 rate) or 25% of the employee's includible compensation (reduced by amounts deferred under a 403[b], 401[k], or SEP-IRA plan).

➤ **Dependent care.** If the church pays or reimburses your child or dependent care services, you can exclude the amount of this benefit from income within certain limits (also, see page 57 for a flexible spending account dependent care plan). The dependent must be (1) under 13 years old, (2) physically or mentally incapable of self-care, or (3) a spouse who is physically or mentally incapable of self-care. The amount excludable is limited to the smaller of

- your earned income,
- your spouse's earned income, or
- $5,000 ($2,500 if married filing separately).

The dependent care assistance must be provided under a separate written plan of your employer that does not favor highly compensated employees and that meets other qualifications.

Dependent care assistance payments are excluded from income if the payments cover expenses that would be deductible if the expenses were not reimbursed. If the minister is married, both spouses must be employed. There are special rules if one spouse is a student or incapable of self-care.

➤ **Dependent educational benefits.** The church may provide educational benefits for the minister's children when they attend college or a pre-college private school. When the church makes the payment to the college, the funds are taxable income to the minister. If the church withholds money from your pay and forwards the funds to a college for the education of your child, the amount withheld does not reduce your taxable compensation. See the 2009 edition of *The Zondervan Church and Nonprofit Tax & Financial Guide* for more information on scholarship funds established by churches.

➤ **Disability insurance.** If the church pays the disability insurance premiums (and the minister is the beneficiary) as a part of the compensation package, the premiums are excluded from income. However, any disability policy proceeds must be included in gross income. This is based on who paid the premiums for the policy covering the year when the disability started. If the premiums are shared between the church and the minister, then the benefits are taxable in the same proportion as the payment of the premiums.

Idea

Statistics suggest that a minister is seven times more likely to need disability insurance than life insurance before age 65. When a church provides the maximum disability insurance as a tax-free benefit, it could reduce the awkwardness of a pastoral transition should the minister become disabled while serving the congregation.

Conversely, if you pay the disability insurance premiums or have the church withhold the premiums from your salary, you receive no current deduction and any disability benefits paid under the policy are not taxable to you.

A third option is for the church to pay the disability premiums. But instead of treating the premiums as tax-free, the church treats the premiums as additional employee compensation. Benefits you receive under this option are tax-free.

How do you determine whether disability benefits are taxable if the disability insurance premiums are paid by the church for some years and by the minister for other years? Taxability of the benefits generally depends on who paid the premiums for the policy year in which the disability benefit payments begin.

Caution

Discretionary funds often serve a useful purpose for the pastoral staff—giving them the flexibility to provide immediate financial assistance, generally in small amounts, to those in need (larger amounts should be handled through a formal benevolence fund). However, an adequate accounting (dates, names, amounts, and need) must be maintained and made available for audit.

➤ **Discretionary fund.** Churches often establish a fund to be disbursed upon the discretion of the pastor. If the funds are used for church business or the needs of individuals associated with the church in a benevolent manner, and if a proper accounting is made, there is no tax impact on the minister. If there is no accounting to the church, and if it is permissible to distribute some of the funds to the minister, money placed in the fund becomes additional taxable income to the minister in the year the money is transferred by the church to the discretionary fund.

➤ **Educational assistance benefit plans.** An educational assistance program is a separate written plan of a church to provide educational assistance to employees. A program may include courses whether or not they are job related. Graduate-level courses are covered under the program. The program must be nondiscriminatory.

No benefits may be provided to the employee's spouse or dependents. The church should exclude from income the first $5,250 of any qualified educational assistance paid for you during the year.

➤ **Educational reimbursement plans.** If your church requires you to take educational courses or you take job-related courses, and your church either pays the expenses directly to the educational organization or reimburses you for the expenses after you make a full accounting, you may not have to include in income the amount paid by your church. (See pages 109-10 for three types of deductions for education expenses and page 12 for three types of education credits.)

Idea

In addition to educational reimbursements, a special $4,000 deduction may be taken for college costs by itemizers and non-itemizers alike. To take this deduction, the education need not be necessary for you to keep your position. The education can even qualify you for a new occupation.

While there are no specific dollar limits on educational expenses paid under a nonqualified reimbursement plan, the general ordinary and necessary business expense rules do apply. These types of payments may be discriminatory.

Though the education may lead to a degree, expenses may be deductible or reimbursable if the education

- ☐ is required by your church to keep your

salary, status, or job (and serves a business purpose of your church), or

- maintains or improves skills required in your present employment.

Even though the above requirements are met, expenses do not qualify if the education is

- required to meet the minimum educational requirements of your present work, or
- part of a program of study that will qualify you for a new occupation.

➤ **Entertainment expenses.** A minister may deduct ministry-related entertainment expenses. Entertainment expenses must be directly related to or associated with the work of the church. Documentation of entertainment expenses must reflect the relationship of entertainment to church ministry. Entertainment expenses are not deductible if they are lavish or extravagant.

If business meal and entertainment expenses are not reimbursed under an accountable plan, only 50% of the expenses are deductible. If the church reimburses the expenses, a 100% reimbursement may be made.

➤ **Equity allowance.** If the church owns the parsonage, only the church is building up equity. If the church provides a cash allowance for the minister to purchase a home, the minister may establish some equity.

An equity allowance is an amount paid to the minister living in a church-owned parsonage. This allowance may partially or fully offset the equity that the minister would have accumulated in a personally owned home.

An equity allowance that you are paid is fully taxable and not excludable as a housing allowance. However, the church could make the equity payments to a tax-sheltered annuity (TSA) or 401(k) plan. This would be consistent with the desire of a congregation to provide funds for housing at retirement. Under current law, the funds received at retirement from church-sponsored TSA or 401(k) plans may be eligible for tax-free treatment as a housing allowance (see pages 83-84).

➤ **Flexible spending account (FSA).** "Cafeteria" or FSAs are plans used to reimburse the employee for certain personal expenses. They are provided by employers to pre-fund dependent care (see next item), medical, or dental expenses (often called a healthcare flexible spending account) in pre-tax dollars (see the 2009 edition of *The Zondervan Church and Nonprofit Tax & Financial Guide* for more information on FSAs).

The only taxable benefit that a cafeteria or FSA can offer is cash. A nontaxable benefit to the participant includes any benefit that is not currently taxable upon receipt. Examples of these benefits are group-term life insurance up to $50,000, coverage under an accident or health plan, and coverage under a dependent care assistance program.

A cafeteria or flexible spending plan cannot discriminate in favor of highly compensated participants for contributions, benefits, or eligibility to participate in the plan. While only larger churches generally offer cafeteria plans because of plan complexity and cost, many churches could feasibly offer an FSA.

The IRS has approved an administrative grace period as a way to provide relief without running afoul of the prohibition on deferred compensation. Under this provision, employees are permitted a grace period of 2½ months immediately following the end of the plan year. Expenses for qualified benefits incurred during the grace period may be paid or reimbursed from benefits or contributions remaining unused at the end of the plan year.

Employers may adopt a grace period for the current plan year (and subsequent plan years) by amending the plan document before the end of the current plan year.

- **Flexible spending account dependent care plan.** Generally, a dependent care flexible spending account (FSA) is designed to pay for the care of dependent children under age 13 by a babysitter, in a day care center, or in a before-school or after-school program. The maximum amount that may be funded through a dependent care FSA is $5,000, earned income, or spouse's earned income, whichever is less.
- **Frequent flyer awards.** Free travel awards used personally that are received as frequent flyer miles on business travel paid by the church are not taxable when the awards are used. However, if these awards are converted to cash, they are taxable.
- **Gifts/personal.** Money that a minister receives directly from an individual is usually considered a personal gift and may be excluded from income if the payments are intended for the personal benefit of the minister and not in consideration of any services rendered. If the gift is a check, it should be made payable directly to the minister to qualify for tax exclusion for the minister. A personal gift of this nature will not qualify as a charitable contribution by the donor.
- **Gifts/special occasion.** Christmas, anniversary, birthday, retirement, and similar gifts paid by a church to its minister are typically taxable compensation. This is true if the gift came from the general fund of the church or from an offering in which tax-deductible contributions were made to the church for the benefit of the minister.

  To qualify as a nontaxable gift, the payment must be based on detached and disinterested generosity, out of affection, respect, admiration, charity, or like impulses. The transferor's

Idea

For several years, the IRS has taken the position that an individual has tax liability because he or she has received or used frequent flyer miles or other promotional benefits related to the individual's business travel. However, the IRS threw in the towel, saying these benefits are generally tax-free.

Filing Tip

Checks payable to the church designated for the benefit of the minister typically represent taxable income when paid to the minister. Such payments may not qualify as charitable contributions because of their possible appearance as conduit payments. It is highly preferable for payments of this nature to be made directly to the minister instead of "running them through the church" to try to get a tax deduction.

intention is the most critical factor. Also, it must be made without consideration of services rendered.

The church may announce an all-cash offering with a clear understanding that all proceeds will be paid directly and personally to the minister and that amounts given will not be receipted as charitable contributions. If the amounts given are not entered on the church books as contributions, they may qualify as tax-free gifts to the minister.

If the church gives you a turkey, ham, or other item of nominal value at Christmas or other holidays, the value of the gift is not income. But if the church gives you cash or an item that you can easily exchange for cash, such as a gift certificate, the gift is extra compensation regardless of the amount involved.

Caution

Certain non-insurance arrangements, often called "newsletter" plans, are used by some ministers. Since such plans are typically described as non-insurance, the payments by a church to these plans (or to reimburse a minister's payments to these plans) are generally fully taxable.

➤ **Health insurance.** If the church pays the medical insurance premiums directly to the insurance carrier or reimburses the minister-employee for the premiums based on substantiation, the premiums are tax-free to the minister. However, if similar payments are made for a minister who the church considers to be self-employed for income tax purposes, the payments represent additional taxable income.

Tax law and regulations are not clear if church payments to reimburse health insurance premiums deducted from a spouse's payroll are tax-free.

Churches are *exempt* from the requirements imposed on other employers to refrain from discriminating in favor of more highly paid individuals for health insurance programs handled through an insurance carrier.

Caution

An HRA may reimburse healthcare expenses under a plan in which the employer decides how much will be available for each employee. This amount is generally the same for all eligible employees because the nondiscrimination rules apply. Account balances may be carried forward to increase the maximum reimbursement amount in subsequent coverage periods.

➤ **Health reimbursement arrangement (HRA).** A properly designed, *written* employee HRA under which the church pays the medical expenses of the minister, spouse, and dependents, not covered by health insurance, may be nontaxable to the minister-employee. (Also see the 2009 edition of *The Zondervan Church and Nonprofit Tax & Financial Guide* for a sample plan and other requirements for an HRA.)

HRAs may only be funded by church-provided funds. Funding by a salary reduction election is not permitted. Excess money in a church-funded HRA can be carried over to a future year without any tax implications to the minister. Because benefits can be carried over indefinitely, the only danger of losing the balance in an HRA account is at retirement or other separation of employment.

Typical expenses covered by such a plan are deductibles, coinsurance, and noncovered amounts paid by the individual. An HRA may be an excellent supplement to a high-deductible health insurance plan.

HRAs may not discriminate in favor of highly compensated employees with regard to either benefits or eligibility. HRAs are only available to employees.

➤ **Health savings account (HSA).** HSAs are individual, portable, tax-free, interest-bearing accounts (typically held by a bank or insurance company) through which individuals with a high-deductible health plan (HDHP) save for medical expenses. The purpose of an HSA is to pay what basic coverage would ordinarily pay.

Within limits, HSA contributions made by employers are excludable from income tax and social security wages and do not affect the computation of the earned income credit. HSA contributions may not be funded through salary reduction. Earnings on amounts in an HSA are not currently taxable, and HSA distributions used to pay for medical expenses are not taxable.

Tip

HSAs are confidential. Employees are not required to provide medical bills to their employer or the trustee or custodian of the plan. The employee is responsible to reconcile withdrawals from the HSA with unreimbursed medical expenses.

In addition to coverage under a high-deductible health plan, a person who is eligible to participate in an HSA is generally one who

- □ is not covered by any other health plan that is not a high-deductible health plan (however, insurance for one or more specific diseases, such as cancer, diabetes, asthma, or congestive heart failure, is permitted as long as the principal health coverage is provided by the HDHP),
- □ is not entitled to benefits under Medicare (this means both eligibility *and* enrollment in Medicare), and
- □ may not be claimed as a dependent on another person's tax return.

HSAs can be funded up to $2,900 for 2008 for individuals and $5,800 for families to cover healthcare costs (these amounts will be indexed annually for inflation). In addition to the maximum contribution amount, catch-up contributions may be made by or on behalf of individuals age 55 or older and younger than 65. Individuals who have reached age 55 by the end of the tax year are allowed to increase their annual contribution limit by $900 for 2008 and $1,000 for 2009 and thereafter.

Funding of an HSA by the employer may fluctuate from one month to the next. This is unlike a cafeteria or flexible spending account, under which changes in contributions are generally only available on each January 1.

Only employees who are enrolled in qualifying high-deductible plans may participate in an HSA. A high-deductible health insurance plan has at least $1,100 annual deductible for self-only coverage and $2,200 deductible for family coverage (2008 limits). Additionally, annual out-of-pocket expenses for HSAs must be limited to $5,600 for self-covered and $11,200 (2008 limit) for families. A state high-risk health insurance plan (high-risk pool) qualifies as an HDHP if it does not pay benefits below the minimum annual deductible under the HSA rules. (Also see the 2009 edition of *The Zondervan Church and Nonprofit Tax & Financial Guide* for a sample plan and other requirements for an HSA.)

➤ **Home office.** If their home is the principal place of business, certain taxpayers can deduct a portion of their home expenses (for example, depreciation, utilities, and repairs). However, a home provided by a minister does not generate any home-office deductions if the church designates a housing allowance and all housing expenses are excluded. With the exclusion of the housing allowance from salary, the housing expenses—including the housing element of home-office expenses—have already been treated as tax-free.

The status of a home office as a regular or principal place of business may have a direct bearing on the status of commuting vs. business transportation expenses (see pages 107-8).

➤ **Housing allowance.** A properly designated housing allowance may be excluded from income subject to certain limitations. The fair rental value of a parsonage provided to a minister is not taxable for income tax purposes but is includible for social security tax purposes.

Any housing allowance paid to a minister that is more than the excludable amount is taxable compensation. The excess must be determined by the minister and reported on Form 1040, page 1. The church does not have a reporting requirement to the minister or the IRS regarding any portion of the designated housing allowance that exceeds the amount actually excluded.

Caution

If the church pays the premium on a whole life or universal life policy on the life of the minister and the minister names personal beneficiaries, all the premiums paid are taxable income to the minister.

➤ **Life insurance/group-term.** If the group life coverage provided under a nondiscriminatory plan does not exceed $50,000 for the minister, the life insurance premiums are generally tax-free to the minister-employee. Group-term life insurance coverage of more than $50,000 provided to the minister-employee by the church is taxable under somewhat favorable IRS tables. Group-term life insurance is term life insurance protection that

- provides a general death benefit that can be excluded from income,
- covers a group of employees (a "group" may consist of only one employee),
- is provided under a policy carried by the employer, and
- provides an amount of insurance for each employee based on a formula that prevents individual selection.

If you pay any part of the cost of the insurance, your entire payment reduces, dollar for dollar, the amount the church would otherwise include in income.

If your group-term life insurance policy includes permanent benefits such as a paid-up or cash surrender value, you must include in income the cost of the permanent benefits, reduced by the amount you pay for them.

If you are a retired minister, you also should include in income any payments for group-term life insurance coverage over $50,000 made by a former employing church, unless you otherwise qualify to exclude the payments.

➤ **Loan-grants.** Churches may provide a loan-grant to a minister relating to moving expenses, the purchase of a car, or the purchase of other property. In these instances, compensation is reported on Form W-2 for the minister based on the amount of the loan forgiven in a calendar year. The rules on compensation-related loans (see below) apply to loan-grants over $10,000.

➤ **Loans.** If the church provides a below-market, compensation-related loan to a minister-employee or to a self-employed minister, the employer may be required to include the additional compensation for the foregone interest on the minister's Form W-2.

If the loan proceeds are used for housing, the loan is secured and properly recorded, and you itemize your deductions, you may be able to deduct the imputed interest as mortgage interest. However, term loan interest must be prorated over the term of the loan. The interest is also eligible for inclusion in housing expenses for housing allowance purposes.

A "compensation-related" loan is any direct or indirect loan of over $10,000 made below market interest rates that relates to the performance of services between a church and a minister. There is an exception for certain employee-relocation loans.

For term loans, additional compensation equal to the foregone interest over the entire term of the loan is considered as received on the date the loan was made. For demand loans, the foregone interest is added to compensation each year that the loan is outstanding.

Loans to ministers may be prohibited by state law. Employers should check with legal counsel before making such a loan.

- **Long-term care insurance.** Long-term care or nursing home insurance premiums paid or reimbursed by the church are tax-free. If the premiums are paid by the minister and not reimbursed by the church, they are deductible as medical expenses subject to annual limits based on your age.

- **Meals.** If meals provided to you by the church are a means of giving you more pay and there is no other business reason for providing them, their value is extra income to you.

  If the meals are furnished by the church for the church's convenience (*e.g.,* such as having a minister on call) and as a condition of employment, a minister-employee does not include their value in income if the benefits are nondiscriminatory. However, the benefits are taxable for social security purposes.

- **Minimal fringe benefits.** If the fringe benefits are so small *(de minimis)* in value that it would be unreasonable or impractical to account for them, the minister does not have to include their value in income. If the value of the benefit is not small, you must include its entire value in your income.

  De minimis fringe benefits include traditional holiday gifts with a low fair market value, occasional typing of personal letters by the church secretary, or occasional personal use of the church copy machine.

  Example: You use the church copy machine for personal items. The machine is used at least 85% of the time for business purposes since the church restricts personal use of the copy machine. Though you use the machine for personal purposes more than other employees, your use is *de minimis* and not taxable.

> **Caution**
>
> Churches and other employers should review the distance and timing tests to determine if moving expenses paid or reimbursed are includible in or excludable from gross pay. For example, the new principal place of work must be at least 50 miles farther from the minister's old residence than the old residence was from the minister's old place of work.

- **Moving expenses** (paid by the church). Moving expenses paid directly or reimbursed by the church are excludable from gross income (reported on Form W-2, only in Box 12, using Code P to identify them as nontaxable reimbursements) for minister-employees. Amounts are excludable only to the extent that they would be deductible as moving expenses; *i.e.,* only the cost of moving household goods and travel, other than meals, from the old residence to the new residence. Distance and timing tests must also be met.

  Moving expenses do not qualify as business expenses. Therefore, moving expenses are not deductible in computing self-employment tax on Schedule SE for ministers considered to be self-employed for income tax purposes. For ministers filing as employees for income tax purposes, there is no requirement to add moving expense reimbursements, excluded on Form W-2, to Schedule SE income.

➤ **Parking.** You do not have to include in income the value of free parking facilities provided to you on or near the church premises if it is $220 or less per month for 2008. This also applies for reimbursements from the church for renting a parking space on or near the church premises. A church can also sell transit passes or tokens to ministers at discounts of up to $115 (2008 limit) per month tax-free or give cash up to $115 for passes and tokens tax-free.

➤ **Pre-employment expense reimbursements.** Prospective ministers may be reimbursed for expenses related to seeking a position with a particular church. Substantiated expenses related to interviews (meals, lodging, and travel) are not includible in the prospective employee's gross income whether or not the minister is subsequently employed.

➤ **Property transfers/restricted.** To reward good work, a church may transfer property to a minister subject to certain restrictions. The ultimate transfer of the property will occur only if the restrictions are met at a later date.

Property that is subject to substantial risk of forfeiture and is nontransferable is substantially not vested. No tax liability will occur until title to the property is vested with the minister. This simply represents a deferral of the tax consequences.

When restricted property becomes substantially vested, the minister must include in income, for both income and social security tax purposes, an amount equal to the excess of the fair market value of the property at the time it becomes substantially vested, over the amount the minister pays for the property. The church should report the additional income on the minister's Form W-2 or 1099-MISC.

For tax planning purposes, the "vesting" of a restricted property transfer to a minister may be staggered over several years. The reporting of a sizable restricted gift in one year may have significant tax consequences.

Example: A church transfers a house to a minister subject to the completion of 20 years of pastoral service to the church. The minister does not report any taxable income from the gift until the year that includes the twentieth anniversary of the agreement.

Caution

If property is transferred by the church to a minister at no charge or less than fair market value, the church should report the additional income on the minister's Form W-2 or 1099-MISC.

➤ **Property transfers/unrestricted.** If a church transfers property (for example, a car, equipment, or other property) to a minister at no charge, this constitutes taxable income to the minister. The amount of income is generally the fair market value of the property transferred as of the date of the transfer.

If you buy property from the church at a price below its fair market value, you must include in compensation the difference between the property's fair market value and the amount you paid for it and liabilities that you assumed.

- **Rabbi trust.** Deferred compensation plans that use a trust are commonly referred to as "rabbi trusts." If the model trust issued by the IRS is used, contributions to the trust will generally not be taxed currently for federal income tax purposes.

- **Recreational expenses.** A minister may incur expenses that are primarily recreational; *e.g.*, softball or basketball league fees, greens fees, and so on. Even if there is an element of ministry purpose, the deduction or reimbursement of such fees as business expenses is generally not justified.

- **Retirement gifts.** Gifts made to a minister at retirement by the employing church are usually taxable compensation. This is particularly true for minister-employees. Retirement gifts made by an individual directly to a minister may be tax-free to the minister, but they will not qualify as charitable contributions by the donor.

- **Retirement plans**

  - **401(k) plans.** A church may offer a 401(k) plan to its employees. Under a 401(k) plan, an employee can elect to have the church make tax-deferred contributions, up to $15,500 for 2008 (in addition to catch-up contributions). See the 2009 edition of *The Zondervan Church and Nonprofit Tax & Financial Guide* for a comparison between 401(k) and tax-sheltered annuity plans.

  - **403(b) plans (also called tax-sheltered annuities).** Ministers who are employees for income tax purposes may have a Section 403(b) salary reduction arrangement based on a written plan. Payments to a 403(b) contract by chaplains filing as self-employed for income tax purposes must be deducted on Form 1040, line 36. Such payments are not eligible for pre-tax treatment.

    A minister's housing allowance or the fair rental value of church-provided housing is not included in gross income for income tax reporting purposes. Thus, the definition of computing the limit on 403(b) contributions is generally considered to exclude the portion of a minister's housing allowance excluded for income tax purposes or the fair rental value of church-provided housing.

    Compliance with special nondiscrimination rules may be a condition to a minister benefiting from the Section 403(b) exclusion allowance (see pages 50-51 for more information on these rules). Churches and elementary or secondary schools controlled, operated, or principally supported by a church or convention or association of churches are not subject to the nondiscrimination rules.

    Both nonelective (for example, payments by your church into a denominational

> **Caution**
>
> A designated housing allowance generally must be excluded from compensation when calculating TSA contribution limits.

403[b] other than funded through a salary reduction agreement) and elective (funded through a salary reduction agreement) contributions for a minister to a 403(b) are excludable for income and social security tax (SECA) purposes. While permissible, after-tax employee contributions are the exception.

There are two separate, yet interrelated limitations on the amount of contributions to a 403(b) plan that are excludable from gross income:

- **Salary reduction limitation.** This limitation is $15,500 for 2008. Employees over age 50 will also be able to make a "catch-up" contribution of $5,000 in 2008.

- **Maximum exclusion allowance.** For 2008, the maximum exclusion allowance is $46,000 or 100% of compensation, whichever is less.

A minister can roll funds tax-free from one 403(b) to another 403(b) and from a 403(b) to an IRA. Rollovers are not subject to annual limits.

Withdrawals from a denominationally sponsored 403(b) plan qualify for designation as a housing allowance and are not subject to social security (SECA) tax (see pages 83-84).

For a comparison between 403(b) and 401(k) plans, see the 2009 edition of *The Zondervan Church and Nonprofit Tax & Financial Guide.*

☐ **Individual Retirement Accounts.** Amounts contributed by a church for a minister-employee's Individual Retirement Account (IRA) are includible in the employee's compensation on the Form W-2 and are subject to self-employment tax. IRA contributions may fall into one of the following categories:

- **Contributions to a regular IRA.** Each spouse may, in the great majority of cases, make deductible contributions to his or her IRA up to the dollar limitation (*e.g.,* $3,000 reduced by adjusted gross income limits). The adjusted gross income phaseout ranges for 2008 are $83,000 to $103,000 for married taxpayers and $52,000 to $62,000 for singles. (The phaseout amounts are different if you are not an active participant but your spouse is.) Catch-up contributions may be made by taxpayers age 50 and over.

- **Contributions to a Roth IRA.** Nondeductible contributions may be made to a Roth IRA. The buildup of interest and dividends within the account may be tax-free depending on how and when you withdraw the money from the account.

☐ **Keogh plans.** If a minister has self-employment income for income tax purposes, a Keogh plan may be used. Amounts contributed to a Keogh plan are not taxed until distribution if the contribution limits are observed. If you withdraw money from your Keogh plan before you reach the age of 59½, you will be subject to a 10% early withdrawal penalty.

☐ **Pension plans.** Contributions to certain pension and retirement plans are excludable or deductible by a minister for income tax purposes. In these instances, there is generally no tax consequence until the funds are distributed to the minister.

- **Denominational plans.** When the church makes contributions to a denominational pension plan for you, the contributions are not included in your taxable income. Upon retirement, the benefits represent taxable income for income tax purposes unless excluded as a parsonage allowance. Pension benefits are tax-free for social security purposes.
- **Nonqualified deferred compensation plans.** (See Deferred compensation.)
- **Pension payroll deductions.** The amounts provided by salary reductions to 403(b) tax-sheltered annuities or 401(k) plans are excluded from income for income tax purposes. However, you cannot generally exclude from income amounts that you pay directly or pay into a pension plan through payroll deductions.
- **Other.** (See Individual Retirement Accounts, Keogh plans, Simplified Employee Pension plan, and 403[b] plans.)

➤ **Sabbatical pay.** Unless payments qualify as a tax-free scholarship, sabbatical pay generally represents taxable income. To achieve treatment as a scholarship, the recipient must be a candidate for a degree at an educational institution and the scholarship must be used for tuition.

➤ **Salary.** The cash salary (less the properly designated and excludable housing allowance amount) is taxable income.

➤ **Severance pay.** A lump-sum payment for cancellation of your employment contract is income in the tax year you receive it and must be reported with your other compensation.

➤ **Sick or disability pay.** Amounts you receive from your employer while you are sick or disabled are part of your compensation (sick or disability pay is distinguished from payments for injury provided under Workers' Compensation insurance, which are normally not taxable). You must also include in income any payments made by an insurance company if the employer paid the premiums.

If you paid the premiums on an accident or health insurance policy or if the premiums paid by your employer were treated as part of your taxable compensation, the benefits you receive under the policy are not taxable.

➤ **Simplified Employee Pension plan (SEP).** Through an SEP, your employer may contribute amounts to your IRA if you are an employee or self-employed for income tax purposes. But there are many nondiscriminatory limitations on SEP contributions that

Caution

An allowance to cover the minister's self-employment social security tax provides absolutely no tax benefit since the amount is fully taxable. However, paying at least one-half of the minister's social security tax is important so this amount can be properly shown as a fringe benefit for compensation analysis purposes.

most churches will find insurmountable.

➤ **Social security tax reimbursement.** Churches and other employers commonly reimburse ministers for a portion or all of their self-employment social security (SECA) tax liability. Any social security reimbursement must be reported as taxable income.

Because of the deductibility of the self-employment tax in both the income tax and self-employment tax computations, a full reimbursement is effectively less than the gross 15.3% rate:

Your Marginal Tax Rate	Effective SECA Rate
0%	14.13%
10	13.42
15	13.07
27	12.22
30	12.01

It is usually best to reimburse the minister for self-employment tax on a monthly or quarterly basis. An annual reimbursement may leave room for misunderstanding between the church and the minister if the minister moves to another church before the reimbursement is made.

For missionaries who are not eligible for the income tax deduction of one-half of the self-employment tax due to the foreign earned income exclusion, the full reimbursement rate is effectively 14.13%.

➤ **Subscriptions.** A church may reimburse a minister for ministry-related magazine subscriptions as a tax-free benefit. Unreimbursed subscriptions may be deducted on Schedule A or C.

➤ **Telephone.** A minister is denied a business deduction or reimbursement for basic local telephone service charges on the first land line in the residence. Additional charges for ministry-related long-distance calls, equipment, optional services (*e.g.*, call waiting), or additional telephone lines may be deductible.

The ministry-related portion of monthly usage fees for employer-provided cell phones is tax-free to a minister if the minister accounts for each call in a diary, log, or other record; *e.g.*, an accountable plan. Payments for the personal portion of cell phone usage represent taxable income to the minister. If the minister does not account for the ministry portion of cell phone usage, the entire monthly fee is taxable income.

If the minister provides the cell phone, meets the "condition of employment" and "conve-

Caution

The travel expenses of an employee's spouse and children often do not qualify for tax-free reimbursement or as a business tax deduction. There must be a bona fide business purpose for the spousal and children travel in addition to substantiation of expenses.

nience of employer" tests (see page 112 for the definition of these terms), and accounts for the ministry portion of the monthly usage, the expenses qualify for deduction or reimbursement. If these tests are not met, reimbursements by an employer represent taxable income.

- **Travel expenses.** Travel expenses of a minister are deductible as business expenses if they are ordinary and necessary and incurred while traveling away from the minister's tax home for business-related reasons. Expenses that are for personal or vacation purposes, or that are lavish or extravagant, may not be deducted.

  Travel expenses incurred outside the United States may be subject to a special business vs. personal travel-expense allocation of the transportation costs to and from the business destination. This allocation can apply even when foreign travel expenses are incurred primarily for business purposes. Expenses incurred for travel as a form of education, such as a tour of the Holy Land, are generally not deductible (see page 95).

  If a minister incurs travel expenses for a spouse or child, the minister may deduct or receive a tax-free reimbursement for the spouse's and children's expenses if they qualify for employee treatment and

  - the travel is for a bona fide business purpose; and
  - the minister-employee substantiates the time, place, amount, and business purpose of the travel under an accountable business expense reimbursement plan.

Tip

Tax-free tuition and fee discounts are only available to the dependents of an employee of a school. Discounts provided to church employees are taxable. This is true if the school is operated as part of the church, is a subsidiary corporation under the church, or is separately incorporated.

- **Tuition and fee discounts.** If you are an employee of a church-operated elementary, secondary, or undergraduate institution, certain tuition and fee discounts provided to a minister, spouse, or dependent children are generally tax-free. The discounts must be nondiscriminatory and relate to an educational program.

  If you are employed by the church and not by the church-related or church-operated private school, any tuition and fee discounts that you receive are taxable income.

- **Vacation pay.** Payments made by the church to you for vacations are taxable income.

- **Vehicles/personal use of employer-owned vehicle.** One of the most attractive fringe benefits for a minister is for the church or other employer to own or lease a vehicle for the minister. The church generally makes the lease payments or car loan payments, if any, plus paying for all gas, oil, insurance, repairs, and other related expenses. Unless the vehicle is always parked on the church premises (*e.g.,* where business trips start) and never used for personal purposes, the minister must maintain a log to document personal use of the vehicle.

The fair market value of the personal use must be included in the minister's gross income unless the minister fully reimburses the value to the church.

Example: Your church provides a vehicle for your use for a full year. The vehicle cost was $16,000 and the annual lease value for the year is $4,600 (see table in the 2009 edition of *The Zondervan Church and Nonprofit Tax & Financial Guide*). You drive 6,000 miles during the year for the church and 2,000 miles for personal use. The value of the working condition fringe is 6,000 (business miles) divided by 8,000 (total miles) times $4,600 (total value) equals $3,450. The $3,450 value of the working condition fringe is excluded from income. The remaining $1,150 value is for the personal use of the vehicle and must be included in your income. You must also add 5.5 cents per mile unless you paid for the fuel when the vehicle was used for personal purposes.

Many churches use the annual lease value rule to set a value on the use of a church-provided vehicle. (There are also several other valuation rules that are available.) If the church provides the fuel, 5.5 cents per mile must be added to the annual lease value. See IRS Publication 535 for more information.

➤ **Vehicle use/nonpersonal.** The total value of the use of a qualified nonpersonal-use vehicle is excluded from income as a working condition fringe. The term "qualified nonpersonal-use vehicle" means any vehicle that is not likely to be used more than a small amount for personal purposes because of its nature or design.

Example: A church provides you with a vehicle to use for church business. You do not qualify for a home office and leave the car parked at the church when it is not being driven for business purposes. There is a written agreement with the church that prohibits your personal use of the vehicle. Only in an emergency is the car driven for personal benefit. This vehicle should qualify under the nonpersonal-use provision, and the entire value of the vehicle would be excluded from your income.

➤ **Wage continuation.** Generally, payments to an employee from a wage continuation plan are treated as compensation for income tax purposes. For the treatment of special types of wage continuation plans, see the explanations under Disability insurance (see pages 54-55) and Workers' Compensation (below).

➤ **Withholding.** Amounts withheld from your pay or put into your bank account under a voluntary withholding agreement for income tax or savings bonds are compensation as though paid directly to you. These amounts must be included on your Form W-2 in the year they were withheld. The same generally is true of amounts withheld for taxable fringe benefits.

If the church uses your wages to pay your debts, or if your wages are garnished, the full amount is compensation to you. Withholding salary to pay a minister's tithe rarely qualifies for tax-free treatment.

Reporting Compensation, Fringe Benefits, and Reimbursements for Income Tax Purposes

Compensation, fringe benefit, or reimbursement	Minister-Employee
Bonus or gift from church	Taxable income/Form W-2
Business and professional expenses reimbursed with adequate accounting	Tax-free/excluded
Business and professional expense payments without adequate accounting	Deduction on Schedule A, Miscellaneous Deductions. Subject to 2% of AGI and 50% meals and entertainment limits
Club dues paid by the church	Taxable income/Form W-2 (exception for dues for civic and public service groups)
Compensation reported to minister by church	Form W-2
Dependent care assistance payments	Tax-free, subject to limitations
Earned income tax credit (EITC)	May be eligible for EITC
Educational assistance programs	May be eligible to exclude up to $5,250 of qualified assistance
401(k) plan	Eligible for 401(k)
Gifts/personal (not handled through church)	Tax-free/excluded
Housing allowance	Excludable, subject to limitations
Health reimbursement arrangement	Tax-free, if plan is properly established
Health savings account	Tax-free, subject to limitations
Healthcare flexible spending account	Tax-free if plan is properly established
IRA payments by church	Taxable income/Form W-2, may be deducted on Form 1040, Line 25
Insurance, disability, paid by church, minister is beneficiary	Premiums are tax-free, but proceeds are taxable
Insurance, disability, paid by minister, minister is beneficiary	Proceeds are tax-free
Insurance, group-term life, paid by church	First $50,000 of coverage is tax-free
Insurance, health	Tax-free if directly paid by church or reimbursed to minister upon substantiation ("newsletter" plan payments do not qualify) If paid by minister and not reimbursed by church, deduct on Schedule A

Reporting Compensation, Fringe Benefits, and Reimbursements for Income Tax Purposes

Compensation, fringe benefit, or reimbursement	Minister-Employee
Insurance, life, whole or universal, church is beneficiary	Tax-free/excluded
Insurance, life, whole or universal, minister designates beneficiary	Taxable income/Form W-2
Insurance, long-term care	Tax-free if directly paid by church or reimbursed to minister on substantiation. If paid by minister and not reimbursed by church, deduct on Schedule A subject to limitations
Loans, certain low-interest or interest-free to minister over $10,000	Imputed interest (the difference between the IRS-established interest rate and the rate charged) is taxable income/Form W-2
Moving expenses paid by the church (only applies to certain qualified expenses)	Tax-free if directly paid by church or reimbursed to minister on substantiation. Reported on Form W-2, only in Box 12, using Code P
Pension payments to a denominational plan for the minister by the church	Tax-deferred. No reporting required until the funds are withdrawn or pension benefits are paid
Per diem payments for meals, lodging, and incidental expenses	May be used for travel away from home under an accountable reimbursement plan
Professional income (weddings, funerals)	Taxable income/Schedule C (C-EZ)
Property transferred to minister at no cost or less than fair market value	Taxable income/Form W-2
Retirement or farewell gift to minister from church	Taxable income/Form W-2
Salary from church	Report salary on page 1, Form 1040
Section 403(b) tax-sheltered annuity	Eligible for 403(b)
Social security reimbursed by church to minister	Taxable income/Form W-2
Travel paid for minister's spouse by the church	May be tax-free if there is a business purpose
Tuition and fee discounts	May be tax-free in certain situations
Value of home provided to minister	Tax-free/excluded
Vehicles/personal use of church-owned auto	Taxable income/Form W-2
Voluntary withholding	Eligible for voluntary withholding agreement

INTEGRITY**Points**

- **Reimbursing out-of-pocket medical expenses.** A minister's first priority is having good health insurance coverage. Sadly, most ministers do not have one of the four plans under which out-of-pocket medical expenses may be reimbursed on a tax-free basis.

  - **Cafeteria plan.** Generally only very large churches can justify establishing and maintaining a cafeteria plan. These plans can cover much more than medical expenses—for example, dependent care, life insurance, and disability insurance.

  - **Health savings account (HSA).** This concept has grown very slowly.

  - **Health reimbursement arrangement (HRA).** The same HRA benefit must be provided to all employees. This makes this concept very limiting since out-of-pocket costs significantly vary employee-to-employee.

  - **Flexible spending account (FSA).** The FSA should generally be the plan of choice for ministers and churches. The FSA is simple to establish and easy to administer by the church.

- **The impact of the nondiscrimination rules on ministers.** While the nondiscrimination rules impact several fringe benefits (see pages 50-51), these rules do apply to all of the four plans under which out-of-pocket medical expenses (see above) may be reimbursed.

  Often a congregation will reimburse out-of-pocket medical expenses for the staff at varying levels, *i.e.,* up to $1,000 for the senior pastor, up to $500 for the associate pastor and up to $300 for a secretary under an HRA. This arrangement fails the nondiscrimination test.

- **The challenges of cell phone expenses.** The cell phone expense documentation rules (see page 67) are onerous. Whether we like the rules or not, unless cell phone expenses are properly documented, the IRS does not permit the deduction of unreimbursed expenses or the payment of the expenses on a tax-free basis by the congregation (either directly paid by or reimbursed by the congregation).

- **Discretionary funds.** If a congregation provides a minister with discretionary funds (funds to provide benevolence assistance as needs are identified by the minister), the accounting to the church for these funds is vital. Unless a minister documents the date the funds were spent, the recipient of the funds, and the benevolent need, discretionary funds are taxable to the minister as compensation.

Housing Allowance

In This Chapter

- Types of housing arrangements
- Establishing and modifying the housing allowance
- Reporting the housing allowance to the minister
- Accounting for the housing allowance
- Other housing allowance issues
- Housing allowance worksheets

Qualified ministers (see chapter 1 for who is a qualified minister) are eligible to receive lodging from the church free of income tax liability by *excluding* dollars from gross income. Maximizing housing benefits requires careful planning. Used properly, the housing allowance can truly be the minister's best tax friend.

Every qualified minister should have a portion of salary designated as a housing allowance. For ministers living in church-owned housing, a housing allowance covering expenses such as furnishings, personal property insurance on contents, and utilities could save several hundred dollars of income taxes annually. For ministers living in their own homes or rental housing, a properly designated housing allowance may be worth thousands of dollars of income tax saved.

The designated housing allowance should be subtracted from compensation before the church completes the data on Form W-2. The housing allowance designation is not entered on Form 1040 or related schedules, except Schedule SE, since it is not a deduction for income tax purposes. However, any unused portion of the housing designation must be reported as income on page 1, Form 1040.

If the church properly designates a portion of your cash salary for expenses of a home you provide, the exclusion is commonly referred to as a *housing* allowance. If the church properly designates a portion of your cash salary for expenses you incur in relation to church-provided housing, the exclusion is often called a *parsonage* allowance. In either instance, it is an exclusion from income tax, not self-employment tax.

Ministers are eligible to exclude the fair rental value of church-provided housing for income tax

Employer-Provided Housing

The fair rental value of the housing plus utilities (if paid by employer) is

- Excludable for federal income tax purposes
- Includible for social security (SECA) purposes

A housing allowance may be provided to a minister living in employer-provided housing. It is a designation of the cash salary. The housing allowance may cover certain housing expenses paid by the minister (see the worksheet on page 86).

Minister-Provided Housing

The excludable portion of a housing allowance is not taxable for federal income tax purposes. The entire housing allowance is taxable for social security tax (SECA) purposes. See the worksheets on pages 87 and 88 for excludable expenses.

The excludable housing allowance is the lowest of these factors:

- Reasonable compensation
- Amount used from current ministerial income to provide the home
- Amount prospectively and officially designated by the employer
- The fair rental value of the home including utilities and furnishings

If a designated housing allowance exceeds these four factors, the excess is reportable as additional income for income tax purposes.

purposes without any official action by the church. However, a cash housing allowance related to church-provided or minister-provided housing is only excludable under the following rules:

- The allowance must be officially designated by the church. The designation should be stated in writing, preferably by resolution of the top governing body, in an employment contract or—at a minimum—in the church budget and payroll records. If the only reference to the housing allowance is in the church budget, the budget should be formally approved by the top governing body of the church. See the 2009 edition of *The Zondervan Church and Nonprofit Tax & Financial Guide* for examples of housing allowance resolutions.

  Tax law does not specifically say an oral designation of the housing allowance is unacceptable. In certain instances, the IRS has accepted an oral housing designation. Still, the use of a written designation is preferable and highly recommended. The lack of a written designation significantly weakens the defense for the housing exclusion upon audit.

- The housing allowance must be designated prospectively by the church. Cash housing allowance payments made prior to a designation of the housing allowance are fully taxable for income tax purposes. Carefully word the resolution so that it will remain in effect until a subsequent resolution is adopted.

> **Key Issue**
>
> Understanding the distinction between a housing allowance designation and the housing exclusion is fundamental. The designation is officially made by the church or other employer. The exclusion is the amount the minister actually excludes for income tax purposes after applying the limitations outlined in this chapter.

- Only actual expenses can be excluded from income. The source of the funds used to pay for a minister's housing expenses must be compensation earned by the minister in the exercise of ministry in the current year.

- Only an annual comparison by a minister of housing expenses to the housing allowance is required. For example, if the housing allowance designation is stated in terms of a weekly or monthly amount, only a comparison of actual housing expenses to the annualized housing allowance is required.

- The housing allowance exclusion cannot exceed the fair rental value of the housing, including furnishings, plus utilities.

Types of Housing Arrangements

Minister living in church-provided housing

If you live in a church-owned parsonage or housing rented by the church, the fair rental value of the housing is not reported for income tax purposes. The fair rental value is subject only to self-employment tax.

You may request a housing allowance to cover expenses incurred in maintaining the church-owned or church-rented housing. The cash housing allowance excludable for income tax purposes is the *lowest* of (1) reasonable compensation, (2) actual housing expenses paid from current ministerial income, (3) the amount prospectively and officially designated, or (4) the fair rental value of the home including utilities and furnishings. Examples of allowable expenses are utilities, repairs, furnishings, and appliances. If the actual expenses exceed the housing allowance declared by the church, the excess amount cannot be excluded from income. The expenses shown on the worksheet on page 86 qualify as part of the housing allowance for a minister living in housing owned or rented by the church.

Tip

The designation of a housing allowance for a minister living in church-provided housing is often overlooked. While the largest housing allowance benefits go to ministers with mortgage payments on their own homes, a housing allowance of a few thousand dollars is often beneficial to a pastor in a church-provided home.

It is appropriate for the minister's out-of-pocket expenses for the maintenance of a church-owned parsonage to be reimbursed by the church if a full accounting is made. Such reimbursements do not relate to a housing allowance. If such expenses are not reimbursed, they could be excludable from income under a housing allowance.

If the church owns the parsonage, the church may wish to provide an equity allowance to help compensate the minister for equity not accumulated through home ownership. An equity allowance is taxable both for income and social security tax purposes *unless* directed to a 403(b) tax-sheltered annuity, 401(k) plan, or certain other retirement programs.

Minister owning or renting own home

If you own or rent your own home, you may exclude, for income tax purposes, a cash housing allowance that is the *lowest* of (1) reasonable compensation, (2) the amount used to provide a home from current ministerial income, (3) the amount prospectively and officially designated, or (4) the fair rental value of the furnished home, plus utilities.

The expenses shown on the worksheet on page 87 qualify as part of the housing allowance for a minister owning or buying a home. Page 88 shows a similar worksheet for a minister renting a home.

Many ministers make the mistake of automatically excluding from income (for income tax purposes) the total designated housing allowance, even though the fair rental value of the furnished home or actual housing expenses are less than the designation. This practice may cause a significant underpayment of income taxes.

The housing expenses related to a minister-owned house should not be reimbursed by the church. These expenses should be covered by the minister under a cash housing allowance paid by the church.

Example: A minister lives in a personally owned home. The church prospectively designates $18,000 of the salary as housing allowance. The minister spends $17,000 for housing-related items. The fair rental value of the home is $19,000.

Since the amount spent is lower than the designated housing allowance or the fair rental value, the excludable housing is $17,000. Therefore, $1,000 ($18,000 less $17,000) must be added by the minister to taxable income on Form 1040, page 1, line 21. Unless the minister has opted out of social security, the entire $18,000 is reportable for social security purposes on Schedule SE.

Establishing and Modifying the Housing Allowance

Before paying compensation

The employer should take the following steps to designate a housing allowance *before* paying compensation:

- Verify the qualified status of the minister. Does the minister meet the tests found on pages 22-30?
- Verify the qualified nature of the minister's services; *e.g.*, administering sacraments, conducting religious worship, performing management responsibilities for a church, a denomination, or an integral agency (see pages 26-28) of a church or denomination or the services performed for a parachurch or other organization (see pages 28-29).
- Determine the extent to which payment of housing expenses will be the responsibility of the minister. For example, will the utilities for a church-owned parsonage be paid by the church or the minister?
- Request that the minister estimate the housing-related expenses expected in the coming year which are the minister's responsibility.
- Adopt a written designation based on the minister's estimate. This designation may be included in minutes or resolutions of the top governing body, an employment contract, annual budget, or another appropriate document if official action on the document is recorded.

Warning

It is the responsibility of the church or other employer—not the minister—to determine if an individual qualifies as a minister in the eyes of the IRS and, therefore, qualifies for a housing allowance designation. Simply being ordained, licensed, or commissioned is often not enough to qualify for this status.

During the calendar year

The following actions should be taken during the year (after designating the housing allowance):

- The minister should keep records of allowable housing expenses incurred.
- The minister should make payments to the IRS to cover the self-employment tax (SECA) on the entire housing allowance (and other income subject to SECA) plus federal income tax on any anticipated unexpended portion of the allowance and other taxable income. This may be accomplished by submitting quarterly tax installments with Form 1040-ES, voluntary income tax withholding by the minister's employer, or spousal income tax withholding.
- The minister should identify any significant change in housing expenses and estimate the amount by which the total actual expenses may exceed the amount designated as the housing allowance.
- When housing expenses are running higher than anticipated or are expected to do so, the minister should ask the church to *prospectively* increase the housing allowance designation. A *retroactive* housing allowance increase is ineffective.
- The church should *prospectively* amend the minister's housing allowance as appropriate to reflect the anticipated change in housing expenses.

After each calendar year

The following steps should be taken after the close of each calendar year with respect to the housing allowance:

- The church should provide the minister with copies of Form W-2. An approved housing allowance paid to the minister may be included on Form W-2 in Box 14 with the explanation: "Housing Allowance." As an option, the church could provide the minister with a separate statement showing the amount of any housing allowance *paid* to or for the minister and omit the data from Form W-2.
- The minister who provides his or her own housing should compare reasonable compensation, the amount designated for housing, and actual housing expenses. The *lowest* of these amounts is excluded for income tax purposes.

  Ministers living in church-provided housing must compare the amount designated and actual housing expenses, and exclude the lowest of these amounts.

Designation limits

The IRS does not place a limit on how much of a minister's compensation may be *designated* as a housing allowance by the employing church. In a few instances, as much as 100% of the compensation may be designated. But practical and reasonable limits usually apply.

A housing allowance must not represent "unreasonable compensation" to the minister. Unfortunately, neither the IRS nor the courts have provided a clear definition of unreasonable compensation. The IRS considers the total compensation package, including the housing allowance and taxable and nontaxable fringe benefits. This amount is often compared with the church's annual budget and may be compared with other similar-sized churches.

Unless the amount is justified based on anticipated expenses, it is generally unwise for the employing church to exclude 100% of compensation. A 100% exclusion may result in very unusual reporting to the IRS that may draw questions and an audit. Officers of financial organizations often give extra scrutiny to loan or home mortgage applications of ministers where the income reflected on Form W-2 is unusually low.

Caution

How high is too high? Can even 100% of a minister's cash salary be designated as a housing allowance? Yes, but only in a few situations. The fair rental value and actual housing expense limitations usually make the 100% designation inappropriate.

Example 1: A minister provides her own housing. The fair rental value is $15,000. She anticipates spending $18,000 on housing. Should the church designate a housing allowance of $15,000 or at least $18,000? A designation of $15,000 should be made since the minister cannot exclude more than this amount.

Example 2: A minister receives a salary of $10,000 per year and provides his home. Actual housing costs are $12,000. If the church sets the housing allowance at 100% of compensation, or $10,000, the minister may exclude $10,000 for federal income tax purposes. If the church had set the housing allowance at 50% of compensation, or $5,000, only $5,000 could be excluded.

Example 3: A minister-employee has a voluntary withholding arrangement with the church, and the church sets the housing allowance at 100% of compensation. Form W-2 would show no salary (ignoring other compensation factors) but would reflect federal income tax and possibly state income tax withheld. While Form W-2 would be correctly stated, its appearance would be most unusual.

It is often best to overdesignate your parsonage allowance by a reasonable amount, subject to the fair rental value test, to allow for unexpected expenses and increases in utility costs. Any excess housing allowance designated should be shown as income on line 21 of Form 1040.

Amending the housing designation

If a minister's actual housing expenses are or will be higher than initially estimated and designated, the church may *prospectively* amend the designation during the year.

Example: The church sets the housing allowance at $1,000 per month on January 1, but housing expenses are averaging $1,200 per month. On July 1, the church approves an increase in the housing allowance to $1,600 per month. Therefore, the housing allowance for the year totals $15,600 ($6,000 for the first six months and $9,600 for the other six months). Actual housing costs are $14,400 ($1,200 for each month). The minister excludes $13,200 for federal income tax purposes: $6,000 for the first six months (limited by the designation) and $7,200 for the last six months (limited by the actual housing costs).

Remember

The housing allowance designation may be prospectively amended at any time during the year, regardless of whether the church or other employer uses a calendar or fiscal year. Changing the designation to cover expenses that have already been paid (almost all ministers use the cash basis for tax purposes) is not acceptable.

Housing allowance as a percentage of salary

Some churches set the housing allowance by applying a percentage to the total cash salary. Housing allowance percentages are often in a range of 40% to 60% of the total cash salary. Setting the housing designation based on an estimate of housing expenses for each minister is highly preferred to the percentage method. By using the percentage approach, the church may unintentionally permit an excessive housing exclusion from income or preclude a legitimate exclusion.

Housing allowance adopted by denomination

If the local congregation employs and pays you, a resolution by a national or area office of your denomination does not constitute a housing allowance designation for you. The local congregation must officially designate a part of your salary as a housing allowance.

But a resolution of your denomination can designate your housing allowance if you are employed *and* paid by a national or area office or if you are a retired minister receiving retirement funds from a denominational retirement plan.

Reporting the Housing Allowance to the Minister

The designated housing allowance may be reflected on Form W-2 in Box 14 with the notation, "Housing Allowance." Though not required, this reporting method is suggested by Publication 517.

Or, a church can report the designated housing allowance to a minister by providing a statement separate from Form W-2. This may be in a memo or letter. The statement should not be attached to your income tax returns.

Your church may erroneously include the housing allowance on your Form W-2, Box 1. If this happens, the church should prepare a corrected form.

There is no requirement for the minister to account to the church for the actual housing expenses. Many ministers consider this as an intrusion into their personal finances. However, if the church requires this reporting, based on administrative discretion, the church would prepare Form W-2 with the adjusted housing allowance excluded. Under this approach, the excluded housing is always equal to or less than the housing designation.

Tip

The designated housing allowance should always be excluded from Form W-2, Box 1, as compensation. Including the housing allowance in this box could cause unnecessary communication between the IRS and the minister.

Accounting for the Housing Allowance

Determining fair rental value

The determination of the fair rental value of church-provided housing for self-employment social security purposes is solely the responsibility of the minister. The church is not responsible to set the value. The fair rental value should be based on comparable rental values of other similar residences in the immediate neighborhood or community, comparably furnished.

One of the best methods to establish the fair rental value of your housing is to request a local realtor to estimate the value in writing. Place the estimate in your tax file and annually adjust the value for inflation and other local real estate valuation factors.

Housing allowance in excess of actual expenses or fair rental value

Some ministers erroneously believe that they may exclude every dollar of the housing *designation* adopted by the church without limitation. The housing designation is merely the starting point. If reasonable compensation, actual expenses, or the fair rental value is lower, the lowest amount is eligible for exclusion from income.

Example: A minister living in a home owned personally receives cash compensation from the church of $25,000. The church prospectively designates $20,000 as a housing allowance. The fair rental value is $21,000. Actual housing expenses for the year are $14,000. The amount excludable from income is limited to the actual housing expenses of $14,000.

Caution

Even though the fair rental value test is etched into law, there have been no changes in the sketchy guidance provided by the IRS as to how to determine the fair rental value.

Determining actual expenses

The actual amount expended for housing and furnishings is limited to amounts expended in the current calendar year. Amounts expended in a prior year cannot be carried forward to a following year through depreciation or by carrying forward actual current year expenses that exceeded amounts designated in a prior year. Housing expenses that are not used to justify a housing allowance exclusion simply have no value in future years.

Home equity loans and second mortgages

Without a home mortgage, a minister has no mortgage principal and interest amounts to exclude under a housing allowance. Also, there is no double deduction of the mortgage interest as an itemized deduction and as housing expense for purposes of the housing allowance exclusion if there is no mortgage.

What is the treatment of principal and interest payments on a second mortgage or a mortgage that has been refinanced to increase the indebtedness? This issue has not been addressed by the IRS or a court. However, it appears that an allocation of the loan payments between excludable housing expenses and nonexcludable personal expenses would be required based on the use of the additional loan proceeds.

Warning

Loan payments on home equity loans and second mortgages qualify as housing expenses only in certain instances. The use of the loan proceeds as housing expenses vs. nonhousing expenses determines whether the loan payments may be excluded for income tax purposes.

Do principal and interest payments on a home equity loan qualify as excludable housing expenses? The IRS and the Tax Court have ruled that the loan or mortgage payments are excludable as housing expenses *only* if the loan proceeds are used for housing expenses. The exclusion is not available if the loan proceeds are used for personal expenses such as the purchase of an auto or for a child's college education. The interest is only deductible on Schedule A if the note is secured.

Example: A home equity loan of $20,000 was obtained by a minister, secured by the residence. The money was used as follows: $10,000 for a new car and $10,000 to add a deck and screened-in porch to the minister's home. The home equity loan payments relating to funds used to purchase the new car are not excludable as housing expenses. Since the other $10,000 was used for housing, the payments relating to this portion of the loan qualify as housing expenses.

Other Housing Allowance Issues

Payment of the housing allowance to the minister

It is immaterial whether the payment of a properly designated cash housing allowance is a separate payment or is part of a payment that also includes other compensation. A cash housing allowance usually is included with the minister's salary check.

Cost of the housing allowance to the church

Some churches mistakenly believe that providing a housing allowance to their minister will increase the church budget. This is not true. If a portion of the minister's compensation is designated as a housing allowance, it costs the church nothing.

> **Example:** A church is paying a minister $30,000 per year but does not presently designate a housing allowance. The minister provides the home. The minister requests that the church designate a housing allowance of $10,000 per year. The church adopts a resolution reflecting compensation of $30,000 per year, of which $10,000 is a designated housing allowance. Before the designation, Form W-2 for the minister would have shown compensation of $30,000. After the designation, Form W-2 would reflect compensation of $20,000. The cash spent by the church is the same before and after the designation.

Double deduction of interest and taxes

Ministers who own their homes and itemize their deductions are eligible to deduct mortgage interest and property taxes on Schedule A even though these items are excluded from taxable income as part of the housing allowance. This is often referred to as a "double deduction."

Housing allowances for retired ministers

Pension payments, retirement allowances, or disability payments paid to a retired minister from an established plan are generally taxable as pension income. However, denominations often designate a housing allowance for retired ministers to compensate them for past services to local churches of the denomination or to the denomination or in denominational administrative positions. The housing allowance designated relates only to payments from the denominationally sponsored retirement program.

Withdrawals from a denominationally sponsored 403(b) plan, also called a tax-sheltered annuity (TSA), or 401(k) plan qualify for designation as a housing allowance. Withdrawals from a 403(b) or 401(k) plan not sponsored by a local church are not eligible for designation as a housing allowance.

Retired ministers may also exclude the rental value of a home furnished by a church or a rental allowance paid by a church as compensation for past services.

Can a local church (as contrasted with a denomination), or a nondenominational local church, designate a housing allowance for a retired minister for the church's contributions to a minister's 403(b) plan? While IRS rulings in this area are not specific, a

Remember

Payments from denominational retirement plans are generally subject to a housing allowance designation. While a local church may designate a housing allowance for a retired minister, it is unclear if the IRS will honor the designation on the minister's tax return.

church has a reasonable and supportable position to make the designation. However, it is unclear whether the IRS will accept a housing exclusion on the minister's tax return based on such a designation.

If a denomination or church reports the gross amount of pension or TSA payments on Form 1099-R and designates the housing allowance, the recipient may offset the housing expenses and insert the net amount on page 1, Form 1040. A supplementary schedule example should be attached to the tax return as follows:

Pensions and annuity income (Form 1040, line 16a)	$10,000
Less housing exclusion	8,000
Form 1040, line 16b	$2,000

For a retired minister, the amount excluded for income tax purposes is limited to the lowest of (1) the amount used to provide a home, (2) the properly designated housing allowance, or (3) the fair rental value of the furnished home, plus utilities.

A surviving spouse of a retired minister *cannot* exclude a housing allowance from income. If a minister's surviving spouse receives a rental allowance, it is includible in gross income.

Housing allowances for evangelists

Traveling evangelists may treat a portion of an honorarium received as an excludable housing allowance to the extent that the paying church designates all or a portion of the honorarium as a housing allowance in advance of payment. Honoraria payments of $600 or more in a calendar year to an evangelist require the church to issue Form 1099-MISC. The $600 reporting threshold is after excluding any properly designated housing allowances and net of expense reimbursements based on adequate substantiation.

Example: William Dalton, an ordained evangelist, preaches at Westside Church for ten days. Westside Church paid Mr. Dalton $1,500 consisting of $300 documented travel expenses, a properly designated housing allowance of $500, and a $700 honorarium. Since the honorarium exceeded $600, the church issued Mr. Dalton a Form 1099-MISC for $700.

Some itinerant evangelists form nonprofit corporations for their ministries. The nonprofit corporation may designate a housing allowance for the evangelist. This eliminates the need for each church to provide the housing designation. If an evangelist purchases a house and rents it out while traveling, only the housing expenses relating to the time at home are excludable.

Housing allowances for teachers or administrators

If you are a minister employed as a teacher or administrator by a church school, college, or university, you are performing ministerial services for purposes of the housing exclusion. However, if you perform services as a teacher or administrator on the faculty of a nonchurch college, you cannot exclude from your income a housing allowance or the value of a home that is provided to you.

INTEGRITY*Points*

- **Properly determining who qualifies for a housing allowance.** The designation of a portion of cash compensation as a housing allowance is only available to certain ministers. Ordination, licensure, or commissioning of a minister alone is not enough.

  The first integrity step for a church or parachurch organization is to determine whether an individual qualifies for the designation of a housing allowance. The various rules for ministers serving a local church, serving as evangelists or missionaries, members of religious orders, assigned by a church, or in other service positions are discussed in chapter 1.

- **Applying the limits on the exclusion.** The designation of a housing allowance for a qualified minister is an action required by a church, formally and prospectively. However, it is the minister's responsibility to determine how much of the housing allowance designation qualifies for exclusion from federal, and perhaps state, income taxes. Remarkably, the IRS does not require the reporting of the application of the housing exclusion limits. But the law and integrity require the limits be applied.

  For the vast majority of ministers, the most critical test is the fair rental value, including furnishings, plus utilities. The housing allowance designation by the church or parachurch organization (see first IntegrityPoint) is only the starting point.

  The fair rental value, including furnishings, plus utilities is admittedly a "soft" number because the guidance provided by the IRS is vague on this topic. But an honest effort to reasonably determine this number is essential.

  The excess housing allowance, which is the designated housing allowance less the lowest of the four housing exclusion limitations (see page 74), must be reported on Form 1040, Line 21. This results in the excess housing allowance subjected to federal, and perhaps state, income taxes.

Housing Allowance Worksheet

Minister Living in a Parsonage
Owned by or Rented by the Church

Minister's name: ______________________________

For the period ____________________, 200__ to ____________________, 200__

Date designation approved ____________________, 200__

Allowable Housing Expenses *(expenses paid by minister from current income)*

	Estimated Expenses	Actual
Utilities *(gas, electricity, water)* and trash collection	$ ________	$ ________
Local telephone expense *(base charge)*	________	________
Decoration and redecoration	________	________
Structural maintenance and repair	________	________
Landscaping, gardening, and pest control	________	________
Furnishings *(purchase, repair, replacement)*	________	________
Personal property insurance on minister-owned contents	________	________
Personal property taxes on contents	________	________
Umbrella liability insurance	________	________
Subtotal	________	
10% allowance for unexpected expenses	________	
TOTAL	**$** ________	**$** ________ (A)
Properly designated housing allowance		**$** ________ (B)

The amount excludable from income for federal income tax purposes is the *lower* of A or B.

Housing Allowance Worksheet

Minister Living in Home

Minister Owns or Is Buying

Minister's name: ____

For the period ____________________, 200__ to ____________________, 200__

Date designation approved __________________________, 200__

Allowable Housing Expenses *(expenses paid by minister from current income)*

	Estimated Expenses	Actual	
Down payment on purchase of housing	$ ________	$ ________	
Housing loan principal and interest payments	________	________	
Real estate commission, escrow fees	________	________	
Real property taxes	________	________	
Personal property taxes on contents	________	________	
Homeowner's insurance	________	________	
Personal property insurance on contents	________	________	
Umbrella liability insurance	________	________	
Structural maintenance and repair	________	________	
Landscaping, gardening, and pest control	________	________	
Furnishings *(purchase, repair, replacement)*	________	________	
Decoration and redecoration	________	________	
Utilities *(gas, electricity, water)* and trash collection	________	________	
Local telephone expense *(base charge)*	________	________	
Homeowner's association dues/condominium fees	________	________	
Subtotal	________		
10% allowance for unexpected expenses	________		
TOTAL	**$** ________	**$** ________	(A)
Properly designated housing allowance		**$** ________	(B)
Fair rental value of home, including furnishings, plus utilities		**$** ________	(C)

The amount excludable from income for federal income tax purposes is the *lowest* of A, B, or C.

Housing Allowance Worksheet

Minister Living in Home

Minister Is Renting

Minister's name: ____

For the period ____________________, 200__ to ____________________, 200__

Date designation approved ________________________, 200__

Allowable Housing Expenses *(expenses paid by minister from current income)*

	Estimated Expenses	Actual	
Housing rental payments	$ ________	$ ________	
Personal property insurance on minister-owned contents	________	________	
Personal property taxes on contents	________	________	
Umbrella liability	________	________	
Structural maintenance and repair	________	________	
Landscaping, gardening, and pest control	________	________	
Furnishings *(purchase, repair, replacement)*	________	________	
Decoration and redecoration	________	________	
Utilities *(gas, electricity, water)* and trash collection	________	________	
Local telephone expense *(base charge)*	________	________	
Mobile home space rental	________	________	
Subtotal	________		
10% allowance for unexpected expenses	________		
TOTAL	**$** ________	**$** ________	(A)
Properly designated housing allowance		**$** ________	(B)

The amount excludable from income for federal income tax purposes is the *lower* of A or B.

Business Expenses

In This Chapter

- Accountable and nonaccountable expense reimbursement plans
- Substantiating and reporting business expenses
- Travel and transportation expenses
- Auto expense deductions
- Home-office rules
- Other business expenses
- Allocation of business expenses

Most ministers spend several thousands of dollars each year on church-related business expenses. For example, the ministry-related portion of auto expenses is often a major cost. You only have two choices: try to deduct the expenses for tax purposes or have the expenses reimbursed by the church under an accountable expense reimbursement plan. You will almost always save tax dollars if your expenses are reimbursed.

Business and professional expenses fall into three basic categories: expenses reimbursed under an accountable plan, expenses paid under a nonaccountable plan, and unreimbursed expenses. The last two categories are treated the same for tax purposes.

The reimbursement of an expense never changes the character of the item from personal to business. Business expenses are business whether or not they are reimbursed. Personal expenses are always nondeductible and nonreimbursable. If a personal expense is inadvertently reimbursed by the employer, the minister should immediately refund the money to the employer.

To be deductible or reimbursable, a business expense must be both ordinary and necessary. An *ordinary* expense is one that is common and accepted in your field. A *necessary* expense is one that is helpful and appropriate for your field. An expense does not have to be indispensable to be considered necessary.

Key Issue

Combining an accountable expense reimbursement plan with a housing allowance or health reimbursement arrangement (or any other fringe benefit plan) is not permissible. These concepts are each covered under separate sections of the tax law and cannot be commingled.

Accountable and Nonaccountable Expense Reimbursement Plans

An accountable plan is a reimbursement or expense allowance arrangement established by your church that requires (1) a business purpose for the expenses, (2) substantiation of expenses to the employer, and (3) the return of any excess reimbursements. A sample plan is included in the 2009 edition of *The Zondervan Church and Nonprofit Tax & Financial Guide.*

The substantiation of expenses and the return of excess reimbursements must be handled within a reasonable time. The following methods meet the "reasonable time" definition:

- The fixed date method applies if
  - an advance is made within 30 days of when an expense is paid or incurred;
  - an expense is substantiated to the employer within 60 days after the expense is paid or incurred; and
  - any excess amount is returned to the church within 120 days after the expense is paid or incurred.
- The periodic statement method applies if
  - the employer provides employees with a periodic statement that sets forth the amount paid that is more than substantiated expenses under the arrangement;
  - the statements are provided at least quarterly; and
  - the employer requests that the employee provide substantiation for any additional expenses that have not yet been substantiated and/or return any amounts remaining unsubstantiated within 120 days of the statement.

Caution

Documentation for business expenses must be submitted to the church or other employer on a timely basis—within 60 days after the expense was paid or incurred. While the 60 days is a timeliness "safe harbor" vs. a fixed time limit, it is clear that documentation submitted semiannually or annually should not be reimbursed under an accountable plan.

If you substantiate your business expenses and any unused payments are returned, expense reimbursements have no impact on your taxes. The expenses reimbursed are not included on Form W-2 or deducted on your tax return.

Example 1: Your church adopts an accountable reimbursement plan using the "fixed date method." The church authorizes salary of $26,000 and agrees to pay business expenses up to $10,000.

During the year, you substantiate $9,000 of expenses under the accountable guidelines. The church provides you with a Form W-2 reflecting compensation of $26,000. The substantiated expenses of $9,000 are not reported to the IRS by the church or on your tax return.

The church retains the $1,000 difference between the amount budgeted by the church and the amount reimbursed to the minister. (See page 92 for an example where the church pays the balance in the expense reimbursement plan to the minister.)

Example 2: Your church authorizes a salary of $23,000 plus an auto allowance of $5,000 and $3,000 for other business expenses. The church does not require or receive any substantiation for the auto or other business expenses. This is a nonaccountable reimbursement plan.

The church should provide you with a Form W-2 reflecting compensation of $31,000. The auto and other business expenses you incur could be claimed on Form 2106 (2106-EZ) and Schedule A as miscellaneous deductions if you are reporting as an employee for income tax purposes.

The IRS disallows deductions for a portion of unreimbursed business expenses on the premise that the expenses can be allocated to your excludable housing allowance (see allocation of business expenses on pages 112-13). This is another reason that every minister should comply with the accountable expense reimbursement rules. The goal should be to eliminate all unreimbursed business expenses.

Accountable expense reimbursement plans should not be combined with other fringe benefit plans or a housing allowance. Too often, ministers have been advised that the employer can establish a general reimbursement account to cover business expenses, housing expenses, dependent care expenses, out-of-pocket medical expenses, and educational expenses. While all of these items can be handled in a tax beneficial manner for a minister, they are subject to separate rules in the tax law. Some of the items are subject to the nondiscrimination rules, others are not. Dollar limits must be separately established in some instances, and not in others. Housing expenses for a minister-owned home are not reimbursable at all.

The timing of documenting expenses for reimbursement is of utmost importance. Under the fixed date method (see page 90), the IRS provides a safe harbor of 60 days after the expense is paid or incurred. In other words, the IRS will contest a reimbursement, based on timeliness of submitting the documentation, if the documentation is provided to the employer. Does this mean that the IRS will disallow expenses reimbursed within 61 days? Not necessarily. It simply means 60 days is a safe harbor as a "reasonable time."

Example: A church approves $50,000 of compensation for the pastor and tells her to let the church know at the end of the year how much she has spent on business expenses, and they will show the net amount on Form W-2. Is this valid? No. The salary must be established separately from expense reimbursements. Further, even if an accountable expense reimbursement plan is used, the annual submission of expense documentation would fail the timeliness test for expenses incurred in all but the last portion of the year.

Nonaccountable expense reimbursement plans

If you do not substantiate your expenses to the church, or if the amount of the reimbursement exceeds your actual expenses and the excess is not returned to the employer within a reasonable period, your tax life becomes more complicated.

Nonaccountable reimbursements and excess reimbursements over IRS mileage or per diem limits must be included in your gross income and reported as wages on Form W-2. If your church pays you an "allowance" for certain business expenses, it represents taxable compensation. The term "allowance" implies that the payment is not based upon documented expenses, does not meet the adequate accounting requirements for an accountable plan, and must be included in your income.

Warning

Many ministers are paid expense "allowances." These payments accomplish nothing in terms of good stewardship. "Allowances" are fully taxable for income and social security tax purposes. Ministers must then resort to trying to deduct their expenses—much of which will be limited by the tax law—instead of receiving a full reimbursement.

Unreimbursed expenses or expenses reimbursed under a nonaccountable plan can be deducted only as itemized miscellaneous deductions and only to the extent that they, with your other miscellaneous deductions, exceed 2% of your adjusted gross income. Unreimbursed expenses are not deductible if you are an employee for income tax purposes and do not itemize.

The unused "balance" in an accountable expense reimbursement plan

If your church pays you the unused balance in an accountable expense reimbursement plan (perhaps calling the payment of the "balance" a bonus), the expense reimbursement plan becomes nonaccountable for the entire year. (This is also referred to as a "recharacterization of income.") All payments under a nonaccountable plan are reportable as compensation on Form W-2.

Example: Your church sets your salary at $25,000 and agrees to reimburse your business expenses under an accountable plan for up to $10,000. Your reimbursed expenses are $9,000 and the church gave you a bonus for the $1,000 difference. Because of the "bonus" arrangement, all reimbursements made under the plan become nonaccountable. The entire $35,000 must be reported by the church as compensation on Form W-2.

Caution

The best expense reimbursement plan for a minister is one that pays 100% of church-related expenses. Too often, churches place dollar limits on these plans. With a dollar limit, any money left in the plan at the end of the year must stay with the church for the reimbursements to be tax-free. If the balance is paid to the minister, all payments for the year become taxable.

Substantiating and Reporting Business Expenses

Substantiating business expenses

For expenses to be allowed as deductions, you must show that you spent the money and that you spent it for a legitimate business reason. To prove that you spent the money, you generally need to provide documentary evidence that can be confirmed by a third party. Canceled checks, credit card or other receipts are an excellent starting point. To the IRS, third-party verification is important; if business expenses are paid in cash, be sure to get a receipt.

Documenting a business expense can be time-consuming. The IRS is satisfied if you note the five Ws on the back of your credit card slip or other receipt:

- Why (business purpose)
- What (description, including itemized accounting of cost)
- When (date)
- Where (location)
- Who (names of those for whom the expense was incurred; *e.g.*, meals and entertainment)

Remember

When a minister provides a listing of business expenses to the church or other employer—this is only a report, not documentation. Documentary evidence is much more than a report. It involves hard-copy support of the five Ws (why, what, when, where, and who).

The only exception to the documentation rules is if your individual outlays for business expenses, other than for lodging, come to less than $75. The IRS does not require receipts for such expenses, although the five Ws are still required. You always need a receipt for lodging expenses regardless of the amount. An employer may apply a documentation threshold lower than $75.

Use of a church credit card can be helpful to charge church-related business expenses. However, the use of a credit card does not automatically provide substantiation without additional documentation; *e.g.*, business purpose and business relationship.

While you are traveling out of town as an employee, your church may use a per diem for reimbursements instead of actual costs of meals (see pages 96-97). The per diem is not subject to the 50% limitation on meal and entertainment expenses.

For more detailed information, refer to IRS Publication 463, *Travel, Entertainment, Gift and Car Expenses.*

Forms on which expenses are reportable

Only the portion of business and professional expenses directly attributable to your Schedule C (C-EZ) income (self-employment activities) should be deducted on Schedule C (C-EZ). The portion of these expenses related to activities as an employee of the church should be deducted on Form 2106 (2106-EZ). If you receive reimbursement for any business or professional expenses and adequately account to the church under an accountable plan, you should not report the expenses on Form 2106 (2106-EZ) or Schedule C (C-EZ).

Travel and Transportation Expenses

The terms "travel" and "transportation" are often used interchangeably, but each has a distinct meaning for tax purposes. Travel is the broader category, including not only transportation expenses, but the cost of meals, lodging, and incidental expenses as well. To deduct travel expenses—including expenses you incur for meals, phone calls, cab fares, and so forth on the road—the business purpose must take you away from home overnight or require a rest stop. If you do not spend the night, you can deduct only your transportation costs.

> **Key Issue**
>
> Travel expenses must be divided between your self-employment activities reported on Schedule C (C-EZ) and activities as an employee reported on Form 2106 (2106-EZ). Any unreimbursed travel expense that is also a meal or entertainment expense is subject to the 50% limitation for business meals and entertainment.

Travel expenses

Many different expenses can add up on a business trip: air and taxi fares, costs of lodging, baggage charges, rental cars, tips, laundry and cleaning, and telephone expenses. You can deduct 100% of these expenses plus 50% of the meal and entertainment expenses you incurred while you were away, provided you meet certain guidelines:

- The trip must have a business purpose.
- The expenses cannot be "lavish and extravagant."
- You must be away from home long enough to require sleep or rest.

Deriving some personal pleasure from a trip doesn't disqualify it from being deductible. The IRS does, however, apply some important limitations to the tax treatment of foreign travel expenses (see below).

If you are traveling within the United States, you can deduct all transportation costs, plus the costs of business-related meals (subject to the 50% limit) and lodging, if business was the primary reason for the trip. If you need to stay over Saturday night to get a lower airfare, the hotel and meal expenses for Saturday will generally be deductible. If the trip is primarily personal, none of your transportation costs can be deducted, but you can deduct other business-related travel expenses.

If you are reimbursed for travel expenses and adequately account to the church, you should not report your travel expenses on Form 2106 (2106-EZ). Further, you are not subject to the 50% limitation for business meals and entertainment.

International travel

Costs are deductible if you take an international trip for business reasons. If your trip is seven days or less, you can deduct your entire airfare even if you spend most of your time on personal activities. If you spend some days for personal reasons, your hotel, car rental, and meal costs are not deductible for those days. If your trip is more than seven days and you spend more than 25% of your time on personal activities, you must allocate all your expenses between business and personal time.

Trips to the Holy Land

Ministers often travel to the Holy Land to more closely identify with the area where Christ taught, preached, and ministered. In spite of all the obvious ministerial advantages of visiting the Holy Land, the applicability of tax deductions or tax-free reimbursements for such trips is not as clear.

Generally, no deduction or reimbursement is allowed for travel as a form of education. However, travel expense may be deductible or reimbursable if the travel is necessary to engage in an activity that gives rise to a business deduction relating to education.

A number of factors must be considered before the tax status of a Holy Land trip may be determined. To qualify as a deductible or reimbursable ministry-related expense, the trip must meet the general educational expense rules outlined on pages 109-10. Holy Land trips are also subject to the international travel rules as described above.

If you can answer "Yes" to the following questions, your expenses are more likely to qualify for reimbursement or as a deduction:

- Did the employing church require or strongly suggest that you make the trip to the Holy Land?
- Is this your first trip to the Holy Land? If you have a pattern of making the pilgrimage every few years, the trip is less likely to qualify as education expense.
- Will you be receiving college credit for the trip from a recognized educational institution? Is there a course syllabus?
- Is the trip organized for the purpose of study in the Holy Land and led by a Bible scholar?
- Did you take notes and pictures of places visited? If most of your photos include family members, the trip is less likely to qualify as education expense.

A tax deduction or reimbursement by a church for a minister's trip to the Holy Land should be made only after careful consideration of the facts and circumstances and the applicable tax rules.

Furlough travel

A missionary on furlough may qualify for travel status. The purpose of the travel must be primarily business, such as deputation, reporting to constituents, or education, and the missionary's primary residence must remain in another country. Incidental costs for personal travel such as vacation, nonbusiness spousal costs, and travel costs of children are not deductible. If these expenses are paid by a church or missions organization, they should be included in compensation on Form W-2.

Travel expenses of your spouse or children

If your spouse or children accompany you on your business trip, their expenses are non-reimbursable and nondeductible unless they qualify for employee treatment and

- the travel of the spouse or dependent is for a bona fide business purpose; and
- the employee substantiates the time, place, amount, and business purpose of the travel under an accountable business expense reimbursement plan.

If there is not a bona fide purpose or the payments are not made under an accountable plan, the expenses are includible as income on the your Form W-2.

The IRS and the courts evaluate the following criteria to determine whether a bona fide business purpose exists:

- The spouse's function must be necessary; *i.e.,* result in desired business (ministry) benefits to the church.
- The spouse's contributions to the church must be those which cannot efficiently be performed (or performed at all) by the minister-employee alone.
- The spouse's services must augment the minister's purpose for the trip.
- The benefit to the church must be substantial.

> **Remember**
>
> Spouses and children often accompany ministers to Christian conferences and other work-related meetings. Their expenses are reimbursable under an accountable plan or deductible only if you can document a business (ministry) purpose. For example, a minister's wife attends certain meetings at a conference and reports to the church on those meetings.

Per diem allowance

The IRS has provided per diem allowances under which the amount of away-from-home meals and lodging expenses may be substantiated. These rates may not be used to claim deductions for unreimbursed expenses. Higher per diem rates apply to certain locations annually identified by the IRS. For more information on these rates, see IRS

Publication 1542. The per diem rates for travel inside the continental United States (based on a October 1 to September 30 fiscal period):

	Lodging	Meals and Incidentals	Total
2008-09 standard method	$70	$39	$109
2007-08 standard method	70	39	109

Federal per diem rates for travel outside the continental United States, including Alaska, Hawaii, Puerto Rico, the northern Mariana Islands, U.S. possessions, and all other foreign localities, are published monthly at http://www.state.gov/m/a/als/prdm/.

Travel expenses for pastors with interim appointments

Many ministers accept or are appointed to temporary ministerial positions with churches. For example, a semiretired minister may own his or her own home and decide to not relocate for a temporary assignment. So, the minister drives 60 miles each week to serve a church that does not have a resident minister. Or, a minister may have secular employment in a city where he or she lives and is invited to preach each Sunday on an interim basis for a church located 30 miles from his or her home. The minister is able to maintain the secular job and fill the ministerial assignment with periodic trips to the church.

If a minister temporarily changes his or her job location, his or her tax home does not change to the new location. This means that the minister can deduct or be reimbursed for his or her travel expenses (auto or public transportation expense and meals) to and from the temporary location. If the minister stays overnight at the temporary location, food and lodging expenses at the temporary location become deductible or reimbursable.

When is a job location temporary? A minister will be treated as being temporarily away from home during any period of employment that is realistically expected to last and actually does last a year or less. Daily transportation expenses are deductible or reimbursable by the church if the minister qualifies for temporary work status. These rules may also apply to a minister serving more than one church (a circuit arrangement).

> **Caution**
>
> Ministers often drive significant distances each week to serve their churches. Auto expenses become a major issue. The transportation expenses are deductible or reimbursable only if the period of employment is for an indefinite period. Simply being classified as an "interim" minister by a church does not justify indefinite status.

However, if employment away from home is realistically expected to last for more than one year or there is no realistic expectation that the employment will last for one year or less, the employment will be treated as indefinite, regardless of whether it actually exceeds one year. In this case, daily transportation expenses are not deductible or reimbursable by the church.

Example 1: A minister lives in town A and accepts an interim pulpit assignment in town B, which is 60 miles away from town A. The assignment in town B is realistically expected to be completed in 18 months, but in fact it was completed in 10 months. The employment in town B is indefinite because it was realistically expected that the work in town B would last longer than one year, even though it actually lasted less than a year. Accordingly, travel expenses paid or incurred in town B are nondeductible.

If employment away from home in a single location initially is realistically expected to last for one year or less, but at some later date the employment is realistically expected to exceed one year, that employment will be treated as temporary (in the absence of facts and circumstances indicating otherwise) until the date that the minister's realistic expectation changes.

Example 2: An interim assignment began as a temporary assignment (a six-month assignment that was extended for a second six-month period), but at the 365th day of employment it was apparent that the contract would be extended for an additional period. At that time, the minister no longer has a realistic expectation that his or her employment would last for one year or less. Thus, the expenses the minister incurred after that 365th day were not deductible.

When a minister's realistic expectation changes—*i.e.,* when the minister realistically expects the initially temporary employment to exceed one year—the employment becomes indefinite for the remaining term of employment. In other words, the employment can become indefinite before the end of the one-year period if, before the end of that period, the minister realistically expects that his or her employment will exceed one year.

Example 3: A minister accepted a temporary ministerial assignment, which the minister realistically expected would be completed in nine months. After eight months, the minister was asked to remain for seven more months (for a total stay of 15 months). Although the minister's employment is temporary for the first eight months and travel expenses during that period are deductible, the minister's employment for the remaining seven months is indefinite, and the minister's travel expenses for that seven-month period are not deductible. If, after working on the assignment only three months, the minister was asked to extend his or her employment for 10 months, only the travel expenses incurred during the first three months would be deductible.

In effect, the IRS takes the position that part of a period of employment that is more than a year will still be treated as temporary if the taxpayer reasonably expected that the employment would last for a year or less when the employment started. The employment won't be treated as indefinite until the taxpayer's expectations change.

If a minister is not told how long an assignment is expected to last, other factors will have to be taken into account to determine whether it can reasonably be expected to last more than one year. Merely being classified as an interim minister by a church does not justify indefinite status. Also, the fewer connections that a minister keeps with his or her former work location, the less likely it is that the new assignment will be treated as merely temporary.

Auto Expense Deductions

A minister's car expenses are deductible or reimbursable to the extent they are for business (or income producing) rather than personal use. Generally, only those expenses that are necessary to drive and maintain a car that is used to go from one workplace to another are deductible. However, in some limited situations, the expense of driving between home and a workplace is deductible (see pages 106-8).

Auto expenses incurred by an employee and reimbursed under an accountable plan are offset against the reimbursement, which is excludable from the employee's gross income. Generally, unreimbursed employee auto expenses may be claimed only as a miscellaneous itemized deduction on Schedule A, subject to the 2% floor.

Mileage and actual expense methods

In determining your deduction for the business use of a personal car, you can use one of two methods to figure your deduction: the standard mileage rate or the actual expense method. Generally, you can choose the method that gives you the greater deduction. If you use the actual expense method and accelerated depreciation for the first year your car was placed in service, you may not use the standard mileage method in a subsequent year. However, if you use the standard mileage method for the first year your car was placed in service, you may use either method in subsequent years.

Standard mileage rate method

If you are paid the maximum mileage rate of 50.5 cents per mile for January 1 to June 30 and 58.5 cents per mile for July 1 to December 31, 2008, and you provide the time, place, and business purpose of your driving, you have made an adequate accounting of your automobile expenses.

If the church does not reimburse you for auto expenses or reimburses you under a nonaccountable plan, you may deduct business miles on Form 2106 (2106-EZ). The total from Form 2106 (2106-EZ) is carried to Schedule A, Miscellaneous Deductions.

The standard mileage rate, which includes depreciation and maintenance costs, is based on the government's estimate of the average cost of operating an automobile. Depending upon the make, age, and cost of the car, the mileage rate may be more or less

Remember

The standard mileage rate may generate a lower deduction than using actual expenses in some instances. But the simplicity of the standard mileage method is a very compelling feature.

than your actual auto expense. If you use the mileage rate, you also may deduct parking fees and tolls and the business portion of personal property tax. All auto-related taxes must be claimed on Schedule A for employees.

If you used the standard mileage rate for the business use of your car, depreciation was included in that rate. The rate of depreciation that was allowed in the standard mileage rate may be found in IRS Publication 463.

The standard mileage rate may also be used for leased autos (see page 104 for additional information, "Leasing your car").

- **Conditions on use of mileage rate.** You may not use the mileage rate if
  - you have claimed depreciation under MACRS, ACRS, or another accelerated method, or
  - you have claimed first-year expenses under Section 179.
- **Use of mileage rate in first year.** If you choose the standard mileage rate for the first year the car is in service, you may use the standard mileage rate or actual expense method in later years. If you do not choose the standard mileage rate in the first year, you may not use it for that car in any year.

  By choosing to use the mileage rate in the first year your car is in service, you may not use the MACRS method of depreciation for the car in a later year. Also, you may not claim a deduction under Section 179. If you switch to the actual expense method in a later year before your automobile is fully depreciated, you must use the straight-line method of depreciation.

Actual expense method

The actual expense method is a permitted alternative method for ministers. This method may be preferential when operating costs exceed the deduction allowed under the standard mileage rate method. However, even when the actual expense method exceeds the mileage method, the simplicity of the mileage method may outweigh the tax savings.

If you have kept accurate records, determining your deduction for most expenses should be straightforward. Generally, the amount of depreciation you may claim and the method you use to calculate it depend on when you purchased your auto and began to use it for ministerial purposes.

Under the actual expense method, you can use either accelerated or straight-line depreciation. As the names imply, the accelerated method front-loads the depreciation, giving you larger deductions sooner. The straight-line method gives you the same depreciation deduction every year.

With either method, you calculate your depreciation deduction just as you would for any other asset used for business purposes. Your "depreciable basis" is the purchase price of the car multiplied by the percentage you use it for business purposes.

Allowable expenses under the actual expense method include

gas and oil	interest on auto loan
repairs	lease payments
tires	automobile club membership
batteries	car washes and waxes
insurance	supplies, such as antifreeze
license plates	parking fees and tolls

Warning

You have an important decision to make the first year you put a car into service. You will generally want to use the standard mileage rate in that first year. If you do not use the standard mileage rate in the first year, you may not use it for that car in any year.

Depreciating your car

Depreciation is an allowance for wear and tear on your car. To compensate for this loss of value, the tax law allows you to recover the cost of your car over a period of five years.

The first step in computing depreciation is to determine the business basis of the car. This is generally the purchase price multiplied by the business use percentage. The purchase price includes any carrying charges that are not identifiable as interest or insurance, as well as destination and dealer preparation charges, reduced by the amount of any rebate paid to a customer by a car manufacturer.

Typical vehicle depreciation is computed using the 200% declining balance method. You take only half a year's depreciation in the first year, no matter when actual use began, and half a year when the car is sold or traded in. This is the half-year convention. This rule spreads the depreciation deduction over six years.

The following percentages represent the allowed depreciation by year:

Year one	20.00%
Year two	32.00%
Year three	19.20%
Year four	11.52%
Year five	11.52%
Year six	5.76%
	100.00%

The so-called "luxury auto limit" places a ceiling on the annual depreciation deduction you can claim for a passenger automobile based on the date you place the automobile in service. Some large vehicles are not classified as passenger vehicles and are not subject to the luxury auto limits, but are still covered by the business-use substantiation rules. Examples of vehicles that do not meet the passenger vehicle definition include minivans or sport utility

Tip

While the actual method is one of your options for obtaining a reimbursement or taking a deduction for auto expenses, it requires significantly more record-keeping than the mileage method. For example, you still need to maintain a mileage log so you can prorate costs between business and personal miles.

vehicles, with a gross weight rating, when loaded to capacity, above 6,000 pounds. For luxury vehicles placed in service in 2008, the depreciation deduction cannot exceed the dollar limits indicated below:

Tax Year	Used Passenger Autos	New Passenger Autos
1st Tax Year	$3,060	$4,800
2nd Tax Year	4,900	4,800
3rd Tax Year	2,850	2,960
Each Succeeding Year	1,775	1,775

The luxury car limitations do not permanently deprive you from recovering the cost of your car. They merely postpone a portion of depreciation deductions to later years by placing a cap on the amount of depreciation that may be claimed in any year. The part of an otherwise allowable deduction may be taken after the normal recovery period.

If your car is used for both business and personal driving, depreciation is computed only on the business portion of the car's basis. Because depreciation is computed on the business portion of your car, your basis can change each year if your percentage of business use varies.

Example: You purchased a used car on May 15, 2008, for $20,000. During 2008, you drove the car a total of 10,000 miles. Ministerial miles were 6,000. Your depreciation deduction is $1,740 using the 200% declining balance method. Bonus depreciation was not elected.

- Percentage of business use

Business miles	6,000	
Total miles	10,000	= 60%

- Business portion of basis

Purchase price	$20,000
Business percentage	60%
	$12,000

- Depreciation deduction

Business portion of basis	$12,000
Depreciation percentage/year one	20%
	$ 2,400

- Maximum allowable depreciation

$3,060 x 60% business	= $ 1,836

Driving an employer-provided vehicle

When a congregation provides a car to a minister, the congregation must report the personal use of the car as income on Form W-2 or 1099-MISC. However, when a minister pays the congregation the fair market value of the personal use of the car, no income results to the minister. Partial payment to the congregation reduces the minister's income by the amount of the payment.

When a car is used for both business and personal purposes, an allocation between the two types of use must be made on the basis of the number of miles driven. The amount included in the minister's compensation is generally based on one of the following valuation rules (for more information, see the 2009 edition of *The Zondervan Church and Nonprofit Tax & Financial Guide*):

> **Caution**
>
> One of the best fringe benefits for a minister is when the church or other employer provides a vehicle. However, unless the car is parked at the church when not in use, it still requires maintaining a mileage log. Personal (including commuting) miles driven must either be reimbursed to the employer or the tax-value must be placed on Form W-2.

➤ **Cents-per-mile valuation rule.** Generally, this rule may be used if the employer reasonably expects that the vehicle will be regularly used in the employer's trade or business, and if the vehicle is driven at least 10,000 miles a year and is primarily used by employees. This valuation rule is available only if the fair market value of the vehicle, as of the date the vehicle was first made available for personal use by employees, does not exceed a specified value set by the IRS. For 2008, this value is $15,000.

The value of the personal use of the vehicle is computed by multiplying the number of miles driven for personal purposes by the current IRS standard mileage rate (50.5 cents per mile for January 1 to June 30 and 58.5 cents per mile for July 1 to December 31, 2008). For this valuation rule, personal use is "any use of the vehicle other than use in the employee's trade or business of being an employee of the employer."

➤ **Commuting valuation rule.** This rule may be used to determine the value of personal use only where the following conditions are met:

- ☐ The vehicle is owned or leased by the employer and is provided to one or more employees for use in connection with the employer's trade or business and is used as such.
- ☐ The employer requires the employee to commute to and/or from work in the vehicle for bona fide noncompensatory business reasons. One example of a bona fide noncompensatory business reason is the availability of the vehicle to an employee who is on-call and must have access to the vehicle when at home.
- ☐ The employer has a written policy that prohibits employees from using the vehicle for personal purposes other than for commuting or *de minimis* personal use such as a stop for a personal errand on the way home from work.
- ☐ The employee required to use the vehicle for commuting is not a "control" employee of the employer. A control employee is generally defined as any employee who is an officer of the employer whose compensation equals or exceeds $50,000 or is a director of the employer whose compensation equals or exceeds $100,000.

The personal use of an employer-provided vehicle that meets the above conditions is valued at $1.50 per one-way commute, or $3.00 per day.

- **Annual lease valuation rule.** Under this rule, the fair market value of a vehicle is determined and that value is used to determine the annual lease value amount by referring to an annual lease value table published by the IRS. The annual lease value corresponding to this fair market value, multiplied by the personal use percentage, is the amount to be added to the employee's gross income. If the organization provides the fuel, 5.5 cents per mile must be added to the annual lease value. Amounts reimbursed by the employee are offset.

  The fair market value of a vehicle owned by an employer is generally the employer's cost of purchasing the vehicle (including taxes and fees). The fair market value of a vehicle leased by an employer generally is either the manufacturer's suggested retail price less 8%, the dealer's invoice plus 4%, or the retail value as reported in a nationally recognized publication that regularly reports automobile retail values.

Leasing your car

A minister who leases a car and uses it in connection with the work of the church is generally able to deduct part or all of lease payments as a rental deduction. However, business use is typically less than 100%. Therefore, the rental deduction is scaled down in proportion to the personal use. For example, a minister who uses a leased car 80% for business may deduct only 80% of the lease payments.

Additionally, the tax law is designed to bring lease payments in line with the "luxury auto" limits placed on depreciation deductions for purchased cars. For cars first leased in 2008, a "luxury auto" is one that costs more than $15,000. So, leasing a "luxury" car may not give you a tax break over buying one. However, nontax considerations may be important in the lease vs. buy decision.

The mileage method may also be used for the deduction or reimbursement of expenses for a leased car.

Commuting

Personal mileage is never deductible. Commuting expenses are nondeductible personal expenses.

Unless your home-office qualifies as a home-office under the tax law (see pages 107-8), travel from home to church (a regular work location) and return for church services and other work at the church is commuting and is not deductible or reimbursable. The same rule applies to multiple trips made in the same day.

The cost of traveling between your home and a

> **Key Issue**
>
> Churches (and other employers) and ministers often struggle to define commuting miles. It is a very important issue because commuting miles should not be reimbursed by an employer or deducted by a minister. The key to understanding commuting miles is defining regular and temporary work locations.

temporary work location is generally deductible or reimbursable. Once you arrive at the first work location, temporary or regular, you may deduct trips between work locations.

A regular place of business is any location at which you work or perform services on a regular basis. These services may be performed every week, for example, or merely on a set schedule. A temporary place of business is any location at which you perform services on an irregular or short-term (*i.e.,* generally a matter of days or weeks) basis.

Commuting vs. Business Miles

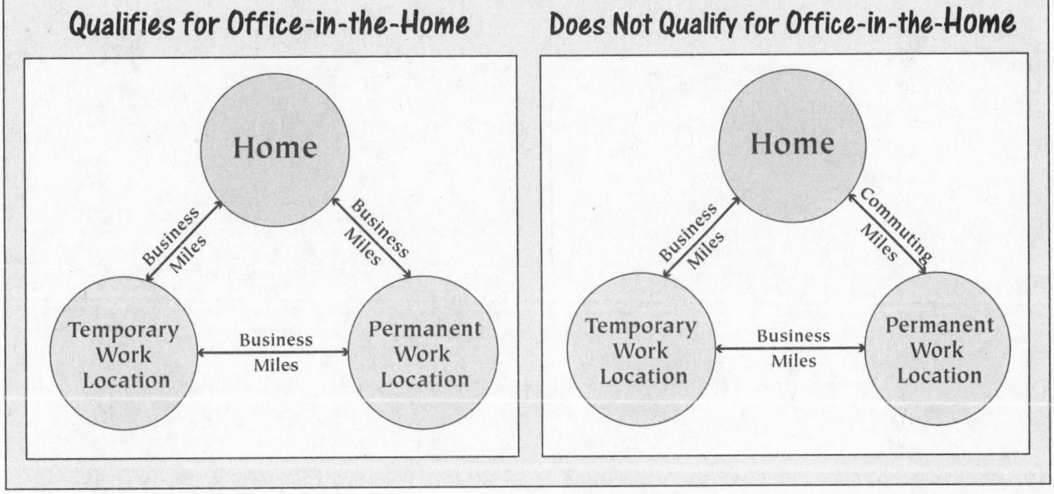

If you make calls in a certain nursing home nearly every day, it would qualify as a regular work location. However, if you only visit the nursing home a few days each month, it would generally qualify as a temporary work location.

Example 1: A minister, not qualifying for an office at home, drives from home to the church. This trip is commuting and treated as personal mileage.

The minister leaves the church and drives to a hospital to call on a member. From the hospital, the minister drives to the home of a prospect to make a call. These trips qualify for business mileage regardless if the hospital qualifies as a regular or a temporary work location.

From the prospect's house, the minister drives home. This trip is also deductible since the minister is driving from a temporary work location.

Example 2: A minister, not qualifying for an office at home, drives from home to a hospital to call on a member. The hospital is typically a temporary work location. This trip is deductible.

The minister then drives to a member's office to make a call and then returns to the minister's office at the church. The trips to this point are deductible as business expenses because they are all trips between work locations. The minister then drives to his home. This trip is commuting and is not deductible because the minister is driving from a regular work location to a nonwork location.

Business Miles Do Not Start at Home If—

- ❐ You have a personal computer in your home office and you or another member of your family occasionally uses the personal computer for personal use.
- ❐ Your home office is in your bedroom, your living room, or any other room where the space is shared for church work and family living.
- ❐ The church has an adequate office. You do most of your work there but work at home once in a while.
- ❐ The church expects you to use the church office for your work, but you prefer to work at home because it is convenient to you.

Documentation of auto expenses

To support your automobile expense deduction or reimbursement, automobile expenses must be substantiated by adequate records. A weekly or monthly mileage log that identifies dates, destinations, business purposes, and odometer readings in order to allocate total mileage between business and personal use is a basic necessity if you use the mileage method. If you use the actual expense method, a mileage log and supporting documentation on expenses is required.

Remember

For your records to withstand an IRS audit, use a daily mileage log to document business vs. personal mileage. Whether you keep a notepad in the car or track the data in a PDA, some type of log is the best approach to submitting data for reimbursement from your employer or taking a tax deduction.

Reporting auto expenses

If you are reimbursed for automobile expenses under an accountable expense plan, you should not report your travel expenses on Form 2106 (2106-EZ). This type of reimbursement eliminates the need for income or social security tax reporting by the church or the minister. If you do not have an accountable expense reimbursement plan, automobile expenses are reported on Form 2106 (2106-EZ) for minister-employees.

Home-Office Rules

Rarely is it advantageous or even appropriate for a minister to claim office-in-the-home deductions (Form 8829). A home office provided by a minister does not generate any deductible or reimbursable expenses if all the housing expenses are already treated as tax-free via a housing allowance. Even if there is no home-office expense deduction or reimbursement available to a minister, qualifying the home-office rules will permit a minister to treat otherwise personal commuting mileage as business mileage (also see IRS Publication 587, *Business Use of Your Home*).

Idea

The tax law provides for a home-office deduction. However, with housing expenses excluded from income by the housing allowance, ministers generally do not qualify for the home-office deduction. The home-office rules may still benefit some ministers by allowing them to start claiming business miles from their home instead of first requiring them to reach the church or other business location.

If a minister qualifies for home-office status, the starting (first business trip of the day) and ending (last business trip of the day) points for business miles can be the home. But ministers not qualifying under the home-office rules can only deduct or be reimbursed for miles from the minister's home to a temporary work location (a hospital, nursing home, member's home, etc.) and/or miles from a temporary work location to the minister's home. The miles between the minister's residence and the church (home to a permanent work location) are personal commuting miles—nondeductible, nonreimbursable—regardless of the number of trips made each day unless home-office status applies. Even without home-office status, when a minister has reached a work location (either permanent or temporary), trips between work locations are deductible or reimbursable.

Another advantage of home-office status for ministers relates to home computers. Without qualifying for a home office, detailed computer use records must be maintained that busy ministers find especially bothersome. However, the home-office rules eliminate these detailed record-keeping rules.

Under the home-office rules, a minister must meet the following qualifications to achieve home-office status:

- A specific portion of the taxpayer's home must be used *exclusively* and on a *regular basis* for business activity.
- The home office is used for the convenience of the employer or is necessary for the business of the employer. Use of the home that is merely appropriate and helpful to the church is not sufficient to meet the convenience test. Similarly, use of the home for the minister's convenience or because the minister can get more work done at home also will not suffice.
- The home office must be the minister's principal place of business. Under the new rules, conducting administrative or management activities of the church in the home office are examples of qualifying work. Under the old standard, the principal place of

business had to be demonstrated under the relative importance or time tests.

- The home office is used for the convenience of the employer, and the employer has no other fixed location where the minister conducts *substantial* administrative or management activities. *Note:* Insubstantial administrative or management activities that take place outside the home office will not necessarily preclude the minister from qualifying.

For many ministers, the key is to determine if they are performing work that is so substantial that they fail the last test (see above). A minister may do minimal paperwork at another fixed location, like the church, and meet the insubstantial test. Also, ministers conducting substantial nonadministrative or nonmanagement business activities at fixed locations other than their home offices will not be prevented from qualifying for a home office. For example, counseling sessions with individuals at the church will not preclude home-office status.

> **Caution**
>
> To qualify for home-office status, there are rigorous tests the minister must pass. One of the toughest is the test that requires a specific portion of the taxpayer's home to be used exclusively and on a regular basis for business activity. This is tough for many ministers when a computer in the office area is not used exclusively for business purposes.

The rules do not define if sermon preparation time qualifies as administrative or management activities. However, it seems that sermon preparation is a program activity of the church and is not administrative or management. The following activities would likely qualify as administrative or management: communication with church vendors; time spent in planning and communication with church staff or congregational leaders regarding issues such as project assignments, personnel issues, financial matters, planning for annual or quarterly congregational meetings; and planning for periodic meetings of the top governing body or committees of the church.

If a minister does not perform substantially all of his or her administrative and management activities in the home office, the relative importance or time tests must be met:

- The relative importance test considers the importance of the activities undertaken at each place of business. The activities are compared to determine which location serves as a base for the most important functions.

- The time test considers the actual time spent at respective business locations. A minister would meet this test if he or she spent more than half of his or her time working in the home office.

Ministers should keep proper records to document the required regular and exclusive business use of the home office, even if the office is only a portion of a room. They should keep a daily log of meetings related to church activities at the home office. They should also make videotapes or take photographs to show there are no personal items in that part of the home. They also need to ensure that no personal or family activities occur in the home office. It will also be helpful if the church has a written policy explaining the need for the minister to have a home office.

Other Business Expenses

In addition to travel and transportation expenses, there are other business and professional expenses that may be deductible if unreimbursed or submitted to the church for reimbursement under an accountable plan:

- **Business gifts.** You can deduct up to $25 per donee for ministry gifts to any number of individuals every year. Incidental costs, such as for engraving, gift wrapping, insurance, and mailing, do not need to be included in determining whether the $25 limit has been exceeded.

  The gifts must be related to your ministry. Gifts to church staff or board members would generally be deductible, subject to the $25 limit. Wedding and graduation gifts generally do not qualify as business expenses.

- **Clothing.** The cost of your clothing is deductible or reimbursable if the church requires the clothes and they are not suitable as normal wearing apparel. For example, a regular suit worn into the pulpit on Sunday is not deductible or reimbursable, but vestments are deductible or reimbursable.

- **Education.** There are three types of deductions for educational expenses. First, up to $2,500 of interest paid during the tax year on any qualified education loan is deductible as an adjustment to gross income on Form 1040, line 33. The debt must be incurred by the taxpayer solely to pay qualified higher educational expenses.

  Second, there is a deduction on Form 1040, assuming the tax provision for this deduction is extended for 2008, for up to $4,000 for tuition and related expense paid for enrollment or attendance by the taxpayer, spouse, or dependent at any accredited post-secondary institution. This deduction must be coordinated with educational credits.

  Thirdly, the taxpayer's own educational expenses may also be deducted as a business expense, even if they lead to a degree, if the education:

  - ☐ is required by your church to keep your salary status or job (and serves a business purpose of your church), or
  - ☐ maintains or improves skills in your present employment.

  Even though the above requirements are met, expenses do not qualify if the education is

  - ☐ required to meet the minimum educational requirements of your work, or
  - ☐ part of a program of study that will qualify you for a new occupation.

  Deductible educational expenses include the

> **Idea**
>
> Many taxpayers do not have their education expenses reimbursed by their employer. A special deduction may be taken on Form 1040, page 1, line 27 even if you do not itemize deductions on Schedule A.

cost of tuition, books, supplies, laboratory fees, correspondence courses, and travel and transportation expenses. Expenses under a written "qualified educational assistance program" are discussed on page 55.

- **Entertainment.** Meal and entertainment expenses are deductible or reimbursable if they are ordinary and necessary and are either directly related to or associated with your ministerial responsibilities.

  Do personal meals qualify when you are entertaining? Personal expenses are not deductible or reimbursable since you would be eating anyway. Granted, you might not be spending $10 for your lunch, but you would be eating. Only the amount over what you normally spend for breakfast, lunch, or dinner is deductible or reimbursable. But the IRS has decided not to enforce this part of the tax law. Unless a taxpayer is deducting outrageous amounts of personal expenses, 50% of the cost of the meals while entertaining will be allowed.

  Certain entertainment expenses incurred in your home may be deductible or reimbursable if you can show a ministry relationship. Since it is difficult to precisely document the cost of meals served in the home, a reasonable cost per meal is generally allowable (for you and your guests). Keep a log including date(s), names of guests, ministry purpose, and estimated cost. Some ministers claim deductions or reimbursements for providing overnight lodging for church-related guests based on the value of motel lodging. Such deductions or reimbursements are not allowable.

- **Interest expense.** For a minister-employee, all auto-related interest expense is personal interest, which is not deductible.

- **Moving expenses.** Certain moving expenses reimbursed by a church to a minister-employee are excludable from gross income.

  For minister-employees, when moving expense reimbursements have been excluded from income, there is no requirement to add these amounts to determine a minister's net earnings from self-employment, and therefore they are not subject to self-employment tax.

  Moving expense reimbursements or payments are excludable only to the extent that they would qualify for a moving expense deduction if they had been paid by the minister and not reimbursed. The definition of deductible moving expenses is very restrictive. For example, meals while traveling and living in temporary quarters near the new workplace are not deductible. If a minister is reimbursed for nondeductible moving expenses, the amounts paid are additional taxable compensation.

- **Personal computers.** Personal computers you own and use more than 50% for ministry may be depreciated (or reimbursed) as five-year recovery property or deducted (but not reimbursed) under Section 179 up to the annual limit of $125,000 on a joint return (2008 rate). The business portion of depreciation may be reimbursed under an accountable expense reimbursement plan if the 50% business, "convenience of the church," and "condition of employment" tests are met (see the discussion of these topics under "Telephones/cellular" on page 112).

If a computer is provided by the church in the church office but you prefer to work at home on your personal computer, it is not being used for the church's convenience. If you meet the "convenience of employer" and "condition of employment" tests but do not use your computer (and related equipment) more than 50% of the time for your work, you must depreciate these items using the straight-line method and you cannot take the Section 179 write-off. If you qualify under the home-office rules (see pages 106-8), the 50% test does not apply to you.

Adequate records of the business use of your computer or cellular telephone should be maintained to substantiate your deductions (see page 112).

Warning

If a minister purchases a computer and uses it primarily for church work and meets the "condition" and "convenience" tests, only the depreciation on the business portion of the computer can be reimbursed by the church, not the business portion of the cost, based on the Section 179 first-year write-off rules.

- **Section 179 deductions.** In the year of purchase, you may choose to deduct up to $125,000 (for 2008) on a joint return of the cost of tangible personal property used for business. Section 179 generally has limited use for automobiles because of the $4,800 (2008 rate) luxury auto limit on annual auto depreciation. While Section 179 may be used by ministers to deduct expenses, the deduction is not includible under an accountable expense reimbursement plan.

Warning

The one-time equipment write-off cannot be used as part of a minister's accountable expense reimbursement plan. If a minister personally owns a computer that is partially used for his or her employer, the business portion of the computer can be reimbursed under an accountable plan based on annual depreciation. The business portion of the cost of the computer cannot be reimbursed in one year under the one-time write-off rules.

- **Subscriptions and books.** Subscriptions to ministry-related periodicals are deductible or reimbursable. If the information in a periodical relates to your ministerial preparation, news magazines may even qualify.

  The cost of books related to your ministry with a useful life of one year or less may be deducted. The cost of books (such as commentaries) with a useful life of more than one year may be depreciated over the useful life. Books with a useful life of more than one year may generally be deducted in the year of purchase under Section 179, but they are not eligible for reimbursement by your church (also see page 51).

- **Telephone.** You may not deduct, as a business expense, any of the basic local service charge (including taxes) for the first telephone line into your home. Ministry-related long-distance calls, a second line, special equipment, and services (such as call-waiting) used for business are deductible. If you are out of town on a business trip, the IRS generally will not challenge a reasonable number of telephone calls home.

Although your basic local telephone service (including taxes) for the first telephone line into your home is not deductible for tax purposes, it is includible as housing expense for housing allowance purposes.

- **Telephones/cellular.** Cellular telephones you own and use more than 50% for ministry may be depreciated (or reimbursed) as five-year recovery property or deducted under Section 179 up to the annual limit of $125,000 on a joint return. The business portion of depreciation may be reimbursed under an accountable expense reimbursement plan, if the 50% business, "convenience of the church," and "condition of employment" tests are met.

Remember

For monthly cellular phone user fees to qualify for reimbursement or deduction, the phone must be required for the minister to perform duties properly and the business usage must exceed 50%. Written records are required to prove that the 50% level of usage has been attained.

As a minister-employee, your use of a cellular telephone must be for the "convenience of the church," and required as a "condition of employment." The "convenience of the church" test will generally be met if the cellular telephone is furnished for substantial "noncompensatory business reasons." Whether a minister (or other church employee) passes the "condition of employment" test is based on all the facts and circumstances and is not determined merely by an employer's statement that the use of the cellular telephone is a condition of employment.

If you meet the "convenience of employer" and "condition of employment" tests but do not use your cellular telephone more than 50% of the time for your work, you must depreciate it using the straight-line method. You may be reimbursed (or deduct as unreimbursed business expenses on Schedule A) the business-related telephone call charges and the business-related portion of the monthly fees. If you qualify under the home-office rules (see pages 107-8), the 50% test does not apply to you.

A log or similar documentation of the business use of your cellular telephone should be maintained to substantiate your deduction.

Allocation of Business Expenses

The IRS will often limit the deduction of unreimbursed business expenses to the extent that they are "allocable" to an excluded housing allowance or the fair rental value of church-provided housing, applying what is often referred to as the "Deason" rule. Tax Court cases clearly document their position. IRS Publication 517 (*Social Security and Other Information for Members of the Clergy and Religious Workers*) explains this topic in detail and includes the concept in a completed tax return example. The *Tax Guide for Churches and Other Religious Organizations* and the *MSSP Audit Guide for Ministers' Returns,* both issued by the IRS, clearly apply the expense allocation concept.

Since the housing allowance is not tax-exempt for self-employment purposes, it has generally been assumed that the Deason rule does not apply to the computation of a minister's self-employment taxes. However, in a Tax Court ruling that cannot be cited as a precedent, the Court applied the Deason concept to self-employment taxes.

Under the Deason guidelines, if you exclude a parsonage allowance or are provided housing by your church, you cannot deduct expenses that are allocable to your excluded rental or parsonage allowance. This rule does not apply to your deductions for home mortgage interest or real estate taxes.

A statement containing all the following information must be attached to your tax return:

- A list of each item of taxable ministerial income by source (such as wages, salary, honoraria from weddings, baptisms, etc.) plus the amount
- The amount of your excluded housing allowance or the fair rental value of church-provided housing
- A list of each item of unreimbursed ministerial expense plus the amount
- A statement that the other deductions on your tax return are not allocable to your excluded housing allowance

Key Issue

Tax Court cases have reinforced the power of the IRS to reduce unreimbursed expense deductions for income tax purposes. In one case, the IRS also reduced the deductions for social security purposes—a first!

This limitation requires the following calculation:

1. Amount of tax-exempt income (the fair rental value of a church-provided parsonage and the housing allowance excluded from gross income; this may be less than the church-designated housing allowance) $ ____________
2. Total income from ministry:
   Salary (including the fair rental value of a church-provided parsonage and the housing allowance excluded from gross income) $ ____________
   Fees ____________
   Allowances (nonaccountable plan) ____________
   $ ____________
3. Divide line 1 amount by line 2 amount = % of nontaxable income ____________%
4. Total unreimbursed business and professional expenses, less 50% of meals and entertainment expenses $____________
5. Multiply line 4 total by line 3 percentage (these are nondeductible expenses allocable to tax-exempt income) $ ____________
6. Subtract line 5 amount from line 4 amount (these are deductible expenses for federal income tax purposes on Form 2106 [2106-EZ] or Schedule C [C-EZ]) $____________

INTEGRITY*Points*

- **Personal vs. business expenses.** Integrity in expense reimbursements or deductions starts by determining if the expenses are truly business expenses. A business expense must be ordinary (one that is common and accepted in a particular field) and necessary (one that is helpful and appropriate for a particular field). The law and integrity require the faithful application of the "ordinary" and "necessary" rule.

  The reimbursement of an expense never affects the character of the expense. Simply by reimbursing an expense does not change its character from personal to business. Personal expenses are always nondeductible and not eligible for reimbursement.

- **An accountable expense reimbursement plan.** The reimbursement of business expenses is much better stewardship for the minister and the employing congregation or parachurch organization. A reimbursement is a dollar-for-dollar tax-free payment. A deduction only benefits the minister if he or she reaches the itemized deduction threshold, and then, only by the marginal income tax rates.

  A formal plan is the fundamental starting point. The plan provides the boundaries for compliance with the tax law for business expense reimbursements.

- **Substantiation vs. reporting of expenses.** Substantiating business expenses, either for reimbursement or deduction, is much more rigorous than simply reporting expenses. Substantiation generally involves providing documentary evidence that can be confirmed by a third party. Cancelled checks, credit card or other receipts are an excellent starting point. But the substantiation is not complete without the "why" (business purpose), "what" (description, including itemized account of cost), "when" (date), "where" (location), and "who" (names of those for whom the expense was incurred: *e.g.,* meals and entertainment).

Retirement and Social Security

In This Chapter

- Preparing for retirement
- The fundamentals of social security
- Taking out your retirement money
- The two social security tax systems
- Computing the self-employment tax
- Both spouses are ministers
- Self-employment tax deductions
- Use of income tax withholding to pay social security taxes
- Opting out of social security
- Working after you retire
- Canada Pension Plan

Age 65 was entrenched as the finish line for our careers. But this false endpoint is gradually being removed. We are living longer, the social security retirement age is increasing, and stock market fluctuations have significantly impacted our retirement plans. In fact, the stock market slump has left many ministers focused on their nest eggs to the exclusion of all else in their retirement planning.

Medicare still becomes effective at age 65. But this program for the elderly and disabled doesn't pay for prescription drugs and it does not pay for long-term care costs.

For many ministers, the word "retirement" means freedom. Retirement is the end to stressful deadline pressure and setting your alarm clock. But it's also the end to regular paychecks. For ministers who have lived in church-owned parsonages all their lives, retirement brings significant housing challenges.

Retirement is a transition period. God never intended for retirement to be an end in itself. And instead of kicking back at age 60 or 65, by starting a second career, shifting to part-time work, or simply continuing to work full-time, you can allow your retirement portfolio to expand by compounding for a greater period of time.

There is a danger in trying to be too precise in planning your nest egg with elaborate worksheets or powerful computer programs. Life isn't that precise. Think about what will constitute a successful retirement for you. Most people would be better off investing more of their efforts in the things money cannot buy:

- Deepening your relationship with the Lord,
- Building relationships with family and friends,
- Remaining in good health—weight and stress management are vital, and
- Participating in gratifying and fulfilling activities.

Preparing for Retirement

How much income will you need?

Being financially prepared for retirement is simply a function of time and money: the less you have of one, the more you need of the other.

What is the biggest excuse ministers use who are not saving for retirement? They say they need every penny to pay their bills now—but they'll start saving once the bills are paid off. Paying off your debts is a worthy goal, but most people never pay them all off.

Most ministers cannot save a fortune by the time they reach retirement. On a minister's pay, it is difficult to squirrel away as much as many experts insist is needed for a comfortable retirement. But there is one inescapable truth: the sooner you start saving, the better. Saving for retirement isn't like climbing one great peak. It's really like climbing several smaller ones.

Many financial planners suggest that you will need 70% to 80% of your preretirement income. But you may be able to significantly reduce your income requirement just by moving from an area with a high cost of living to a lower-cost one.

How long is retirement going to be?

The major concern of retirees today is the fear of outliving their income. Today, a 66-year-old male is expected to live 18 more years, and a female is expected to live 24 more years. But life expectancies are averages, and planning on an "average" retirement can be dangerously shortsighted for anyone in good health. It makes sense for healthy people from long-lived families to plan for a retirement stretching at least to age 85, and women are likely to live longer than men.

Investing for retirement

The best advice for ministers is the simplest—put as much into your 403(b) tax-sheltered annuity plan as you can. Whether the payments are church funded or funded by a salary reduction from your pay, the contributions are tax-deferred for income tax purposes and are not subject to self-employment social security taxes. When you

Idea

Few ministers contribute up to the limits of their retirement plans. With the changes in retirement plan contribution limits, ministers can contribute more than ever before. Check out these limits on page 4.

receive benefits from your tax-sheltered annuity plan in retirement, the payments are not subject to self-employment social security taxes.

If your plan was sponsored by a church denomination, your benefits qualify for housing allowance treatment, subject to the regular housing allowance limitations (see pages 83-84). Most financial planners recommend paying off your mortgage before you retire. But if you are a good money manager, you may want to arrange your indebtedness so you have mortgage payments during at least the early years of your retirement.

What if you have already contributed the maximum to your tax-sheltered annuity plan? A $3,000 contribution to a nondeductible Roth IRA or a regular deductible IRA is a good option for your next retirement savings dollars. How do you decide? Young ministers will tend to benefit more from a Roth IRA because it thrives on long-term compounding. If you are nearing retirement and in a 25% or higher income tax bracket but believe you will drop to the 10% bracket when you retire, stay with a deductible IRA.

When you've exhausted these options, consider a taxable investment. The key to choosing taxable investments for your retirement savings is to keep your expenses down and get the most benefit from the 15% maximum capital gains rate (5% if you are in the 10% or 15% income tax bracket).

Asset allocation—the division of your savings among different investment vehicles—is a key part of any retirement strategy. Not only do you have to decide what kind of investment account to use, you also have to decide which of your specific investments go into which account.

Proper diversification entails much more than simply spreading your contributions evenly among the choices open to you. It is influenced strongly by how long you will continue to work and how much you already have invested elsewhere. In general, the more time you have, the more aggressive you can afford to be in your asset allocation.

Insurance choices as you approach retirement

When you are approaching retirement, your insurance needs often are different from when you were in your 30s and 40s. Here are some insurance policies that you may need and policies you can probably do without:

- **Life insurance.** The need for life insurance usually declines or disappears once you are in or near retirement. Your children are probably financially independent. And by now you may have accumulated enough assets to cover your spouse's future needs. This means you might want to drop some of your insurance coverage.

  If you need life insurance for estate planning, or to protect dependents financially for at least 15 years, you should probably buy cash-value insurance so you can lock in the premium. If you own a term life policy you no longer need, you can stop paying premiums and let the policy lapse.

Countdown to Retirement

This table can help you make the timely decisions that ensure a comfortable retirement. Since only you know when you plan to call it quits, it is organized according to the number of years you have until then. If you have to move up your plans, you can compress this checklist into the time you have available.

CATEGORY	FIVE YEARS BEFORE RETIREMENT	TWO YEARS BEFORE RETIREMENT	THREE MONTHS BEFORE RETIREMENT	IN RETIREMENT
BUDGET	Draw up two budgets, current expenses and expected expenses in retirement. Plan to pay off debts by retirement.	Update your current and future budgets.	Merge your two budgets, deleting career expenses and adding any new retiree expenses.	Fine-tune your budget every year so that your projected spending matches your actual spending.
PENSION Defined-benefit plan	Ask your pension office to project your pension monthly and in a lump sum.	Decide how to take your pension; if as a lump sum, decide how to invest it.	Set up the investments you have chosen for your lump sum.	Invest your lump sum immediately to avoid the tax consequences.
403(b), 401(k) plans	Put the maximum in your plan. Wait as long as possible to tap the money so earnings grow tax deferred.	Keep contributing the maximum. If you will take a lump sum, ask an accountant how to minimize taxes.	Decide how to take your money. At 59½ you may start penalty-free lump-sum withdrawals.	At 70½ you may have to start minimum withdrawals from tax-deferred retirement plans.
SOCIAL SECURITY	Send Form 7004 to your local social security office to check your earnings and be sure your employers contributed the right amounts.	Double-check your account by sending your local social security office another Form 7004.	Decide when after age 62 to start receiving social security.	At retirement age, there is no limit on the income you can earn without reducing your social security benefits.
INVESTMENTS	Meet with a financial planner to discuss your goals and adjust your asset mix to meet them.	Adjust the balance between growth and income investments to reduce your market risk and increase income.	Make further reductions in market risk.	Generally, keep some of your money in stocks to offset inflation.
EMERGENCY FUND	Stash an amount equal to three months' expenses in a money market fund.	Set up (or renew) a home-equity line of credit that you can tap in case of an emergency.	Your cash and home-equity line of credit should amount to one full year of expenses.	Keep one year's expenses in the fund; tap it only when you must.
HOUSE Sell vs. keep	Decide whether to keep your present house or sell it. If you sell, decide whether to buy another or rent.	If you plan to move after retiring, visit potential locations during vacations.	If you are selling, put your house on the market three to six months before retirement.	Your gain on the house is tax-free up to $500,000 (married), $250,000 (single).
Repairs and improvements	Renovate now; it's easier to borrow if you're employed.	Budget now for any big-ticket repairs you may need after you retire.		
MEDICAL INSURANCE	Ask your pension office what your medical benefits will be in retirement.	If you need individual coverage, start shopping for it now.	Apply for the coverage one month prior to retiring.	Medicare starts at 65. Six months before then, shop for Medigap insurance.

- **Long-term care insurance.** Long-term care (LTC) insurance is a way to pay for nursing home costs while protecting your financial assets. LTC policies have improved significantly in recent years, but they are expensive, averaging more than $2,000 a year for policies purchased at age 65.

  Long-term care policies cover nursing home stays only, home care only, or both. A good LTC policy will cover skilled or intermediate care, or custodial help in any type of facility, with no prior hospitalization required.

Remember

Nursing home stays are typically short but the need for home health care is often longer. Consider long-term care plans that provide the same coverage for home health care and nursing facilities. Your employer can pay or reimburse your LTC premiums tax-free. The premiums are generally your responsibility from after-tax dollars after you retire.

- **Medical insurance.** Your medical insurance may stop when you become eligible for Medicare at your full retirement age, currently age 65. If you're old enough for Medicare, call social security to enroll. You may be eligible to remain in your group policy for 18 months after you leave your current employment, if the plan is based on COBRA rules.

The Fundamentals of Social Security

Ignore scare stories about social security not being there when you retire. The truth is, the benefits for most ministers will survive largely intact for many years. And Congress is likely to take steps to shore up the program in the next few years.

The age for collecting your full social security benefit used to be 65—but no longer. Full retirement gradually increases from age 65 to 67. Here, by year of birth, is the age at which you can expect to collect your full social security retirement benefit:

Year of Birth	Age for Collecting Full Retirement Benefit
Before 1938	65
1938	65 and two months
1939	65 and four months
1940	65 and six months
1941	65 and eight months
1942	65 and ten months
1943-1954	66
1955	66 and two months
1956	66 and four months
1957	66 and six months
1958	66 and eight months
1959	66 and ten months
1960 and later	67

Filing Tip

If you work while receiving social security benefits, you still pay social security and Medicare taxes regardless of your age. Additional earnings can result in increasing your benefit if the earnings are higher than those of an earlier year used in the previous calculation.

Income taxes on benefits

Social security benefits are income tax free for the majority of beneficiaries. However, those with high total incomes must include up to 85% of their benefits as income for federal income tax purposes. Special step-rate "thresholds" determine the amount on which you may be taxed:

- Single persons: $25,000 and $34,000
- Married couples filing a joint return: $32,000 and $44,000

Working after you reach retirement age

If you are under full retirement age (FRA), you lose $1 of social security benefits for every $2 you earn over a certain limit, which increases annually ($13,560 in 2008). Once you reach FRA, you can earn as much as you like with no cut in benefits. The earnings test looks only at money you earn from a job or self-employment, not income from investments or other sources. Dollars from income excluded because of the housing allowance are included in the earnings test.

Checking on your benefits

Complete a Request for Earnings and Benefit Estimate Statement (Form SSA-7004) every three years. You can order a free copy of the form at http://www.ssa.gov/online/ssa-7004.html. Complete the form and the SSA will mail you a statement of your earnings along with a projection of your future benefits. Notify the SSA of any discrepancies.

And don't overlook the possibility of errors in your church retirement plan, either. Get a summary plan description from your church pension board, and look over your annual statement summary.

Taking Out Your Retirement Money

Ministers spend their entire lives putting money into retirement plans. When and how you withdraw money from your tax-deferred retirement plans are among the most important financial decisions of your life.

Capital builds up in your retirement plans, free of taxes. But the federal, state, and local governments are looking for their share when you pull out your money. And Congress has devised a host of hurdles and penalties:

- You cannot start withdrawing until you retire at age 55 or reach 59½. If you do, you have to pay a 10% tax penalty on top of the standard income tax rates. The Roth IRA is an exception because money can be withdrawn without penalty if you leave the funds in the Roth IRA for at least five years.
- For church plans, you must start withdrawals at age 70½ or your date of retirement, whichever is later. For other retirement plans, you must start withdrawals when you

How long will $100,000 last?

Withdrawals starting at*	Years money will last invested at the following yields				
	4%	6%	8%	10%	12%
$ 2,000	50	151	FOREVER		
$ 6,000	17	20	25	43	FOREVER
$10,000	10	11	12	14	17
$14,000	7	8	8	9	10

*Single withdrawal at first of year, increasing each year by 4% to cover inflation

reach age 70½. If you don't, you have to pay a walloping 50% penalty tax. There is no age requirement for starting to withdraw funds from your Roth IRA.

The Two Social Security Tax Systems

Social security taxes are collected under two systems. Under the Federal Insurance Contributions Act (FICA), the employer pays one-half of the tax and the employee pays the other half. Under the Self-Employment Contributions Act (SECA), the self-employed person pays all the tax (self-employment tax) as calculated on the taxpayer's Schedule SE. IRS Publications 517 and 1828 provide information on social security taxes.

Ministers are always self-employed for social security purposes under the tax law with respect to services performed in the exercise of their ministry, whether employed by a church, integral agency of a church, or a parachurch organization. Ministers are self-employed for social security purposes regardless of how their employer categorizes them for income tax purposes. Ministers are not subject to FICA-type social security taxes, even though they report their income taxes as employees and receive a Form W-2 from their employer.

When FICA is inappropriately withheld (7.65%) from a minister's pay and matched (7.65%) by the employer, it subjects the minister and the employer to possible action by the IRS because:

- the minister has often underpaid his or her income taxes. The 7.65% match that was withheld from the church is really compensation that is avoiding income tax because it is not being reported in Box 1 of the Form W-2. Additionally, the minister is paying FICA instead of SECA, and the IRS could require that this be corrected retroactively.

Warning

Churches and other employers commonly subject ministers to the wrong type of social security. If a minister qualifies for a housing allowance, he or she is not subject to FICA-type social security. The inappropriate use of FICA instead of SECA may result in the underpayment of a minister's income taxes.

➤ the employer is underreporting the employee's income by the 7.65% FICA match. Also, the employer is reporting FICA social security taxes when it should not. The IRS could require the employer to retroactively correct Forms 941 and W-2.

Example: A church hires and pays you to perform ministerial services for it, subject to its control. Under the common-law rules (pages 31-32), you are an employee of the church while performing those services. The church reports your wages on Form W-2 for income tax purposes, but no social security taxes are withheld. You are self-employed for social security purposes. You must pay self-employment tax (SECA) on those wages yourself unless you request and receive an exemption from self-employment tax. On Form W-2, Boxes 3 through 6 are left blank.

Many churches reimburse ministers for a portion or all of their SECA liability. SECA reimbursements represent additional taxable compensation in the year paid to the minister for both income and social security tax purposes.

Because of the SECA deductions (see pages 66-67), a full SECA reimbursement is effectively less than the gross 15.3% rate.

Example: A church provides a cash salary of $35,000 and provides a parsonage that has an annual fair rental value of $15,000. Even though a full reimbursement of the minister's SECA is slightly less than 15.3%, the church decides to reimburse at the 15.3% rate for simplicity. Since the minister has entered into a voluntary withholding arrangement with the church for federal income taxes, the church grosses up the monthly pay by $637.50 (15.3 times $50,000, or $7,650 divided by 12) and withholds federal income tax of $637.50 plus a sufficient amount to cover the minister's estimated federal income tax.

SOCIAL SECURITY SYSTEMS

FICA (Federal Insurance Contributions Act)	**SECA** (Self-Employment Contributions Act)
Nonminister employees of a church are all subject to FICA.	All qualified ministers are subject to SECA (unless they have opted out of social security).
Employee pays 7.65% Employer pays 7.65% 15.30%	Self-employed individuals pay the full 15.3%.
The 15.3% is paid on a wage base of up to $102,000 for 2008.	The 15.3% is paid on a wage base of up to $102,000 for 2008.
Both the employer and employee pay a 1.45% tax rate on all wages above $102,000.	The individual pays a 2.9% tax rate on all wages above $102,000.

Computing the Self-Employment Tax

When computing the self-employment tax, your net earnings include the gross income earned from performing qualified services minus the deductions related to that income.

This includes church compensation reported in Box 1 of Form W-2 (the designated housing allowance should not be shown in this box), the net profit or loss from Schedule C or C-EZ (relating to clergy income), any housing allowance excluded from Box 1 of Form W-2, the fair rental value of church-provided housing, and amounts that should have been included in Box 1 of Form W-2, such as business expense reimbursements made under a non-accountable plan, a self-employment social security tax reimbursement or allowance, love offerings, etc.

Key Issue

Unless a minister has opted out of social security, the net ministerial income plus the excluded housing allowance and the fair rental value of church-provided housing is subject to self-employment social security tax. This is true even if the minister is retired and receiving social security benefits. There is no age limit on paying social security tax.

The following tax rates apply to net earnings from self-employment of $400 or more each year:

	Tax Rate		Maximum Earnings Base	
Year	OASDI	Medicare	OASDI	Medicare
2006	12.4%	2.9%	94,200	no limit
2007	12.4%	2.9%	97,500	no limit
2008	12.4%	2.9%	102,000	no limit
2009	12.4%	2.9%	106,500 (est.)	no limit

OASDI = Old-age, survivors, and disability insurance, or social security

Only business expenses are deductible in determining income subject to SECA. The minister may deduct unreimbursed business expenses for the SECA computation even if deductions are not itemized on Schedule A.

Moving expenses do not qualify as business expenses. Therefore, moving expenses are not deductible in computing self-employment tax. However, for minister-employees, reimbursed moving expenses are excludable from Form W-2. Therefore, the reimbursements are not included for income or social security tax purposes.

Example: You have the following ministerial income and expenses: church salary $30,000 (of which the housing allowance is $12,000); net Schedule C (C-EZ) income related to special speaking engagements, weddings, funerals, etc. $1,350; Schedule A employee business expenses (after offsetting 50% of nondeductible meal and entertainment) $1,800. You do not itemize your deductions on Schedule A since the standard deduction is more beneficial.

Self-Employment Social Security Tax Worksheet

Inclusions:

Salary paid by church as reflected on Form W-2, Box 1	$	________
Net profit or loss as reflected on Schedule C or C-EZ (includes speaking honoraria, offerings you receive for marriages, baptisms, funerals, and other fees)		________
Housing allowance excluded from salary on Form W-2		________
Fair rental value of church-provided housing (including paid utilities)		________
Nonaccountable business expense reimbursements (if not included on Form W-2)		________
Reimbursement of self-employment taxes (if not included on Form W-2)		________
Other amounts that should have been included on Form W-2, Box 1, such as love offerings		________
Total inclusions		________

Deductions:

Unreimbursed ministerial business and professional expenses or reimbursed expenses paid under a nonaccountable plan

A. Deductible on Schedule A before the 2% of AGI limitation whether or not you itemized[1] or		________
B. Not deductible on Form 2106/2106 EZ or Schedule C/C-EZ because expenses were allocated to taxable/nontaxable income		________
Total deductions		________
Net earnings from self-employment (to Schedule SE)	$	________

[1] The 50% unreimbursed meal and entertainment expense limitation applies to amounts subject to social security tax. In other words, if some of your meal and entertainment expenses were subjected to the 50% limit, the remainder cannot be deducted here.

Note 1: Your net earnings from self-employment are not affected by the foreign earned income exclusion or the foreign housing exclusion or deduction if you are a U.S. citizen or resident alien who is serving abroad and living in a foreign country.

Note 2: Amounts received as pension payments or annuity payments related to a church-sponsored tax-sheltered annuity by a retired minister are generally considered to be excluded from the social security calculation.

Your self-employment income is

Salary from church	$18,000
Church-designated housing allowance	12,000
Schedule C (C-EZ) net earnings	1,350
Schedule A employee business expenses	(1,800)
Total	$29,550

Use the worksheet on page 124 to calculate net earnings from self-employment. Net earnings are transferred to Form SE, page 1, line 2, to calculate the SECA.

Both Spouses Are Ministers

If a husband and wife who are both duly ordained, commissioned, or licensed ministers have an agreement with a church that each will perform specific services for which they will receive pay, jointly or separately, they must divide the compensation according to the agreement. Such a division of income would have no impact on their income tax if they filed a joint return. But each of them could obtain social security coverage by dividing the compensation and subjecting the compensation to social security tax.

If the agreement for services is with one spouse only and the other spouse receives no pay for any specific duties, amounts paid for services are included only in the income of the spouse having the agreement.

If you have already filed a return and incorrectly divided, or failed to divide, the income for self-employment tax purposes, you may file an amended return showing the corrected amount as self-employment income for each spouse.

Caution

A minister's spouse who is not duly ordained, commissioned, or licensed as a minister of a church but who receives pay for performing services for the organization should not include the earnings with the minister's self-employment income. The nonminister spouse is generally an employee of the church for federal income tax and social security (FICA) tax purposes.

If one spouse is ordained, commissioned, or licensed and the other is not, the "qualified" minister under the tax law generally receives 100% of the compensation from the church, and the spouse is considered a volunteer. This is true even though they may have been hired as a team and each spouse provides significant services to the church.

However, it may be legitimate to split the compensation from the church based on the duties of each spouse. Pay should never be split merely for the purpose of allowing a spouse to qualify for social security or to avoid exceeding the social security earnings limit for one spouse.

Self-Employment Tax Deductions

You can take an income tax deduction equal to one-half of your self-employment tax liability. The deduction is claimed against gross income on line 27 of Form 1040, page 1.

You also may deduct a portion of your self-employment tax liability in calculating your self-employment tax. This deduction is made on Schedule SE, Section A, line 4 or Section B, line 4a, by multiplying self-employment income by .9235.

The purpose of these deductions is to equalize the social security (and income) taxes paid by (and for) employees and self-employed persons with equivalent income.

Idea

Because of the deductibility of the self-employment tax in both the income tax and self-employment tax computations, if your church desires to reimburse your entire social security tax obligation, it is effectively less than the gross 15.3% rate. See pages 66-67 for the effective rate at various marginal income tax rates.

Use of Income Tax Withholding to Pay Social Security Taxes

Under a voluntary withholding agreement, a minister-employee may ask the church to withhold a sufficient amount to cover federal income taxes plus enough for the self-employment taxes (SECA). The church must report all amounts withheld under such an arrangement as federal income taxes. The other option for the payment of income and social security taxes is to use the Form 1040-ES in paying quarterly estimated taxes.

Example: A minister projected that he will owe $1,000 of federal income tax for 2009 and $3,000 of self-employment social security tax for a total tax obligation of $4,000. The minister and his spouse will not have withholding from nonchurch employment. He will not qualify for the earned income tax credit. The minister could enter into a voluntary withholding agreement whereby the church would withhold federal income tax from each paycheck so that by the end of 2009, $4,000 was withheld (this would be reported on Form W-2, Box 2). No FICA-type social security tax is withheld from the minister's pay since he is not subject to that type of social security. Alternately, the minister could file Forms 1040-ES on April 15, 2009, June 15, 2009, September 15, 2009, and January 15, 2010 and submit payments of $1,000 per filing.

Key Issue

Take advantage of opportunities to enter into a voluntary withholding arrangement with your employer to withhold enough federal income tax to cover both your federal income tax and self-employment social security tax obligation. Withholding the proper amount each week of payday is a very efficient way to pay your taxes. You do not run the risk of filing Forms 1040-ES late and incurring underpayment penalties.

Opting Out of Social Security

All ministers are automatically covered by social security (SECA) for services in the exercise of ministry unless an exemption has been received based on the filing with and approval by the IRS of Form 4361. You must certify that you oppose, either conscientiously or because of religious principles, the acceptance of any public insurance (with respect to services performed as a minister), including social security coverage. Either opposition must be based on religious belief. This includes an opposition to insurance that helps pay for or provide services for medical care (such as Medicare) and social security benefits.

Warning

Opting out of social security is relatively simple. Form 4361 must be filed by the due date of the minister's tax return for the second year with $400 or more of ministerial income. But the simplicity of opting out should not be confused with the significant difficulty of complying with the requirements for opting out.

To claim the exemption from self-employment tax, you must

- file Form 4361;
- be conscientiously opposed to public insurance (which includes insurance systems established by the Social Security Act) because of your individual religious considerations (not because of your general conscience), or because of the principles of your religious denomination;
- file for *other than* economic reasons;
- inform the ordaining, commissioning, or licensing body of your church or order that you are opposed to public insurance if you are a minister;
- establish that the religious organization that ordained, commissioned, or licensed you or your religious order is a tax-exempt religious organization;
- establish that the organization is a church or a convention or association of churches; and
- sign and return the statement the IRS mails to you to verify that you are requesting an exemption based on the grounds listed on the statement.

Tip

Even though a minister signs Form 4361 and certifies that he or she is opposed to accepting public insurance benefits which is based on earnings from services performed in his or her capacity as a minister, the minister can still purchase life insurance or participate in retirement programs administered by non-governmental institutions.

Deadline for filing for an exemption

The application for exemption from self-employment tax must be filed by the date your tax return is due, including extensions, for the second year in which you had net ministerial income of $400 or more. These do not have to be consecutive tax years.

Example 1: A minister ordained in 2007 has net earnings of $400 in 2007 and $500 in 2008. An application for exemption must be filed by April 15, 2009, if no extension has been filed. If the minister does not receive the approved exemption by April 15, 2009, the self-employment tax for 2008 is due by that date.

Example 2: A minister has $300 in net clergy earnings in 2007 but earned $400 in both 2006 and 2008. An application for exemption must be filed by April 15, 2009, if no extension has been filed. If the minister does not receive the approved exemption by April 15, 2009, the self-employment tax for 2008 is due by that date.

Example 3: A minister, ordained in 2006, earned $700 net for that year. In 2007, ministerial compensation was $1,000 and related expenses were $1,000. Therefore, the 2007 net earnings were zero. Also in 2007, $7,000 in net self-employment earnings was received from nonministerial sources. In 2008, net ministerial earnings were $1,500 and self-employment income of $12,000 was received from nonministerial sources.

Because the minister had ministerial net earnings in 2006 and 2008 that were more than $400 each year, the application for exemption must be filed by April 15, 2009. If the minister does not receive the approved exemption by April 15, 2009, the self-employment tax for 2008 is due by that date.

Example 4: A minister was ordained in 2007 with $1,000 and $2,000 of net ministerial earnings for 2007 and 2008, respectively. The minister filed Form 4361 in 2008 (this was a timely filing since the last day to file without extensions is April 15, 2009) and the application was approved by the IRS. The minister paid self-employment social security tax on the $1,000 of net ministerial earnings for 2007 since the Form 4361 had not yet been filed. Based on the approval of Form 4361, the minister can file an amended income tax return for 2007 using Form 1040X (see pages 143-44) and receive a refund of the social security tax paid on the net ministerial earnings for that year.

Tip

If the exemption is approved, it does not apply to nonministerial wages or to any other self-employment income. For example, a bivocational pastor who is employed part-time in a secular job is subject to FICA on the wages from the secular job. If a minister performs independent contractor services unrelated to his ministry, this net profit is subject to social security.

A minister must include with Form 4361 a statement that he has informed the ordaining body of his church of his opposition to the coverage.

Form **4361** (Rev. November 2007) Department of the Treasury Internal Revenue Service

Application for Exemption From Self-Employment Tax for Use by Ministers, Members of Religious Orders and Christian Science Practitioners

OMB No. 1545-0074

File Original and Two Copies

File original and two copies and attach supporting documents. This exemption is granted only if the IRS returns a copy to you marked "approved."

Please type or print

1 Name of taxpayer applying for exemption (as shown on Form 1040): Harold T. Baldwin

Social security number: 603 ⁝ 42 ⁝ 8941

Number and street (including apt. no.): PO Box 183

Telephone number (optional): ( )

City or town, state, and ZIP code: Milton, PA 17647

2 Check **one** box: ☐ Christian Science practitioner ☒ Ordained minister, priest, rabbi ☐ Member of religious order not under a vow of poverty ☐ Commissioned or licensed minister (see line 6)

3 Date ordained, licensed, etc. (Attach supporting document. See instructions.) 7 / 1 / 05

4 Legal name of ordaining, licensing, or commissioning body or religious order: Christian General Conference

Employer identification number: 48-9017682

Number, street, and room or suite no.: PO Box 5002

City or town, state, and ZIP code: Nashville, AR 71852

5 Enter the first 2 years, after the date shown on line 3, that you had net self-employment earnings of $400 or more, any of which came from services as a minister, priest, rabbi, etc.; member of a religious order; or Christian Science practitioner . . . . . ▶ 05 | 06

6 If you apply for the exemption as a licensed or commissioned minister, and your denomination also ordains ministers, please indicate how your ecclesiastical powers differ from those of an ordained minister of your denomination. Attach a copy of your denomination's bylaws relating to the powers of ordained, commissioned, and licensed ministers.

7 I certify that I am conscientiously opposed to, or because of my religious principles I am opposed to, the acceptance (for services I perform as a minister, member of a religious order not under a vow of poverty, or a Christian Science practitioner) of any public insurance that makes payments in the event of death, disability, old age, or retirement; or that makes payments toward the cost of, or provides services for, medical care. (Public insurance includes insurance systems established by the Social Security Act.)

I certify that as a duly ordained, commissioned, or licensed minister of a church or a member of a religious order not under a vow of poverty, I have informed the ordaining, commissioning, or licensing body of my church or order that I am conscientiously opposed to, or because of religious principles, I am opposed to the acceptance (for services I perform as a minister or as a member of a religious order) of any public insurance that makes payments in the event of death, disability, old age, or retirement; or that makes payments toward the cost of, or provides services for, medical care, including the benefits of any insurance system established by the Social Security Act.

I certify that I have never filed Form 2031 to revoke a previous exemption from social security coverage on earnings as a minister, member of a religious order not under a vow of poverty, or a Christian Science practitioner.

I request to be exempted from paying self-employment tax on my earnings from services as a minister, member of a religious order not under a vow of poverty, or a Christian Science practitioner, under section 1402(e) of the Internal Revenue Code. I understand that the exemption, if granted, will apply only to these earnings. Under penalties of perjury, I declare that I have examined this application and to the best of my knowledge and belief, it is true and correct.

Signature ▶ Harold T. Baldwin Date ▶ 6/30/08

Caution: *Form 4361 is* **not proof** *of the right to an exemption from federal income tax withholding or social security tax, the right to a parsonage allowance exclusion (section 107 of the Internal Revenue Code), assignment by your religious superiors to a particular job, or the exemption or church status of the ordaining, licensing, or commissioning body, or religious order.*

For Internal Revenue Service Use

☐ Approved for exemption from self-employment tax on ministerial earnings

☐ Disapproved for exemption from self-employment tax on ministerial earnings

By .... (Director's signature) .... (Date)

Section references are to the Internal Revenue Code unless otherwise noted.

General Instructions

Purpose of form. File Form 4361 to apply for an exemption from self-employment tax if you are:

- An ordained, commissioned, or licensed minister of a church;
- A member of a religious order who has not taken a vow of poverty;
- A Christian Science practitioner; or
- A commissioned or licensed minister of a church or church denomination that ordains ministers, if you have authority to perform substantially all religious duties of your church or denomination.

This application must be based on your religious or conscientious opposition to the acceptance (for services performed as a minister, member of a religious order not under a vow of poverty, or Christian Science practitioner) of any public insurance that makes payments for death, disability, old age, or retirement; or that makes payments for the cost of, or provides services for, medical care, including any insurance benefits established by the Social Security Act.

If you are a duly ordained, commissioned, or licensed minister of a church or a member of a religious order not under a vow of poverty, prior to filing this form you must inform the ordaining, commissioning, or licensing body of your church or order that you are opposed to the acceptance of public insurance benefits based on ministerial service on religious or conscientious grounds.

For Privacy Act and Paperwork Reduction Act Notice, see page 2 Cat. No. 41586H Form **4361** (Rev. 11-2007)

Caution: Very few ministers qualify to file Form 4361. The filing must be based on the minister's conscience or religious principles, not because of a preference to invest retirement funds elsewhere.

A second ordination with a second church generally does not provide a second opportunity for a minister to opt out by filing Form 4361.

Basis of filing for exemption

Neither economics nor any other nonreligious reason is a valid basis for the exemption. Many ministers are improperly counseled to opt out of social security because it may not be a "good investment." Your view of the soundness of the social security program has absolutely no relationship to the application for exemption.

Your first consideration is your ability to sign Form 4361 with a clear conscience. Key words in qualifying for exemption from social security coverage on ministerial earnings are "religious principles" and "conscientiously opposed to the acceptance of any public insurance." Religious principles do not simply consist of the conviction that perhaps social security will not be there when you retire or that a better retirement can be purchased through an annuity or other retirement program. The belief must be an integral part of your religious system of beliefs, your theology.

Caution

Opting out of social security is one of the most abused provisions of the tax law that applies to ministers. Too often ministers have opted out because they are concerned about long-term safety of the program or they feel they have a better way to invest the funds. These reasons do not provide a basis to sign Form 4361.

Further, this religious principle must be one that would prevent you from ever asking for the benefits from such a plan based on your church salary. No basis exists for an objection related to paying the taxes or to the level of the taxes to be paid.

If you opt out and do not have sufficient credits from prior employment or from future nonministerial employment, neither you nor your dependents will be covered under social security benefits, survivors' benefits, or Medicare. If you opt out of social security, you should make alternate plans to provide for catastrophic illness, disability, or death, as well as for retirement.

This is not a decision to be taken lightly. First, you must act on religious convictions. Second, you must be prepared financially with alternatives to the benefits of social security coverage.

Although a minister may opt out of social security with respect to ministerial income, the minister may still receive social security benefits related to nonministerial wages or other self-employment income.

Opting back into social security

Until April 15, 2002, ministers could opt back into social security by filing Form 2031. This was a special two-year window based on a law passed in 1999. With the window to opt back into social security closed, there is currently no formal method available for ministers to opt back into social security.

Working After You Retire

There is no retirement earnings test for persons who have attained full retirement age (FRA). But for individuals who have not attained FRA, there is a limit on earnings from current work. The earnings limit is a retirement test and is a separate issue from income taxes.

If you earn more than the exempt amount (see below), your benefits and your family members' benefits that are based on your work record will be reduced. If a family member earns more than the exempt amount, only that person's benefit is reduced.

If you are under FRA throughout 2008, you can earn $13,560. If your earnings exceed this, then $1 of benefits is withheld for every $2 you earn above $13,560. If your earnings exceed this limit, some benefits may still be payable.

If you attain FRA in 2008, you can earn $36,120 in the period before the month in which you attain FRA with no reduction in benefits. If your earnings exceed this, then $1 in benefits is withheld for every $3 you earn above $36,120.

After you retire, you may receive special payments for work you did before you started getting social security benefits. Usually, these special payments will not affect your social security benefit if they are compensation for work done before you retired. Examples of special payments include bonuses, accumulated vacation or sick pay, and severance pay.

> **Tip**
>
> Individuals who turn 65 in 2008 must wait until they are 66 years old (FRA) to get full benefits.

Canada Pension Plan

Under an agreement between the United States and Canada, a minister is subject to the laws of the country in which the services are performed for the purposes of United States social security and Canada Pension Plan, respectively. In other words, a Canadian citizen who moves to the United States to pastor a church generally must pay United States social security (SECA) tax.

There is one exception to the general rule: if the minister is required by a Canadian employer to transfer to a related organization in the United States on a temporary basis for a period not exceeding 60 months, with the intention of returning to the employment with the Canadian employer at the end of the temporary assignment. In this case, the Canadian employer must complete Form CPT56, *Certificate of Coverage Under the Canada Pension Plan Pursuant to Article V of the Agreement on Social Security Between Canada and the United States,* which may be obtained at www.ccra-adrc.gc.ca.

Some ministers may work in both the United States and Canada (see Publication IC84-6 *Canada-United States Social Security Agreement issued by the Canada Revenue Agency*). Each country issues "certificates of coverage" to confirm a particular work is covered under the social security laws of that country.

INTEGRITY*Points*

- **Improperly opting out of social security.** The improper (actually, the word is "illegal," but it is such a harsh word) opting out of social security by ministers is one of the dirty little secrets of the profession.

  If I had $100 for every minister with whom I have communicated that has opted out of social security for invalid reasons, I would have a tidy nest egg. Shame on those who have promoted ministers opting out of social security for reasons that are inconsistent with federal law! And, shame on the ministers, many naively by their own admission, who accepted faulty advice.

  It's not a matter of whether it makes good money-sense for a minister to pay into social security. It's simply the right thing to do. Ministers are required to pay social security unless they are one of the rare ministers who are opposed to receiving public insurance (including social security) based on conscientious opposition or religious principles.

  In speaking and otherwise communicating with thousands of ministers across American during my career, I have only found a handful of ministers who opted out of social security for legal reasons. What a blight on the profession and what a poor example for congregations!

- **Correctly calculating the social security tax.** Paying the self-employment social security tax is often a bitter pill to swallow for ministers—the social security tax usually dwarfs the amount of income tax. But calculating the correct amount of social security tax due is also very challenging.

  The IRS certainly does not give a minister much help in calculating the social security tax. One might think the IRS would have developed a form to help ministers—there's an IRS form for nearly every other purpose! And, tax return software doesn't help too much in this area either.

  Far too many ministers do not include the housing allowance excluded from salary on Form W-2 and/or the fair rental value of congregation-provided housing and the reimbursement of social security tax. On the flip side of the equation of the amount subject to social security, many ministers forget to exclude unreimbursed ministerial business and professional expenses (or reimbursed expenses paid under a nonaccountable plan [see page 124]).

Paying Your Taxes

In This Chapter

- Tax withholding
- Estimated tax
- Excess social security withheld (FICA)
- Earned income credit
- Extension of time to file
- Extension of time to pay
- Offers in compromise
- Filing an amended tax return

The federal income tax is a pay-as-you-go tax. You must pay the tax as you earn or receive income during the year. Employees usually have income tax withheld from their pay. However, the pay of qualified ministers is not subject to federal income tax withholding. Ministers who are employees for income tax purposes may enter into a voluntary withholding agreement with the church to cover any income tax and self-employment social security tax that are due. IRS Publication 505 provides additional information on tax withholding and estimated taxes.

Tax Withholding

Federal income tax withheld from earnings as an employee should be reported to you on your Form W-2. The total amount withheld from all sources should be entered on line 64, Form 1040, page 2.

Churches are *not required* to withhold income taxes from wages paid to ministers for services performed in the exercise of their ministry. The exemption does not apply to nonministerial church employees such as a secretary, organist, or custodian.

A minister-employee may have a *voluntary* withholding agreement with the employing church to cover income taxes (the amount may be set high enough to also cover the self-employment social security tax liability). An agreement to withhold income taxes from wages should be in writing. There is no required form for the agreement. It may be as simple as a letter from the minister to the church requesting that a specified amount be withheld as federal income taxes. Or a minister may request voluntary withholding by submitting Form W-4 (Employee's Withholding Allowance Certificate) to the church and indicate an additional amount to be withheld in excess of the tax table amount.

If federal income taxes are withheld sufficient to cover both the minister's income and self-employment social security (SECA) taxes, it is very important that the amounts be reported as "federal income taxes withheld" when the church completes quarterly Form 941 and annual Forms W-2 and W-3. FICA social security taxes should never be withheld or remitted relating to qualified ministers.

Idea

Though not required, churches should offer to withhold federal (and state and local, where applicable) income taxes (never FICA taxes!) from a minister's pay. Filing Forms 1040-ES often means saving up money for the 4/15, 6/15, 9/15, and 1/15 deadlines. Withholding the proper amount each week or payday is so much more efficient.

For personal budgeting purposes, a minister may request the church to withhold amounts from compensation. Coinciding with the Form 1040-ES due dates (April 15, June 15, September 15, and January 15), the church pays the withheld amounts directly to the minister and then the minister uses the funds to make the appropriate estimated tax payments to the IRS. The withholding has no impact on Form W-2.

Example 1: A minister's cash compensation is $40,000 for 2009, and the anticipated income and self-employment social security tax obligation for 2009 is $4,800. The minister uses the estimated tax method to pay income and self-employment social security tax.

Based on an agreement with the minister, a church withholds $400 per month from the minister's compensation in relation to the minister's tax obligation. The church pays the minister $12,000 on April 15, June 15, October 15, and January 15 to provide the amount the minister needs to submit with Form 1040-ES. The $4,800 withheld does not impact the reporting on Form W-2, *e.g.,* Box 1 of Form W-2 shows $40,000. The $4,800 is not included in Box 2 as Federal Income Tax Withheld because no funds were remitted to the IRS for payroll tax purposes.

Example 2: A minister's cash compensation is $40,000 for 2009, and the church and the minister enter into a voluntary withholding arrangement for federal income tax purposes.

Based on the agreement, the church withholds $400 of federal income taxes per month and remits the withheld amounts to the IRS through the payroll tax reporting process. The Form W-2 for 2009 shows compensation in Box 1 of $40,000 and Federal Income Tax Withheld in Box 2 of $4,800.

Estimated Tax

Estimated tax is the method used to pay income and self-employment taxes for income that is not subject to withholding. Your estimated tax is your expected tax for the year minus your expected withholding and credits.

If you are filing a declaration of estimated tax, complete the quarterly Forms 1040-ES. If your 2009 estimated taxes are $1,000 or less, no declaration of estimated tax is required.

If your estimated tax payments for 2009 equal 90% of your 2008 tax liability, you will avoid underpayment penalties. An option is to make the 2009 estimated tax payments equal 100% of your 2008 federal and social security taxes (Form 1040, page 2, line 64). This method generally avoids underpayment penalties and is easier to calculate. The estimated tax payments for certain higher income taxpayers must be 110% of the prior year tax.

> **Filing Tip**
>
> When using the estimated tax method of submitting income and social security tax money to the IRS, pay at least as much as your previous year's total taxes (before offsetting withholding, estimated tax payments, etc.). Spread the payments equally over the four Forms 1040-ES. This will generally avoid underpayment penalties.

Ministers with an adjusted gross income of over $150,000 ($75,000 for married individuals filing separately) may fall under special rules requiring larger estimated tax payments. At this income level, if your estimated tax payments for 2009 equal 110% of your 2008 tax liability, you will avoid underpayment penalties.

In estimating 2009 taxes, net earnings from self-employment should be reduced by 7.65% before calculating the self-employment tax of 15.3%. There also is an income tax deduction for one-half of your self-employment tax (Form 1040, page 1, line 27).

You pay one-fourth of your total estimated taxes in installments as follows:

For the Period		Due Date
January 1 -	March 31	April 15
April 1 -	May 31	June 15
June 1 -	August 31	September 15
September 1 -	December 31	January 15

Estimated tax payments are counted as paid when the IRS receives them. Thus, paying more later does not offset shortfalls from prior installments. Withheld tax is considered as paid evenly throughout the year. Therefore, increasing withholding late in a year offsets earlier underpayments.

Excess Social Security Withheld (FICA)

If you worked for two or more employers during 2008 and together they paid you more than $102,000 in wages, too much FICA tax was probably withheld from your wages. You can claim the extra amount as a credit on line 67 of Form 1040, page 2, to reduce your income tax when you file your return. If the social security tax withholding shown in Box 4

Three Ways to Pay Your Taxes

1

Estimated Taxes

The minister pays federal income taxes and social security taxes (SECA) directly to the IRS.

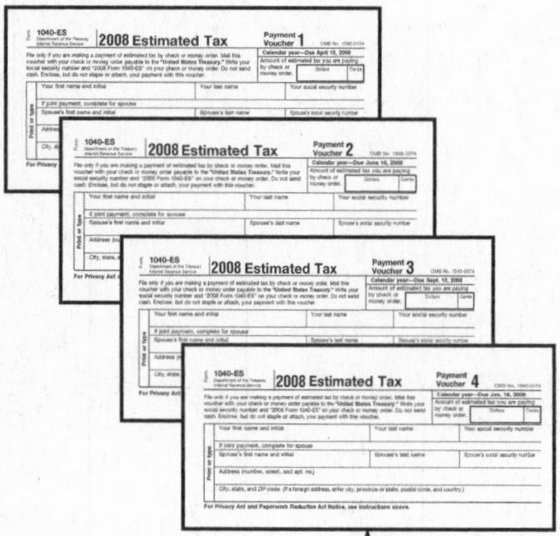
1040-ES 2008 Estimated Tax Payment Voucher 1
1040-ES 2008 Estimated Tax Payment Voucher 2
1040-ES 2008 Estimated Tax Payment Voucher 3
1040-ES 2008 Estimated Tax Payment Voucher 4

Forms 1040-ES are filed by the minister on 4/15, 6/15, 9/15, and 1/15.

2

Voluntary Withholding

The church withholds federal income tax and pays quarterly to the IRS. Additional federal income tax may be withheld to cover the minister's social security tax (SECA) liability.

Forms 941 filed with the IRS quarterly by the church.

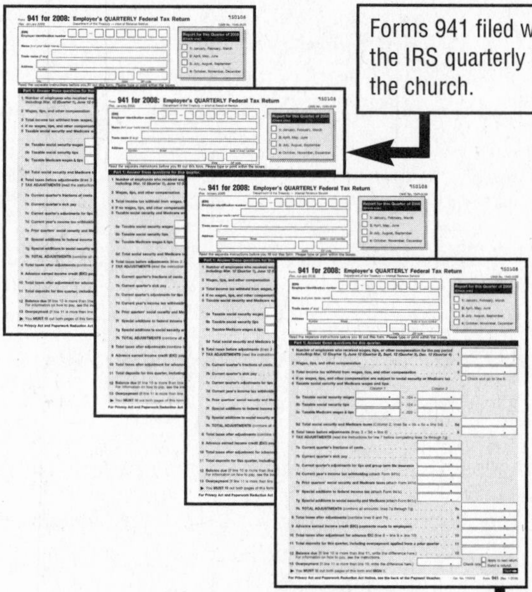
941 for 2008: Employer's QUARTERLY Federal Tax Return

Form 941 data are annually summarized on Form W-2. The W-2 is provided to the minister and the IRS.

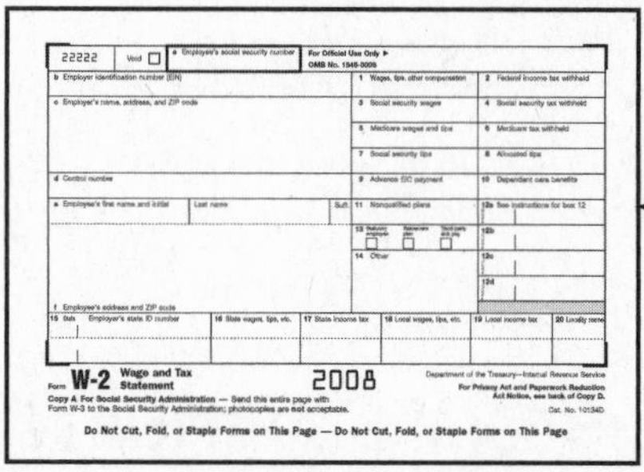
Form W-2 Wage and Tax Statement 2008

3

Payroll withholding from the minister's pay. The church does not remit the amounts withheld to the IRS. The amounts are paid directly to the minister on or before 4/15, 6/15, 9/15, and 1/15. The minister then files Form 1040-ES and remits the money to the IRS.

Calculate Your Most Important Tax Planning Number of 2008

You only have to pay by December 31 (January 15 if you are paying estimates) the smallest of the "safe harbor" amounts. Use this worksheet to calculate them so you will know how much to withhold or pay in estimated taxes.

100% of your 2008 tax liability
(the number on line 63 on your Form 1040): ___________

90% of your estimated 2009 tax (federal income tax and self-employment social security tax) liability. Recalculate this number at least three times before October to update changes in your tax circumstances. (The October date gives you enough time to make changes in withholdings or your final estimated payment.)

Estimated 2009 tax liability: ___________ x 90% = ___________

You can also avoid a penalty if you owe less than $1,000 on April 15 after considering withholdings. But be careful using this loophole—if you miscalculate just a little bit, you could be facing a penalty. So recalculate this at least three times a year as well.

Estimated 2009 tax liability: ___________

Minus Projected 2009 Federal Income Tax
Withholdings: ___________

Equals: (must be less than $1,000) ___________

Fill in the smallest of these numbers: ___________

You only have to pay this amount by the end of the year.

A special rule applies to individuals with adjusted gross income for the previous year in excess of $150,000.

of all your Forms W-2 exceeds $6,324 for 2008, you are entitled to a refund of the excess.

If you are filing a joint return, you cannot add any social security withheld from your spouse's income to the amount withheld from your income. You must figure the excess separately for both you and your spouse to determine if either of you has excess withholding.

Earned Income Credit

Many ministers qualify for the earned income credit (EIC). The program currently furnishes a basic benefit for families even when there are no dependent children. There are three supplemental benefits to adjust for families with two or more children, those with a newborn child, and those that incur certain health insurance costs for their children.

Employees may be eligible for the EIC if their 2008 taxable and nontaxable earned income was less than $15,880 if there is no qualifying child; less than $$36,995 if there is one qualifying child; and less than $41,646 if there are two or more children (these rates are based on married filing jointly). You cannot claim the EIC unless your investment income is $2,600 or less.

Your child is a qualifying child if your child meets three tests: relationship, age, and residency.

> **Tip**
>
> For 2008, a qualifying child was at the end of 2008 under age 19 or under age 24 and a student or any age and permanently and totally disabled and who lived with you in the United States for more than half of 2007. If the child was married or meets the conditions to be a qualifying child of another person (other than your spouse if filing a joint return), special rules apply. See IRS Publication 596.

- **Relationship.** Your child must be either your son, daughter, adopted child, grandchild, stepchild, or eligible foster child.
- **Age.** Your child must be under age 19 at the end of 2008, a full-time student under age 24 at the end of 2008, or permanently and totally disabled at any time during 2008, regardless of age.
- **Residency.** Your child must have lived with you in the United States for more than half of 2008 (all of 2008 if an eligible foster child).

The fair rental value of a parsonage provided by the congregation is includible in the earned income calculation. Plus, a housing allowance designated by the congregation in relation to either a parsonage or minister-provided housing counts as earned income. (Exception: if the minister has opted out of social security, neither the fair rental value of a parsonage or housing allowances designated is includible.) However, fees received from activities such as weddings and funerals are not includible.

If you can claim the EIC, you can either have the IRS figure the amount of your credit, or you can figure it yourself (you must complete and attach Schedule EIC to your return if you have at least one qualifying child). If you calculate it, complete a worksheet found in the IRS instructions that determines whether your earned income credit is based on your earned income or modified adjusted gross income (generally equal to your adjusted gross income after disregarding certain losses). Then look up the amount of your credit in an IRS table.

Advance EIC payments

Do you expect to be eligible for the EIC in 2009 and to have a qualifying child? If so, you can choose to get payments of the EIC in your paycheck instead of waiting to get your EIC all at once in 2010 when you file your tax return for the year 2009. These payments are called advance EIC payments. If you qualify for advance EIC payments, complete Form W-5 and give it to your church or other employer.

Extension of Time to File

Your 2008 return should be filed with the IRS service center and payment made by April 15, 2009, to avoid penalties and interest.

If you have filed an extension of time to file your return, remember that your final payment is still due by April 15, 2009, with the extension application. *The extension of time to file is not an extension of your time to pay.*

Six-month extension

To receive a six-month extension of time, you should file Form 4868, Application for Automatic Extension of Time to File U.S. Individual Income Tax Return. The form must be filed by April 15, 2009.

As an option to filing a paper Form 4868, you can electronically file Form 4868 using your tax software package, through a tax professional, or through one of two service providers approved by the IRS:

- Link2Gov Corporation — 1-888-PAY-1040,
  1-888-658-5465 (Customer Service), www.PAY1040.com

Form **4868**
Department of the Treasury
Internal Revenue Service (99)

Application for Automatic Extension of Time
To File U.S. Individual Income Tax Return

OMB No. 1545-0074

2008

For calendar year 2008, or other tax year beginning , 2008, ending , 200 .

Part I Identification

1 Your name(s) (see instructions)
Milton L. Brown

Address (see instructions)
418 Trenton Street

City, town, or post office	State	ZIP code
Springfield	OH	45504

2 Your social security number	3 Spouse's social security number
541 16 8194	238 49 7209

Part II Individual Income Tax

4	Estimate of total tax liability for 2008 . . $	2,000
5	Total 2008 payments	1,500
6	**Balance due.** Subtract line 5 from line 4 (see instructions)	500
7	Amount you are paying (see instructions) . ▶	500
8	Check here if you are "out of the country" and a U.S. citizen or resident (see instructions) . . . . . . ▶	☐
9	Check here if you file Form 1040NR or 1040NR-EZ and did not receive wages as an employee subject to U.S. income tax withholding . . . . ▶	☐

For Privacy Act and Paperwork Reduction Act Notice, see page 4. Cat. No. 13141W Form **4868** (2008)

- Official Payments Corporation — 1-800-2PAY-TAX, 1-877-754-4413 (Customer Service), www.official payments.com

Each service provider will charge a convenience fee based on the amount of the tax payment you are making. Fees may vary between service providers. You will be told what the fee is during the transaction and will have the option to continue or cancel the transaction. You may also obtain the convenience fee by calling the providers' toll-free automated customer service numbers or visiting their websites. Do not add the convenience fee to your tax payment.

> **Remember**
>
> Obtaining a six-month extension is easy. No reason for late filing is needed. The IRS will automatically grant the extension. However, this is not an extension of time to pay—only an extension of time to file. If the amount you owe on your return will generate an underpayment penalty, filing 4868 will not help you.

Penalties

An elaborate system of penalties exists to make sure that tax returns are filed correctly and tax liabilities are paid on time. In addition, interest is charged on many penalties, including the late filing penalty, substantial understatement penalty, overvaluation penalty, negligence penalty, and fraud penalty.

- **Failure to pay penalty.** Even if the IRS grants an extension of time to file, if 90% of your tax is not paid on time, you will be subject to a penalty of one-half of 1% of the unpaid tax for each month or part of a month that the tax is not paid, to a maximum of 25% of the tax. You can avoid the penalty only if you can show that your failure to pay is due to reasonable cause and not willful neglect.
- **Penalty computed by the IRS.** If you do not want to figure your penalty and pay it when you file your tax return, you do not have to. The IRS will figure it for you and send you a bill. In certain situations you must complete Form 2210 and attach it to your return.
- **Form 2210.** If you want to figure your penalty, complete Part I and either Part II or Part III of Form 2210, Underpayment of Estimated Tax by Individuals and Fiduciaries.

> **Tip**
>
> Ask a professional to look over tax due notices from the IRS. It is not unusual for the IRS to send a penalty notice when no penalty is actually due. Demonstrating that you do not owe a penalty may be as simple as completing Form 2210.

You will not generally have to pay a penalty if any of the following situations applies to you:

- ☐ The total of your withholding and estimated tax payments was at least as much as your 2007 tax, you are not subject to the special rule limiting use of prior year's tax, and all required estimated tax payments were on time.
- ☐ The tax balance on your return is no more than 10% of your total 2008 tax, and all required estimated tax payments were on time.

- ☐ Your total 2008 tax minus withholding is less than $1,000.
- ☐ You did not owe tax for 2008.

Interest

If you have not paid the entire tax due by April 15, 2009, you must pay interest from then until the date you pay your tax liability. Receiving an automatic extension of time to file your tax return will not relieve you of the burden of interest.

State extensions

For states that have a state income tax, check the instruction forms that come with your return to determine how to file an extension. In some states, if you owe no additional tax, you need not file a separate state extension. Instead, the state will allow the same extensions that the IRS grants, and you just attach a copy of your federal extension to your state return for filing. Other states may require their own forms.

Extension of Time to Pay

File your return on time even if it is impossible to pay the tax. Filing on time will avoid late filing penalties which are one-half of 1% per month based on the balance of tax due, up to a maximum penalty of 25%. Filing stops the penalties, not the interest.

If you can't pay the full amount due, pay as much as possible when filing the return. Generally, you should not charge your taxes directly to a credit card unless it's a small amount that can be paid off shortly. While you might earn frequent flyer miles, you'll pay interest charges to the credit card company, plus a credit card cost to the IRS of up to 3%, and none of that is deductible.

Installment payments

The IRS may permit you to pay your taxes on the installment plan. Your request for an installment agreement cannot be turned down if the tax you owe is not more than $10,000 and all three of the following apply:

- ➤ During the past five tax years, you have timely filed all income tax returns and paid any income tax due, and have not entered into an installment agreement for payment of income tax,
- ➤ The IRS determines that you cannot pay the tax owed in full when it is due and you give the IRS any information needed to make that determination, and

> **Tip**
>
> If you want to pay your taxes on the installment plan, ask for a six-month extension of time to pay or make the IRS an offer in compromise. Consider obtaining professional assistance. These are very specialized forms.

- You agree to pay the full amount you owe within three years and to comply with the tax laws while the agreement is in effect.

When you file your tax return, include Form 9465, Installment Agreement Request. Within a month, the IRS will notify you whether the installment payment plan has been approved. But the IRS requires you to start paying within a month. If approved, you will have up to 60 months to pay and will still owe the IRS the late-payment penalty plus interest including interest on the penalty. To limit interest and penalty charges, file your return on time and pay as much of the tax as possible with your return. The IRS charges a user fee of $43 for an installment agreement.

If the IRS approves your request, they will send you a letter telling you how to pay the fee and make your first installment payment. They will usually let you know within 30 days after they receive your request whether it is approved or denied.

Six-month extension

Even if you get a six-month extension of time until October 15, 2009 to file your 2008 return by filing Form 4868 (see pages 139-40), you must generally pay your taxes by April 15, 2009.

You may be able to put off paying your taxes for six months until October 15, 2009 without a penalty by using Form 1127, Application for Extension of Time for Payment of Tax. Getting this extension is not easy. You will have to prove to the IRS that you do not have the money to pay the taxes, cannot borrow, and, if forced to pay up, you and your family will suffer "undue hardship."

Hardship means more than inconvenience. You must show that you will have substantial financial loss if you pay your tax on the date it is due. This loss could be caused by selling property at a sacrifice price.

If you file for this extension, you must include a complete statement of all your assets and liabilities and an itemized list of money you received and spent for three months prior to your request. Plus, the IRS may require security such as a notice of lien, mortgage, pledge, deed of trust of specific property, or personal surety.

Offers in Compromise

An Offer in Compromise (OIC) is an agreement between the taxpayer and the government that settles a tax liability for payment of less than the full amount owed. The IRS will generally accept an OIC when it is unlikely that the tax liability can be collected in full and the amount offered reasonably reflects collection potential.

The IRS may legally compromise for one of the following reasons:

- Doubt as to liability—doubt exists that the assessed tax is correct.
- Doubt as to collectibility—doubt exists that you could ever pay the full amount of

tax owed. The IRS will generally consider a doubt as to collectibility offer when the taxpayer is unable to pay the taxes in full either by liquidating assets or through current installment agreement guidelines.

- Effective tax administration—there is no doubt the tax is correct and no doubt the amount owed could be collected, but an exceptional circumstance exists that allows the IRS to consider the offer. To be eligible for compromise on this basis, you must demonstrate that collection of the tax would create an economic hardship or would be unfair and inequitable.

To work out an offer in compromise, you must show that paying the whole tax would cause a severe or unusual economic hardship. Examples of economic hardship include:

- Incapability of earning a living because of long-term medical condition.
- Liquidation of assets would render the taxpayer unable to pay his or her basic living expenses.

File Form 656, Offer in Compromise, with the district director's office where the liability is pending.

Filing an Amended Tax Return

There may still be time to revise your 2005 and 2006 and 2007 income tax returns by filing Form 1040X (see page 144). Review these tax returns to determine if you missed out on any tax savings. Or if you find you owe more money, you can pay before the IRS catches up with you and the interest due has increased. Do not include any interest or penalties on Form 1040X; the IRS will adjust them.

File Form 1040X only after you have filed your original return. Generally, Form 1040X must be filed within three years, plus extensions, after the date you filed the original return or within two years after the date you paid the tax, whichever is later. If Form 1040 was filed early (before April 15), it is considered filed on the due date. If you are correcting your wages or other employee compensation, attach a copy of all additional or corrected Forms W-2 you received after you filed your original return. File a separate Form 1040X for each year you are amending.

Tip

You may need to amend your tax return to pay more taxes or to get a refund from the IRS. Your tax returns can generally be amended if you file Form 1040X within three years of the due date, plus extensions, of the year you are amending.

Don't forget to amend your state return, if appropriate. The IRS and the state tax authorities exchange information. If you file an amended federal return and do not file an amended state return when required to do so, the state is likely to find out about the amended data from the IRS.

Form **1040X** (Rev. November 2008)

Department of the Treasury—Internal Revenue Service

Amended U.S. Individual Income Tax Return

▶ See separate instructions.

OMB No. 1545-0074

This return is for calendar year ▶ 2008, or fiscal year ended ▶ ________, ____.

Note. Allow 8-12 weeks to process Form 1040X.

Please print or type

Your first name and initial: Milton L.	Last name: Brown	Your social security number: 541 16 8194
If a joint return, spouse's first name and initial: Alessia S.	Last name: Brown	Spouse's social security number: 238 49 7209
Home address (no. and street) or P.O. box if mail is not delivered to your home: 418 Trenton Street	Apt. no.	Phone number ( )
City, town or post office, state, and ZIP code. If you have a foreign address, see page 3 of the instructions.: Springfield, OH 45504		

A If the address shown above is different from that shown on your last return filed with the IRS, would you like us to change it in our records? ▶ ☐ Yes ☒ No

B Filing status. Be sure to complete this line. **Note.** You cannot change from joint to separate returns after the due date.

On original return ▶ ☐ Single ☒ Married filing jointly ☐ Married filing separately ☐ Head of household ☐ Qualifying widow(er)

On this return ▶ ☐ Single ☐ Married filing jointly ☐ Married filing separately ☐ Head of household* ☐ Qualifying widow(er)

* If the qualifying person is a child but not your dependent, see page 3 of the instructions.

Use Part II on the back to explain any changes		A. Original amount or as previously adjusted (see page 3)	B. Net change—amount of increase or (decrease)—explain in Part II	C. Correct amount
Income and Deductions (see instructions)				
1 Adjusted gross income (see page 3)	1	32,000	(3,000)	29,000
2 Itemized deductions or standard deduction (see page 4)	2	11,300	300	11,600
3 Subtract line 2 from line 1	3	20,700	(3,300)	17,400
4 Exemptions. If changing, fill in Parts I and II on the back (see page 4)	4	10,500		10,500
5 Taxable income. Subtract line 4 from line 3	5	10,200	(3,300)	6,900
Tax Liability				
6 Tax (see page 5). Method used in col. C Tax Table	6	1,023	(330)	693
7 Credits (see page 5)	7			
8 Subtract line 7 from line 6. Enter the result but not less than zero	8			
9 Other taxes (see page 5)	9	5,500		5,500
10 Total tax. Add lines 8 and 9	10	6,523	(330)	6,193
Payments				
11 Federal income tax withheld and excess social security and tier 1 RRTA tax withheld. If changing, see page 5	11			
12 Estimated tax payments, including amount applied from prior year's return	12			
13 Earned income credit (EIC)	13			
14 Additional child tax credit from Form 8812	14			
15 Credits: Recovery rebate; federal telephone excise tax; or from Forms 2439, 4136, 8885, or 8801 (refundable credit only)	15			
16 Amount paid with request for extension of time to file (see page 5)	16			
17 Amount of tax paid with original return plus additional tax paid after it was filed	17			
18 Total payments. Add lines 11 through 17 in column C	18			8,000
Refund or Amount You Owe				
19 Overpayment, if any, as shown on original return or as previously adjusted by the IRS	19			291
20 Subtract line 19 from line 18 (see page 6)	20			7,709
21 **Amount you owe.** If line 10, column C, is more than line 20, enter the difference and see page 6	21			
22 If line 10, column C, is less than line 20, enter the difference	22			1,516
23 Amount of line 22 you want **refunded to you**	23			1,516
24 Amount of line 22 you want **applied to your** estimated tax	24			

Sign Here

Joint return? See page 2. Keep a copy for your records.

Under penalties of perjury, I declare that I have filed an original return and that I have examined this amended return, including accompanying schedules and statements, and to the best of my knowledge and belief, this amended return is true, correct, and complete. Declaration of preparer (other than taxpayer) is based on all information of which the preparer has any knowledge.

Milton L. Brown — Your signature — Date 6/18/09

Alessia S. Brown — Spouse's signature. If a joint return, **both** must sign. — Date 6/18/09

Paid Preparer's Use Only

Preparer's signature	Date	Check if self-employed ☐	Preparer's SSN or PTIN
Firm's name (or yours if self-employed), address, and ZIP code		EIN	
		Phone no. ( )	

For Paperwork Reduction Act Notice, see page 7 of instructions. Cat. No. 11360L Form **1040X** (Rev. 11-2008)

Amended returns must be filed within three years of the return due date plus approved extensions (see page 143).

INTEGRITY*Points*

- **Filing your income tax returns and paying the tax due.** Unfortunately many ministers do not file their tax returns when they are due and/or do not pay the amount of tax due. Few things will bring more shame to a minister and the congregation.

  One of the few things worse than getting behind on filing tax returns and paying taxes is taking the position that it is not required to file tax returns—an approach taken by tax protesters. There is no validity to such a position.

- **Withholding of income tax by the church.** Take advantage of income tax withholding by the employing congregation. This is one of the most important decisions a minister can make to ensure timely payment of income tax (and additional income tax may be withheld to cover social security tax).

  True, a congregation is not required to withhold federal (and state) income tax from the minister's pay—it's voluntary for both the congregation and the minister. But most congregations will gladly handle the small additional paperwork to assist the minister with tax withholding. And if taxes are timely withheld, underpayment penalties can be eliminated, and the minister is more likely to file his or her return—and on time!

- **Properly calculating the earned income tax credit.** While it is sad that a minister would ever qualify for the earned income tax credit (confirming the minister is being paid below the poverty line) from the perspective of adequate compensation, there is no shame in claiming the credit.

  However, there is shame in computing the earned income tax credit based on inaccurate data. The fair rental value of a parsonage provided by the congregation plus a housing allowance (parsonage or minister-owned housing) is includible in the earned income calculation for this credit (unless the minister has opted out of social security).

Sample Return No. 1

- Accountable expense reimbursement plan
- Minister owns residence
- Pays federal taxes through voluntary withholding
- Church reimbursed nonqualifying moving expenses
- Housing fair rental value test applied
- 403(b) contribution by salary reduction and employer contributions

Minister considered to be an employee for income tax purposes with an accountable business expense plan.

The Browns live in a home they are personally purchasing. Pastor Brown has entered into a voluntary withholding agreement with the church, and $15,500 of federal income taxes are withheld.

Income, Benefits, and Reimbursements:

Church salary	$64,850
Christmas and other special occasion gifts paid by the church based on designated member-gifts to the church	750
Honoraria for performing weddings, funerals, and baptisms	650
Honorarium for speaking as an evangelist at another church	1,000
Mutual fund dividend income:	
Capital gain distributions	150
Ordinary	954
Interest income:	
Taxable	675
Tax-exempt	1,200
Reimbursement of self-employment tax	12,000

Business Expenses, Itemized Deductions, Housing, and Other Data:

100% of church-related expenses (including 9,412 business miles) paid personally ($7,593) were reimbursed by the church under an accountable expense plan, based on timely substantiation of the expenses.

Expenses related to honoraria income:	
Parking	$ 25
Travel – 849 x 58.5 cents per mile	497 [1]
Meals and entertainment	50
Other	200
Potential itemized deductions:	
Unreimbursed doctors, dentists, and drugs	1,500
State and local income taxes:	
2007 taxes paid in 2008	400
Withheld from salary	1,600
Real estate taxes on home	1,000
Home mortgage interest	15,000
Cash contributions	8,200
Noncash contributions – household furniture/ fair market value	266
Tax preparation fee	200
Student loan interest	1,125
Housing data:	
Designation	26,000
Actual expenses	25,625
Fair rental value including utilities	25,000
403(b) pre-tax contributions for Pastor Brown:	
Voluntary employee contributions made under a salary reduction agreement	500
Nonvoluntary employer contributions	2,000
Moving expenses reimbursed under a nonqualified plan (see page 155)	6,750

[1] These miles were all driven in the second half of 2008 when the business mileage rate was 58.5 cents per mile

Form **1040** Department of the Treasury—Internal Revenue Service
U.S. Individual Income Tax Return 2008 (99) IRS Use Only—Do not write or staple in this space

For the year Jan. 1-Dec. 31, 2008, or other tax year beginning , 2008, ending , 20 OMB No. 1545-0074

Label (See instructions on page 12.) **Use the IRS label.** Otherwise, please print or type. LABEL HERE

Your first name and initial: Milton L.	Last name: Brown		**Your social security number** 541 16 8194
If a joint return, spouse's first name and initial: Alessia S.	Last name: Brown		**Spouse's social security number** 238 49 7209
Home address (number and street). If you have a P.O. box, see page 12.: 418 Trenton Street		Apt. no.	▲ You **must** enter your SSN(s) above. ▲
City, town or post office, state, and ZIP code. If you have a foreign address, see page 12.: Springfield, OH 45504			Checking a box below will not change your tax or refund.

Presidential Election Campaign ▶ Check here if you, or your spouse if filing jointly, want $3 to go to this fund (see page 12) ▶ [X] **You** [X] **Spouse**

Filing Status

Check only one box.

1 [ ] Single
2 [X] Married filing jointly (even if only one had income)
3 [ ] Married filing separately. Enter spouse's SSN above and full name here. ▶
4 [ ] Head of household (with qualifying person). (See page 13.) If the qualifying person is a child but not your dependent, enter this child's name here. ▶
5 [ ] Qualifying widow(er) with dependent child (see page 14)

Exemptions

6a [X] **Yourself.** If someone can claim you as a dependent, **do not** check box 6a
b [X] **Spouse**

Boxes checked on 6a and 6b: 2

c **Dependents:**

(1) First name	Last name	(2) Dependent's social security number	(3) Dependent's relationship to you	(4) ✓ if qualifying child for child tax credit (see page 15)
Charles	Brown	514 43 9196	Son	[ ]
				[ ]
				[ ]
				[ ]

If more than four dependents, see page 15.

No. of children on 6c who:
- **lived with you**: 1
- **did not live with you due to divorce or separation (see page 16)**:

Dependents on 6c not entered above:

d Total number of exemptions claimed — Add numbers on lines above ▶ 3

Income

Attach Form(s) W-2 here. Also attach Forms W-2G and 1099-R if tax was withheld.

If you did not get a W-2, see page 19.

Enclose, but do not attach, any payment. Also, please use **Form 1040-V.**

Line	Description		Amount
7	Wages, salaries, tips, etc. Attach Form(s) W-2	7	57,850
8a	**Taxable** interest. Attach Schedule B if required	8a	675
b	**Tax-exempt** interest. **Do not** include on line 8a — 8b: 1,200		
9a	Ordinary dividends. Attach Schedule B if required	9a	954
b	Qualified dividends (see page 19) — 9b		
10	Taxable refunds, credits, or offsets of state and local income taxes (see page 20)	10	
11	Alimony received	11	
12	Business income or (loss). Attach Schedule C or C-EZ	12	903
13	Capital gain or (loss). Attach Schedule D if required. If not required, check here ▶ [X]	13	150
14	Other gains or (losses). Attach Form 4797	14	
15a	IRA distributions — 15a; b Taxable amount (see page 21)	15b	
16a	Pensions and annuities — 16a; b Taxable amount (see page 22)	16b	
17	Rental real estate, royalties, partnerships, S corporations, trusts, etc. Attach Schedule E	17	
18	Farm income or (loss). Attach Schedule F	18	
19	Unemployment compensation	19	
20a	Social security benefits — 20a; b Taxable amount (see page 24)	20b	
21	Other income. List type and amount (see page 24) Excess housing allowance	21	1,000
22	Add the amounts in the far right column for lines 7 through 21. This is your **total income** ▶	22	61,532

Adjusted Gross Income

Line	Description		Amount		
23	Archer MSA deduction. Attach Form 8853	23			
24	Certain business expenses of reservists, performing artists, and fee-basis government officials. Attach Form 2106 or 2106-EZ	24			
25	Health savings account deduction. Attach Form 8889	25			
26	Moving expenses. Attach Form 3903	26			
27	One-half of self-employment tax. Attach Schedule SE	27	5,988		
28	Self-employed SEP, SIMPLE, and qualified plans	28			
29	Self-employed health insurance deduction (see page 26)	29			
30	Penalty on early withdrawal of savings	30			
31a	Alimony paid b Recipient's SSN ▶	31a			
32	IRA deduction (see page 27)	32			
33	Student loan interest deduction (see page 30)	33	1,125		
34	Jury duty pay you gave to your employer	34			
35	Domestic production activities deduction. Attach Form 8903	35			
36	Add lines 23 through 31a and 32 through 35			36	7,113
37	Subtract line 36 from line 22. This is your **adjusted gross income** ▶			37	54,419

For Disclosure, Privacy Act, and Paperwork Reduction Act Notice, see page 83. Cat. No. 11320B Form **1040** (2008)

Line 21 – See page 153 for calculation of the excess housing allowance.

Line 27 – See pages 125-26 for explanation of the self-employment tax deduction.

Form 1040 (2008) Page **2**

Section	Line	Description	Box	Amount	Line	Amount
Tax and Credits	38	Amount from line 37 (adjusted gross income)			38	54,419
	39a	Check if: ☐ **You** were born before January 2, 1944, ☐ Blind. ☐ **Spouse** was born before January 2, 1944, ☐ Blind. **Total boxes checked** ▶ **39a** ☐				
	b	If your spouse itemizes on a separate return or you were a dual-status alien, see page 31 and check here ▶ **39b** ☐				
	c	If you claim the standard deduction and are deducting real estate taxes, check here (see page 31) ▶ **39c** ☐				
	40	**Itemized deductions** (from Schedule A) **or** your **standard deduction** (see left margin)			40	26,466
	41	Subtract line 40 from line 38			41	27,953
	42	If line 38 is $119,975 or less, multiply $3,500 by the total number of exemptions claimed on line 6d. If line 38 is over $119,975, see the worksheet on page 33			42	10,500
	43	**Taxable income.** Subtract line 42 from line 41. If line 42 is more than line 41, enter -0-			43	17,453
	44	Tax (see page 33). Check if any tax is from: **a** ☐ Form(s) 8814 **b** ☐ Form 4972			44	1,819
	45	**Alternative minimum tax** (see page 36). Attach Form 6251			45	
	46	Add lines 44 and 45 ▶			46	1,819
	47	Credit for child and dependent care expenses. Attach Form 2441	47			
	48	Credit for the elderly or the disabled. Attach Schedule R	48			
	49	Education credits. Attach Form 8863	49			
	50	Foreign tax credit. Attach Form 1116 if required	50			
	51	Child tax credit (see page 39). Attach Form 8901 if required	51	1,000		
	52	Retirement savings contributions credit. Attach Form 8880	52			
	53	Credits from Form: **a** ☐ 8396 **b** ☐ 5695 **c** ☐ 8839	53			
	54	Other credits from Form: **a** ☐ 3800 **b** ☐ 8801 **c** ☐ ____	54			
	55	Add lines 47 through 54. These are your **total credits**			55	1,000
	56	Subtract line 55 from line 46. If line 55 is more than line 46, enter -0- ▶			56	819
Other Taxes	57	Self-employment tax. Attach Schedule SE			57	11,975
	58	Unreported social security and Medicare tax from Form: **a** ☐ 4137 **b** ☐ 8919			58	
	59	Additional tax on IRAs, other qualified retirement plans, etc. Attach Form 5329 if required			59	
	60	Additional taxes: **a** ☐ AEIC payments **b** ☐ Household employment taxes. Attach Schedule H			60	
	61	Add lines 56 through 60. This is your **total tax** ▶			61	12,794
Payments	62	Federal income tax withheld from Forms W-2 and 1099	62	15,500		
	63	2008 estimated tax payments and amount applied from 2007 return	63			
	64a	**Earned income credit (EIC)**	64a			
	b	Nontaxable combat pay election 64b				
	65	Excess social security and tier 1 RRTA tax withheld (see page 59)	65			
	66	Additional child tax credit. Attach Form 8812	66			
	67	Amount paid with request for extension to file (see page 59)	67			
	68	Credits from Form: **a** ☐ 2439 **b** ☐ 4136 **c** ☐ 8801 **d** ☐ 8885	68			
	69	First-time homebuyer credit. Attach Form 5405	69			
	70	Recovery rebate credit (see worksheet on page xx)	70			
	71	Add lines 62 through 70. These are your **total payments** ▶			71	15,500
Refund	72	If line 71 is more than line 61, subtract line 61 from line 71. This is the amount you **overpaid**			72	2,706
	73a	Amount of line 72 you want **refunded to you.** If Form 8888 is attached, check here ▶ ☐			73a	2,706
	▶ b	Routing number ▶ **c** Type: ☐ Checking ☐ Savings				
	▶ d	Account number				
	74	Amount of line 72 you want **applied to your 2009 estimated tax** ▶	74			
Amount You Owe	75	**Amount you owe.** Subtract line 71 from line 61. For details on how to pay, see page 60 ▶			75	
	76	Estimated tax penalty (see page 61)	76			

Standard Deduction for—
- People who checked any box on line 39a, 39b, or 39c **or** who can be claimed as a dependent, see page 31.
- All others:

Single or Married filing separately, $5,450

Married filing jointly or Qualifying widow(er), $10,900

Head of household, $8,000

If you have a qualifying child, attach Schedule EIC.

Direct deposit? See page 59 and fill in 73b, 73c, and 73d, or Form 8888.

Third Party Designee — Do you want to allow another person to discuss this return with the IRS (see page 61)? ☐ **Yes.** Complete the following. ☐ **No**

Designee's name ▶ Phone no. ▶ ( ) Personal identification number (PIN) ▶

Sign Here — Joint return? See page 13. Keep a copy for your records.

Under penalties of perjury, I declare that I have examined this return and accompanying schedules and statements, and to the best of my knowledge and belief, they are true, correct, and complete. Declaration of preparer (other than taxpayer) is based on all information of which preparer has any knowledge.

Your signature	Date	Your occupation	Daytime phone number
Milton L. Brown	4/15/09	Minister	( )
Spouse's signature. If a joint return, **both** must sign.	Date	Spouse's occupation	
Alessia S. Brown	4/15/09	Housewife	

Paid Preparer's Use Only

Preparer's signature	Date	Check if self-employed ☐	Preparer's SSN or PTIN
Firm's name (or yours if self-employed), address, and ZIP code		EIN	
		Phone no. ( )	

Form **1040** (2008)

Line 64 – The minister had income tax withheld under a voluntary withholding agreement with the church. Notice that income tax was withheld relating to both the income and social security tax liability.

SCHEDULES A&B (Form 1040)

Department of the Treasury Internal Revenue Service (99)

Schedule A—Itemized Deductions

(Schedule B is on back)

▶ Attach to Form 1040. ▶ See Instructions for Schedules A&B (Form 1040).

OMB No. 1545-0074 — 2008 — Attachment Sequence No. 07

Name(s) shown on Form 1040: Milton L. and Alessia S. Brown

Your social security number: 541 | 16 | 8194

Section	Line	Description	Box	Amount	Box	Amount
Medical and Dental Expenses		**Caution.** Do not include expenses reimbursed or paid by others.				
	1	Medical and dental expenses (see page A-1)	1	1,500		
	2	Enter amount from Form 1040, line 38 [2] 54,419				
	3	Multiply line 2 by 7.5% (.075)	3	4,081		
	4	Subtract line 3 from line 1. If line 3 is more than line 1, enter -0-			4	0
Taxes You Paid (See page A-2.)	5	State and local income taxes 1,600 + 400	5	2,000		
	6	Real estate taxes (see page A-5)	6	1,000		
	7	Personal property taxes	7			
	8	Other taxes. List type and amount ▶	8			
	9	Add lines 5 through 8			9	3,000
Interest You Paid (See page A-5.)	10	Home mortgage interest and points reported to you on Form 1098	10	15,000		
	11	Home mortgage interest not reported to you on Form 1098. If paid to the person from whom you bought the home, see page A-6 and show that person's name, identifying no., and address ▶	11			
Note. Personal interest is not deductible.	12	Points not reported to you on Form 1098. See page A-6 for special rules	12			
	13	Qualified mortgage insurance premiums (See page A-7)	13			
	14	Investment interest. Attach Form 4952 if required. (See page A-7.)	14			
	15	Add lines 10 through 14			15	15,000
Gifts to Charity If you made a gift and got a benefit for it, see page A-8.	16	Gifts by cash or check. If you made any gift of $250 or more, see page A-8	16	8,200		
	17	Other than by cash or check. If any gift of $250 or more, see page A-8. You **must** attach Form 8283 if over $500	17	266		
	18	Carryover from prior year	18			
	19	Add lines 16 through 18			19	8,466
Casualty and Theft Losses	20	Casualty or theft loss(es). Attach Form 4684. (See page A-9.)			20	
Job Expenses and Certain Miscellaneous Deductions (See page A-9.)	21	Unreimbursed employee expenses—job travel, union dues, job education, etc. Attach Form 2106 or 2106-EZ if required. (See page A-9.) ▶	21			
	22	Tax preparation fees	22	200		
	23	Other expenses—investment, safe deposit box, etc. List type and amount ▶	23			
	24	Add lines 21 through 23	24	200		
	25	Enter amount from Form 1040, line 38 [25] 54,419				
	26	Multiply line 25 by 2% (.02)	26	1,088		
	27	Subtract line 26 from line 24. If line 26 is more than line 24, enter -0-			27	0
Other Miscellaneous Deductions	28	Other—from list on page A-10. List type and amount ▶			28	
Total Itemized Deductions	29	Is Form 1040, line 38, over $159,950 (over $79,975 if married filing separately)? ☐ **No.** Your deduction is not limited. Add the amounts in the far right column for lines 4 through 28. Also, enter this amount on Form 1040, line 40. ☐ **Yes.** Your deduction may be limited. See page A-10 for the amount to enter. ▶			29	26,466
	30	If you elect to itemize deductions even though they are less than your standard deduction, check here ▶ ☐				

For Paperwork Reduction Act Notice, see Form 1040 instructions. Cat. No. 11330X **Schedule A (Form 1040) 2008**

Lines 6 and 10 – The real estate taxes and home mortgage interest are deducted on this form plus excluded from income on line 7, Form 1040, page 1 as a housing allowance.

Line 20 – There are no unreimbursed employee expenses to deduct since the church reimbursed all the professional expenses under an accountable expense reimbursement plan.

Schedules A&B (Form 1040) 2008 — OMB No. 1545-0074 — Page 2

Name(s) shown on Form 1040. Do not enter name and social security number if shown on other side.
Milton L. and Alessia S. Brown

Your social security number: 541 16 8194

Schedule B—Interest and Ordinary Dividends

Attachment Sequence No. 08

Part I Interest

(See page B-1 and the instructions for Form 1040, line 8a.)

Note. If you received a Form 1099-INT, Form 1099-OID, or substitute statement from a brokerage firm, list the firm's name as the payer and enter the total interest shown on that form.

			Amount
1	List name of payer. If any interest is from a seller-financed mortgage and the buyer used the property as a personal residence, see page B-1 and list this interest first. Also, show that buyer's social security number and address ▶		
	State Highway Bonds		1,200
	Ohio, S&L	1	675
	Subtotal		1,875
	Less: Tax-Exempt Interest		-1,200
2	Add the amounts on line 1	2	675
3	Excludable interest on series EE and I U.S. savings bonds issued after 1989. Attach Form 8815	3	
4	Subtract line 3 from line 2. Enter the result here and on Form 1040, line 8a ▶	4	675

Note. If line 4 is over $1,500, you must complete Part III.

Part II Ordinary Dividends

(See page B-1 and the instructions for Form 1040, line 9a.)

Note. If you received a Form 1099-DIV or substitute statement from a brokerage firm, list the firm's name as the payer and enter the ordinary dividends shown on that form.

			Amount
5	List name of payer ▶		
	Vanguard	5	954
6	Add the amounts on line 5. Enter the total here and on Form 1040, line 9a ▶	6	954

Note. If line 6 is over $1,500, you must complete Part III.

Part III Foreign Accounts and Trusts

(See page B-2.)

	You must complete this part if you **(a)** had over $1,500 of taxable interest or ordinary dividends; or **(b)** had a foreign account; or **(c)** received a distribution from, or were a grantor of, or a transferor to, a foreign trust.	Yes	No
7a	At any time during 2008, did you have an interest in or a signature or other authority over a financial account in a foreign country, such as a bank account, securities account, or other financial account? See page B-2 for exceptions and filing requirements for Form TD F 90-22.1.		X
b	If "Yes," enter the name of the foreign country ▶		
8	During 2008, did you receive a distribution from, or were you the grantor of, or transferor to, a foreign trust? If "Yes," you may have to file Form 3520. See page B-2		X

For Paperwork Reduction Act Notice, see Form 1040 instructions. — **Schedule B (Form 1040) 2008**

SCHEDULE C-EZ (Form 1040)

Department of the Treasury Internal Revenue Service (99)

Net Profit From Business

(Sole Proprietorship)

► Partnerships, joint ventures, etc., generally must file Form 1065 or 1065-B.
► Attach to Form 1040, 1040NR, or 1041. ► See instructions on back.

OMB No. 1545-0074

2008

Attachment Sequence No. 09A

Name of proprietor: Milton L. Brown

Social security number (SSN): 541 | 16 | 8194

Part I General Information

You May Use Schedule C-EZ Instead of Schedule C Only If You:

- Had business expenses of $5,000 or less.
- Use the cash method of accounting.
- Did not have an inventory at any time during the year.
- Did not have a net loss from your business.
- Had only one business as either a sole proprietor, qualified joint venture, or statutory employee.

And You:

- Had no employees during the year.
- Are not required to file **Form 4562**, Depreciation and Amortization, for this business. See the instructions for Schedule C, line 13, on page C-4 to find out if you must file.
- Do not deduct expenses for business use of your home.
- Do not have prior year unallowed passive activity losses from this business.

A Principal business or profession, including product or service: Minister

B Enter code from pages C-8, 9, & 10 ► 8 1 3 0 0 0

C Business name. If no separate business name, leave blank.

D Employer ID number (EIN), if any

E Business address (including suite or room no.). Address not required if same as on page 1 of your tax return.

City, town or post office, state, and ZIP code

Part II Figure Your Net Profit

1	**Gross receipts. Caution.** See the instructions for Schedule C, line 1, on page C-3 and check the box if: • This income was reported to you on Form W-2 and the "Statutory employee" box on that form was checked, or • You are a member of a qualified joint venture reporting only rental real estate income not subject to self-employment tax . . . ► ☐	1	1,650
2	**Total expenses** (see instructions on page 2). If more than $5,000, you **must** use Schedule C	2	747
3	**Net profit.** Subtract line 2 from line 1. If less than zero, you **must** use Schedule C. Enter on both **Form 1040, line 12,** and **Schedule SE, line 2,** or on **Form 1040NR, line 13.** (If you checked the box on line 1, **do not** report the amount from line 3 on Schedule SE, line 2.) Estates and trusts, enter on **Form 1041, line 3** . . .	3	903

Part III Information on Your Vehicle. Complete this part **only** if you are claiming car or truck expenses on line 2.

4 When did you place your vehicle in service for business purposes? (month, day, year) ► 1 / 1 / 06

5 Of the total number of miles you drove your vehicle during 2008, enter the number of miles you used your vehicle for:

Schedule C 849

a Business 9,412 b Commuting (see instructions) 1,216 c Other

6 Was your vehicle available for personal use during off-duty hours? . . . ☐ Yes ☒ No

7 Do you (or your spouse) have another vehicle available for personal use? . . . ☐ Yes ☒ No

8a Do you have evidence to support your deduction? . . . ☐ Yes ☒ No

Gross receipts:

Honoraria (weddings, etc.)	$650
Speaking honorarium	1,000
	$1,650

Expenses:

Parking	$ 25
Miles (849 miles x 58.5)	497
Meals & entertainment ($50 x 50%)	25
Other	200
	$ 747

Most ministers considered to be employees for income tax purposes (with that income reported on line 7, Form 1040, page 1) also have honoraria and fee income and related expenses that are reportable on Schedule C (C-EZ).

Schedule SE (Form 1040) 2008 | Attachment Sequence No. **17** | Page **2**

Name of person with **self-employment** income (as shown on Form 1040)	Social security number of person with **self-employment** income ▶	
Milton L.Brown		541 ⁝ 16 ⁝ 8194

Section B—Long Schedule SE

Part I Self-Employment Tax

Note. If your only income subject to self-employment tax is **church employee income,** skip lines 1 through 4b. Enter -0- on line 4c and go to line 5a. Income from services you performed as a minister or a member of a religious order **is not** church employee income. See page SE-1.

A If you are a minister, member of a religious order, or Christian Science practitioner **and** you filed Form 4361, but you had $400 or more of **other** net earnings from self-employment, check here and continue with Part I . . . . ▶ ☐

Line	Description	Box	Amount	
1a	Net farm profit or (loss) from Schedule F, line 36, and farm partnerships, Schedule K-1 (Form 1065), box 14, code A. **Note.** Skip lines 1a and 1b if you use the farm optional method (see page SE-4)	1a		
b	If you received social security retirement or disability benefits, enter the amount of Conservation Reserve Program payments included on Schedule F, line 6b, or listed on Schedule K-1 (Form 1065), box 20, code X	1b	( )	
2	Net profit or (loss) from Schedule C, line 31; Schedule C-EZ, line 3; Schedule K-1 (Form 1065), box 14, code A (other than farming); and Schedule K-1 (Form 1065-B), box 9, code J1. Ministers and members of religious orders, see page SE-1 for types of income to report on this line. See page SE-3 for other income to report. **Note.** Skip this line if you use the nonfarm optional method (see page SE-4)	2	84,753	
3	Combine lines 1a, 1b, and 2	3	84,753	
4a	If line 3 is more than zero, multiply line 3 by 92.35% (.9235). Otherwise, enter amount from line 3	4a	78,269	
b	If you elect one or both of the optional methods, enter the total of lines 15 and 17 here	4b		
c	Combine lines 4a and 4b. If less than $400, **stop**; you do not owe self-employment tax. **Exception.** If less than $400 and you had **church employee income,** enter -0- and continue ▶	4c	78,269	
5a	Enter your **church employee income** from Form W-2. See page SE-1 for definition of church employee income (5a)			
b	Multiply line 5a by 92.35% (.9235). If less than $100, enter -0-	5b		
6	**Net earnings from self-employment.** Add lines 4c and 5b	6	78,269	
7	Maximum amount of combined wages and self-employment earnings subject to social security tax or the 6.2% portion of the 7.65% railroad retirement (tier 1) tax for 2008	7	102,000	00
8a	Total social security wages and tips (total of boxes 3 and 7 on Form(s) W-2) and railroad retirement (tier 1) compensation. If $102,000 or more, skip lines 8b through 10, and go to line 11 (8a)			
b	Unreported tips subject to social security tax (from Form 4137, line 10) (8b)			
c	Wages subject to social security tax (from Form 8919, line 10) (8c)			
d	Add lines 8a, 8b, and 8c	8d		
9	Subtract line 8d from line 7. If zero or less, enter -0- here and on line 10 and go to line 11 ▶	9	97,500	
10	Multiply the **smaller** of line 6 or line 9 by 12.4% (.124)	10	9,705	
11	Multiply line 6 by 2.9% (.029)	11	2,270	
12	**Self-employment tax.** Add lines 10 and 11. Enter here and on **Form 1040, line 57**	12	11,975	
13	**Deduction for one-half of self-employment tax.** Multiply line 12 by 50% (.5). Enter the result here and on **Form 1040, line 27** (13: 5,988)			

Part II Optional Methods To Figure Net Earnings (see page SE-4)

Farm Optional Method. You may use this method **only** if **(a)** your gross farm income[1] was not more than $6,300, **or (b)** your net farm profits[2] were less than $4,548.

Line	Description	Box	Amount	
14	Maximum income for optional methods	14	4,200	00
15	Enter the **smaller** of: two-thirds (⅔) of gross farm income[1] (not less than zero) **or** $4,200. Also include this amount on line 4b above	15		

Nonfarm Optional Method. You may use this method **only** if **(a)** your net nonfarm profits[3] were less than $4,548 and also less than 72.189% of your gross nonfarm income,[4] **and (b)** you had net earnings from self-employment of at least $400 in 2 of the prior 3 years.

Caution. You may use this method no more than five times.

Line	Description	Box	Amount
16	Subtract line 15 from line 14	16	
17	Enter the **smaller** of: two-thirds (⅔) of gross nonfarm income[4] (not less than zero) **or** the amount on line 16. Also include this amount on line 4b above	17	

[1] From Sch. F, line 11, and Sch. K-1 (Form 1065), box 14, code B.

[2] From Sch. F, line 36, and Sch. K-1 (Form 1065), box 14, code A—minus the amount you would have entered on line 1b had you not used the optional method.

[3] From Sch. C, line 31; Sch. C-EZ, line 3; Sch. K-1 (Form 1065), box 14, code A; and Sch. K-1 (Form 1065-B), box 9, code J1.

[4] From Sch. C, line 7; Sch. C-EZ, line 1; Sch. K-1 (Form 1065), box 14, code C; and Sch. K-1 (Form 1065-B), box 9, code J2.

Line 2 – See the worksheet on page 154 for the calculation of this amount.

Line 4 – This line results in the deduction of a portion of the self-employment tax liability.

A minister must use Section B-Long Schedule if he or she received nonministerial wages (subject to FICA) and the total of these wages and net ministerial self-employment earnings (W-2 and Schedule C [C-EZ]-related) is more than $102,000.

Housing Allowance Worksheet

Minister Living in Home

Minister Owns or Is Buying

Minister's Name: Milton L. Brown

For the period January 1, 2008 to December 31, 2008

Date designation approved December 20, 2007

Allowable Housing Expenses *(expenses paid by minister from current income)*

	Estimated Expenses	Actual	
Down payment on purchase of housing	$	$	
Housing loan principal and interest payments	18,117	18,875	
Real estate commission, escrow fees			
Real property taxes	900	1,000	
Personal property taxes on contents			
Homeowner's insurance	500	550	
Personal property insurance on contents	150	200	
Umbrella liability insurance	100		
Structural maintenance and repair		550	
Landscaping, gardening, and pest control		200	
Furnishings *(purchase, repair, replacement)*		400	
Decoration and redecoration			
Utilities *(gas, electricity, water)* and trash collection	3,500	3,500	
Local telephone expense *(base charge)*	150	150	
Homeowner's association dues/condominium fees	219	200	
Subtotal	23,636		
10% allowance for unexpected expenses	2,364		
TOTAL	$ 26,000	$ 25,625	(A)
Properly designated housing allowance		$ 26,000	(B)
Fair rental value of home, including furnishings, plus utilities		$ 25,000	(C)

Note: The amount excludable from income for federal income tax purposes is the *lowest* of A, B, or C.

The $1,000 difference between the designation ($26,000) and the fair rental value ($25,000) is reported as additional income on Form 1040, line 21.

Self-Employment Social Security Tax Worksheet

Inclusions:

Salary paid by church as reflected on Form W-2, Box 1	$ 57,850
Net profit or loss as reflected on Schedule C or C-EZ (includes speaking honoraria, offerings you receive for marriages, baptisms, funerals, and other fees)	903
Housing allowance excluded from salary on Form W-2	26,000
Fair rental value of church-provided housing (including paid utilities)	
Nonaccountable business expense reimbursements (if not included on Form W-2)	
Reimbursement of self-employment taxes (if not included on Form W-2)	
Other amounts that should have been included on Form W-2, Box 1, such as love offerings	
Total inclusions	84,753

Deductions:

Unreimbursed ministerial business and professional expenses or reimbursed expenses paid under a nonaccountable plan	
A. Deductible on Schedule A before the 2% of AGI limitation whether or not you itemized[1] or	
B. Not deductible on Form 2106/2106 EZ or Schedule C/C-EZ because expenses were allocated to taxable/nontaxable income	
Total deductions	
Net earnings from self-employment (to Schedule SE)	$ 84,753

[1] The 50% unreimbursed meal and entertainment expense limitation applies to amounts subject to social security tax. In other words, if some of your meal and entertainment expenses were subjected to the 50% limit, the remainder cannot be deducted here.

Note 1: Your net earnings from self-employment are not affected by the foreign earned income exclusion or the foreign housing exclusion or deduction if you are a U.S. citizen or resident alien who is serving abroad and living in a foreign country.

Note 2: Amounts received as pension payments or annuity payments related to a church-sponsored tax-sheltered annuity by a retired minister are generally considered to be excluded from the social security calculation.

Net earnings from self-employment are entered on Schedule SE, line 2 (see page 152). While the W-2 portion of the self-employment income could be shown on Schedule SE, line 5a, the example shows the simpler approach of transferring the total self-employment income to line 2.

22222	Void ☐	a Employee's social security number 541-16-8194	For Official Use Only ► OMB No. 1545-0008

b Employer identification number (EIN) 38-9418217	1 Wages, tips, other compensation 57850.00	2 Federal income tax withheld 15500.00
c Employer's name, address, and ZIP code Magnolia Springs Church 4805 Douglas Road Springfield, OH 45504	3 Social security wages	4 Social security tax withheld
	5 Medicare wages and tips	6 Medicare tax withheld
	7 Social security tips	8 Allocated tips
d Control number	9 Advance EIC payment	10 Dependent care benefits
e Employee's first name and initial Milton L. / Last name Brown / Suff.	11 Nonqualified plans	12a See instructions for box 12 — E 500
418 Trenton Street Springfield, OH 45504	13 Statutory employee ☐ Retirement plan ☐ Third-party sick pay ☐	12b
	14 Other	12c
f Employee's address and ZIP code		12d

15 State	Employer's state ID number	16 State wages, tips, etc.	17 State income tax	18 Local wages, tips, etc.	19 Local income tax	20 Locality name
OH	627803	57850.00	1600.00			

Form **W-2** Wage and Tax Statement **2008**

Department of the Treasury—Internal Revenue Service

For Privacy Act and Paperwork Reduction Act Notice, see back of Copy D.

Copy A For Social Security Administration — Send this entire page with Form W-3 to the Social Security Administration; photocopies are **not** acceptable.

Cat. No. 10134D

Do Not Cut, Fold, or Staple Forms on This Page — Do Not Cut, Fold, or Staple Forms on This Page

Explanation of compensation reported on Form W-2, Box 1:

Salary ($64,850 less $26,000 housing allowance and $500 403[b] contributions)	$38,350
Special occasion gifts	750
Reimbursement of self-employment tax	12,000
Moving expense reimbursement of nonqualified expenses	6,750
	$57,850

Pastor Brown received reimbursements of $7,593 under an accountable expense reimbursement plan. The reimbursements are not included on Form W-2 or deductible on Form 1040. There is no requirement to add the reimbursements to income taxable for social security purposes on Schedule SE.

Pastor Brown was also reimbursed for $6,750 of nonqualified moving expenses. He failed the distance test in that his new principal place of work was less than 50 miles farther from his old residence than the old residence was from his old place of work.

Sample Return No. 2

- Nonaccountable expense reimbursements
- Minister occupies a church-provided parsonage
- Pays federal taxes using Form 1040-ES
- Qualifies for the Earned Income Credit
- Church did not reimburse moving expenses
- Application of Deason Rule
- Tax Saver's Credit

Minister considered to be an employee for income tax purposes with a nonaccountable business expense plan.

The Halls live in church-provided housing. Pastor Hall files Form 1040-ES to pay income and social security (SECA) taxes and paid $300 each quarter.

Income, Benefits, and Reimbursements:

Church salary – Donald	$ 11,000
Salary – Julie (W-2 not shown)/ Federal withholding of $250	9,150
Christmas and other special occasion gifts paid by the church based on designated member-gifts to the church	500
Honoraria for performing weddings, funerals, baptisms, and outside speaking engagements	5,200
Interest income (taxable)	4,950
Reimbursement of self-employment tax	2,100
Business expense allowance (no accounting provided to church)	1,700

Business Expenses, Itemized Deductions, 403(b) Contributions, Housing Data, and Moving Expense Data:

Church-related expenses paid personally:	
Business use of personally-owned auto (W-2 related) [1]	7,397 miles[1]
Personal nondeductible commuting	2,432 miles
Seminar expenses:	
Airfare	$675 [2]
Meals	233 [2]
Lodging	167 [2]
Subscriptions	200 [2]
Books (less than one-year life)	100 [2]
Supplies	250 [2]
Entertainment expenses	1,207 [2]
Continuing education tuition (related to church employment)	500 [2]
Travel expense related to honoraria (Schedule C):	
Airfare	2,042 [2]
Business use of personally-owned auto [2]	2,601 miles
Lodging	400 [2]
Supplies	700 [2]
Potential itemized deductions:	
Unreimbursed doctors, dentists, and drugs	3,200
State and local income taxes	460
Personal property taxes	300
Cash contributions	3,310
Housing data:	
Designation	2,000
Actual expenses	1,000
Fair rental value, including utilities	11,150
403(b) pre-tax contributions for Pastor Hall: Voluntary employee contributions made under a salary reduction agreement	500
Moving expenses (deductible)	1,000

[1] 1st half of year - 3,212 miles
2nd half of year - 4,185 miles

[2] 5% of these expenses are unallowable (see page 170).

Form **1040** Department of the Treasury—Internal Revenue Service
U.S. Individual Income Tax Return **2008** (99) IRS Use Only—Do not write or staple in this space

For the year Jan. 1-Dec. 31, 2008, or other tax year beginning , 2008, ending , 20 OMB No. 1545-0074

Label (See instructions on page 12.) **Use the IRS label.** Otherwise, please print or type. LABEL HERE

Your first name and initial: Donald L.	Last name: Hall	**Your social security number**: 482 : 11 : 6043
If a joint return, spouse's first name and initial: Julie M.	Last name: Hall	**Spouse's social security number**: 720 : 92 : 1327
Home address (number and street). If you have a P.O. box, see page 12.: 504 Linden Avenue	Apt. no.	▲ You **must** enter your SSN(s) above. ▲
City, town or post office, state, and ZIP code. If you have a foreign address, see page 12.: Wabash, IN 46992		Checking a box below will not change your tax or refund.

Presidential Election Campaign ▶ Check here if you, or your spouse if filing jointly, want $3 to go to this fund (see page 12) ▶ [X] **You** [X] **Spouse**

Filing Status

Check only one box.

1 [ ] Single
2 [X] Married filing jointly (even if only one had income)
3 [ ] Married filing separately. Enter spouse's SSN above and full name here. ▶
4 [ ] Head of household (with qualifying person). (See page 13.) If the qualifying person is a child but not your dependent, enter this child's name here. ▶
5 [ ] Qualifying widow(er) with dependent child (see page 14)

Exemptions

6a [X] **Yourself.** If someone can claim you as a dependent, **do not** check box 6a — Boxes checked on 6a and 6b: 2
b [X] **Spouse**
c **Dependents:**

(1) First name	Last name	(2) Dependent's social security number	(3) Dependent's relationship to you	(4) ✓ if qualifying child for child tax credit (see page 15)
David K.	Hall	514 : 42 : 7465	Son	[X]
Sarah E.	Hall	516 : 49 : 0125	Daughter	[X]
				[ ]
				[ ]

If more than four dependents, see page 15.

No. of children on 6c who: • lived with you: 2
• did not live with you due to divorce or separation (see page 16):
Dependents on 6c not entered above:

d Total number of exemptions claimed — Add numbers on lines above ▶ 4

Income

Attach Form(s) W-2 here. Also attach Forms W-2G and 1099-R if tax was withheld.

If you did not get a W-2, see page 19.

Enclose, but do not attach, any payment. Also, please use **Form 1040-V.**

Line	Description		Amount
7	Wages, salaries, tips, etc. Attach Form(s) W-2	7	21,950
8a	**Taxable** interest. Attach Schedule B if required	8a	4,950
b	**Tax-exempt** interest. **Do not** include on line 8a — 8b		
9a	Ordinary dividends. Attach Schedule B if required	9a	
b	Qualified dividends (see page 19) — 9b		
10	Taxable refunds, credits, or offsets of state and local income taxes (see page 20)	10	
11	Alimony received	11	
12	Business income or (loss). Attach Schedule C or C-EZ	12	963
13	Capital gain or (loss). Attach Schedule D if required. If not required, check here ▶ [ ]	13	
14	Other gains or (losses). Attach Form 4797	14	
15a	IRA distributions — 15a — b Taxable amount (see page 21)	15b	
16a	Pensions and annuities — 16a — b Taxable amount (see page 22)	16b	
17	Rental real estate, royalties, partnerships, S corporations, trusts, etc. Attach Schedule E	17	
18	Farm income or (loss). Attach Schedule F	18	
19	Unemployment compensation	19	
20a	Social security benefits — 20a — b Taxable amount (see page 24)	20b	
21	Other income. List type and amount (see page 24) Excess housing allowance	21	1,000
22	Add the amounts in the far right column for lines 7 through 21. This is your **total income** ▶	22	28,863

Adjusted Gross Income

Line	Description		Amount		
23	Archer MSA deduction. Attach Form 8853	23			
24	Certain business expenses of reservists, performing artists, and fee-basis government officials. Attach Form 2106 or 2106-EZ	24			
25	Health savings account deduction. Attach Form 8889	25			
26	Moving expenses. Attach Form 3903	26	1,000		
27	One-half of self-employment tax. Attach Schedule SE	27	1,399		
28	Self-employed SEP, SIMPLE, and qualified plans	28			
29	Self-employed health insurance deduction (see page 26)	29			
30	Penalty on early withdrawal of savings	30			
31a	Alimony paid b Recipient's SSN ▶	31a			
32	IRA deduction (see page 27)	32			
33	Student loan interest deduction (see page 30)	33			
34	Jury duty pay you gave to your employer	34			
35	Domestic production activities deduction. Attach Form 8903	35			
36	Add lines 23 through 31a and 32 through 35			36	2,399
37	Subtract line 36 from line 22. This is your **adjusted gross income** ▶			37	26,464

For Disclosure, Privacy Act, and Paperwork Reduction Act Notice, see page 83. Cat. No. 11320B Form **1040** (2008)

Line 7 – Julie's W-2, $9,150, plus Donald's W-2, $12,800 (see page 173).

Line 21 – See page 171 for the calculation of the excess housing allowance.

Line 27 – See pages 125-26 for explanation of the self-employment tax deduction.

Form 1040 (2008) Page 2

	Line	Description	Sub-box	Sub-amount	Box	Amount
Tax and Credits	38	Amount from line 37 (adjusted gross income)			38	26,464
	39a	Check if: ☐ You were born before January 2, 1944, ☐ Blind. ☐ Spouse was born before January 2, 1944, ☐ Blind. Total boxes checked ▶ 39a				
	b	If your spouse itemizes on a separate return or you were a dual-status alien, see page 31 and check here ▶ 39b ☐				
	c	If you claim the standard deduction and are deducting real estate taxes, check here (see page 31) ▶ 39c ☐				
	40	**Itemized deductions** (from Schedule A) **or** your **standard deduction** (see left margin)			40	11,308
	41	Subtract line 40 from line 38			41	15,156
	42	If line 38 is $119,975 or less, multiply $3,500 by the total number of exemptions claimed on line 6d. If line 38 is over $119,975, see the worksheet on page 33			42	14,000
	43	**Taxable income.** Subtract line 42 from line 41. If line 42 is more than line 41, enter -0-			43	1,156
	44	Tax (see page 33). Check if any tax is from: a ☐ Form(s) 8814 b ☐ Form 4972			44	116
	45	**Alternative minimum tax** (see page 36). Attach Form 6251			45	
	46	Add lines 44 and 45 ▶			46	116
	47	Credit for child and dependent care expenses. Attach Form 2441	47			
	48	Credit for the elderly or the disabled. Attach Schedule R	48			
	49	Education credits. Attach Form 8863	49			
	50	Foreign tax credit. Attach Form 1116 if required	50			
	51	Child tax credit (see page 39). Attach Form 8901 if required	51	116		
	52	Retirement savings contributions credit. Attach Form 8880	52			
	53	Credits from Form: a ☐ 8396 b ☐ 5695 c ☐ 8839	53			
	54	Other credits from Form: a ☐ 3800 b ☐ 8801 c ☐ ____	54			
	55	Add lines 47 through 54. These are your **total credits**			55	116
	56	Subtract line 55 from line 46. If line 55 is more than line 46, enter -0- ▶			56	-0-
Other Taxes	57	Self-employment tax. Attach Schedule SE			57	2,797
	58	Unreported social security and Medicare tax from Form: a ☐ 4137 b ☐ 8919			58	
	59	Additional tax on IRAs, other qualified retirement plans, etc. Attach Form 5329 if required			59	
	60	Additional taxes: a ☐ AEIC payments b ☐ Household employment taxes. Attach Schedule H			60	
	61	Add lines 56 through 60. This is your **total tax** ▶			61	2,797
Payments	62	Federal income tax withheld from Forms W-2 and 1099	62	250		
	63	2008 estimated tax payments and amount applied from 2007 return	63	1,200		
	64a	**Earned income credit (EIC)**	64a	2,974		
	b	Nontaxable combat pay election 64b				
	65	Excess social security and tier 1 RRTA tax withheld (see page 59)	65	1,779		
	66	Additional child tax credit. Attach Form 8812	66			
	67	Amount paid with request for extension to file (see page 59)	67			
	68	Credits from Form: a ☐ 2439 b ☐ 4136 c ☐ 8801 d ☐ 8885	68			
	69	First-time homebuyer credit. Attach Form 5405	69			
	70	Recovery rebate credit (see worksheet on page xx)	70			
	71	Add lines 62 through 70. These are your **total payments** ▶			71	6,203
Refund	72	If line 71 is more than line 61, subtract line 61 from line 71. This is the amount you **overpaid**			72	3,406
	73a	Amount of line 72 you want **refunded to you.** If Form 8888 is attached, check here ▶ ☐			73a	3,006
	▶ b	Routing number ▶ c Type: ☐ Checking ☐ Savings				
	▶ d	Account number				
	74	Amount of line 72 you want **applied to your 2009 estimated tax** ▶	74	400		
Amount You Owe	75	**Amount you owe.** Subtract line 71 from line 61. For details on how to pay, see page 60 ▶			75	
	76	Estimated tax penalty (see page 61)	76			

Standard Deduction for—
- People who checked any box on line 39a, 39b, or 39c or who can be claimed as a dependent, see page 31.
- All others:

Single or Married filing separately, $5,450

Married filing jointly or Qualifying widow(er), $10,900

Head of household, $8,000

If you have a qualifying child, attach Schedule EIC.

Direct deposit? See page 59 and fill in 73b, 73c, and 73d, or Form 8888.

Third Party Designee Do you want to allow another person to discuss this return with the IRS (see page 61)? ☐ **Yes.** Complete the following. ☐ **No**

Designee's name ▶ Phone no. ▶ ( ) Personal identification number (PIN) ▶

Sign Here Under penalties of perjury, I declare that I have examined this return and accompanying schedules and statements, and to the best of my knowledge and belief, they are true, correct, and complete. Declaration of preparer (other than taxpayer) is based on all information of which preparer has any knowledge.

Joint return? See page 13. Keep a copy for your records.

Your signature	Date	Your occupation	Daytime phone number
Donald L. Hall	4/15/08	Minister	( )
Spouse's signature. If a joint return, **both** must sign.	Date	Spouse's occupation	
Julie M. Hall	4/15/08	Secretary	

Paid Preparer's Use Only Preparer's signature ▶ Date Check if self-employed ☐ Preparer's SSN or PTIN

Firm's name (or yours if self-employed), address, and ZIP code ▶ EIN Phone no. ( )

Form **1040** (2008)

Line 65 – The minister pays federal taxes (income and social security) by quarterly filing Form 1040-ES.

Line 75 – The taxpayers elected to apply $400 of their refund to their 2008 estimated taxes.

SCHEDULES A&B (Form 1040)
Department of the Treasury Internal Revenue Service (99)

Schedule A—Itemized Deductions

(Schedule B is on back)

► Attach to Form 1040. ► See Instructions for Schedules A&B (Form 1040).

OMB No. 1545-0074 **2008** Attachment Sequence No. **07**

Name(s) shown on Form 1040: Donald L. and Julie M. Hall — Your social security number: 482 11 6043

Section	Line	Description	Box	Amount	Line	Amount
Medical and Dental Expenses		**Caution.** Do not include expenses reimbursed or paid by others.				
	1	Medical and dental expenses (see page A-1)	1	3,200		
	2	Enter amount from Form 1040, line 38 [2] 26,464				
	3	Multiply line 2 by 7.5% (.075)	3	1,985		
	4	Subtract line 3 from line 1. If line 3 is more than line 1, enter -0-			4	1,215
Taxes You Paid (See page A-2.)	5	State and local income taxes	5	460		
	6	Real estate taxes (see page A-5)	6			
	7	Personal property taxes	7	300		
	8	Other taxes. List type and amount ►	8			
	9	Add lines 5 through 8			9	760
Interest You Paid (See page A-5.)	10	Home mortgage interest and points reported to you on Form 1098	10			
	11	Home mortgage interest not reported to you on Form 1098. If paid to the person from whom you bought the home, see page A-6 and show that person's name, identifying no., and address ►	11			
Note. Personal interest is not deductible.	12	Points not reported to you on Form 1098. See page A-6 for special rules	12			
	13	Qualified mortgage insurance premiums (See page A-7)	13			
	14	Investment interest. Attach Form 4952 if required. (See page A-7.)	14			
	15	Add lines 10 through 14			15	-0-
Gifts to Charity	16	Gifts by cash or check. If you made any gift of $250 or more, see page A-8	16	3,310		
If you made a gift and got a benefit for it, see page A-8.	17	Other than by cash or check. If any gift of $250 or more, see page A-8. You **must** attach Form 8283 if over $500	17			
	18	Carryover from prior year	18			
	19	Add lines 16 through 18			19	3,310
Casualty and Theft Losses	20	Casualty or theft loss(es). Attach Form 4684. (See page A-9.)			20	-0-
Job Expenses and Certain Miscellaneous Deductions	21	Unreimbursed employee expenses—job travel, union dues, job education, etc. Attach Form 2106 or 2106-EZ if required. (See page A-9.) ►	21	6,552		
	22	Tax preparation fees	22			
(See page A-9.)	23	Other expenses—investment, safe deposit box, etc. List type and amount ►	23			
	24	Add lines 21 through 23	24	6,552		
	25	Enter amount from Form 1040, line 38 [25] 26,464				
	26	Multiply line 25 by 2% (.02)	26	529		
	27	Subtract line 26 from line 24. If line 26 is more than line 24, enter -0-			27	6,023
Other Miscellaneous Deductions	28	Other—from list on page A-10. List type and amount ►			28	-0-
Total Itemized Deductions	29	Is Form 1040, line 38, over $159,950 (over $79,975 if married filing separately)? ☐ **No.** Your deduction is not limited. Add the amounts in the far right column for lines 4 through 28. Also, enter this amount on Form 1040, line 40. ☐ **Yes.** Your deduction may be limited. See page A-10 for the amount to enter. ►			29	11,308
	30	If you elect to itemize deductions even though they are less than your standard deduction, check here ► ☐				

For Paperwork Reduction Act Notice, see Form 1040 instructions. Cat. No. 11330X **Schedule A (Form 1040) 2008**

Line 20 – Because the minister did not have an accountable expense reimbursement plan, the unreimbursed expenses appear on this line. One of the disadvantages of this approach is the 2% deduction (line 26), which costs the minister $529 of deductions.

SCHEDULE C-EZ (Form 1040)

Department of the Treasury Internal Revenue Service (99)

Net Profit From Business

(Sole Proprietorship)

▶ Partnerships, joint ventures, etc., generally must file Form 1065 or 1065-B.
▶ Attach to Form 1040, 1040NR, or 1041. ▶ See instructions on back.

OMB No. 1545-0074

2008

Attachment Sequence No. **09A**

Name of proprietor: Donald L. Hall

Social security number (SSN): 482 ⁝ 11 ⁝ 6043

Part I **General Information**

You May Use Schedule C-EZ Instead of Schedule C Only If You:

- Had business expenses of $5,000 or less.
- Use the cash method of accounting.
- Did not have an inventory at any time during the year.
- Did not have a net loss from your business.
- Had only one business as either a sole proprietor, qualified joint venture, or statutory employee.

And You:

- Had no employees during the year.
- Are not required to file **Form 4562,** Depreciation and Amortization, for this business. See the instructions for Schedule C, line 13, on page C-4 to find out if you must file.
- Do not deduct expenses for business use of your home.
- Do not have prior year unallowed passive activity losses from this business.

A Principal business or profession, including product or service

B Enter code from pages C-8, 9, & 10 ▶ 8 1 3 0 0 0

C Business name. If no separate business name, leave blank.

D Employer ID number (EIN), if any

E Business address (including suite or room no.). Address not required if same as on page 1 of your tax return.

City, town or post office, state, and ZIP code

Part II **Figure Your Net Profit**

1	**Gross receipts. Caution.** See the instructions for Schedule C, line 1, on page C-3 and check the box if: • This income was reported to you on Form W-2 and the "Statutory employee" box on that form was checked, or • You are a member of a qualified joint venture reporting only rental real estate income not subject to self-employment tax . . . ▶ ☐	1	5,200
2	**Total expenses** (see instructions on page 2). If more than $5,000, you **must** use Schedule C	2	4,237
3	**Net profit.** Subtract line 2 from line 1. If less than zero, you **must** use Schedule C. Enter on both **Form 1040, line 12,** and **Schedule SE, line 2,** or on **Form 1040NR, line 13.** (If you checked the box on line 1, **do not** report the amount from line 3 on Schedule SE, line 2.) Estates and trusts, enter on **Form 1041, line 3** . . .	3	963

Part III **Information on Your Vehicle.** Complete this part **only** if you are claiming car or truck expenses on line 2.

4 When did you place your vehicle in service for business purposes? (month, day, year) ▶ 1 / 01 / 04

5 Of the total number of miles you drove your vehicle during 2008, enter the number of miles you used your vehicle for:

a Business 2,601 (1) b Commuting (see instructions) ________ c Other ________

(1) 2,601 miles x 50.5 cents per mile = 1,318 x 95% = 1,252 (travel occurred in the first half of 2008)

6 Was your vehicle available for personal use during off-duty hours? . . . ☒ Yes ☐ No

7 Do you (or your spouse) have another vehicle available for personal use? . . . ☒ Yes ☐ No

8a Do you have evidence to support your deduction? . . . ☒ Yes ☐ No

(1) Expenses have been reduced by 5% as allocable to tax-free income (see calculation on page 170).

Most ministers are employees for income tax purposes (with that income reported on line 7, Form 1040, page 1) and also have honoraria and fee income and related expenses that are reportable on Schedule C (C-EZ).

SCHEDULE SE (Form 1040)

Department of the Treasury Internal Revenue Service (99)

Self-Employment Tax

▶ Attach to Form 1040. ▶ See Instructions for Schedule SE (Form 1040).

OMB No. 1545-0074

2008

Attachment Sequence No. **17**

Name of person with **self-employment** income (as shown on Form 1040)	Social security number of person with **self-employment** income ▶
Donald L. Hall	482 : 11 : 6043

Who Must File Schedule SE

You must file Schedule SE if:

- You had net earnings from self-employment from **other than** church employee income (line 4 of Short Schedule SE or line 4c of Long Schedule SE) of $400 or more, **or**
- You had church employee income of $108.28 or more. Income from services you performed as a minister or a member of a religious order **is not** church employee income (see page SE-1).

Note. Even if you had a loss or a small amount of income from self-employment, it may be to your benefit to file Schedule SE and use either "optional method" in Part II of Long Schedule SE (see page SE-4).

Exception. If your only self-employment income was from earnings as a minister, member of a religious order, or Christian Science practitioner **and** you filed Form 4361 and received IRS approval not to be taxed on those earnings, **do not** file Schedule SE. Instead, write "Exempt—Form 4361" on Form 1040, line 57.

May I Use Short Schedule SE or Must I Use Long Schedule SE?

Note. Use this flowchart **only if** you must file Schedule SE. If unsure, see *Who Must File Schedule SE,* above.

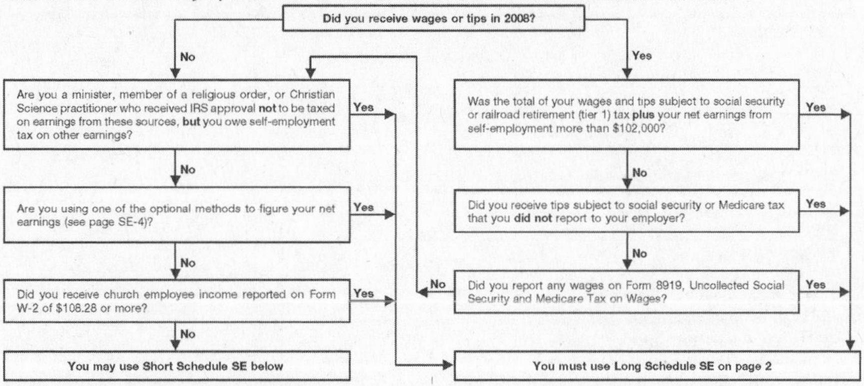

Section A—Short Schedule SE. Caution. Read above to see if you can use Short Schedule SE.

1a	Net farm profit or (loss) from Schedule F, line 36, and farm partnerships, Schedule K-1 (Form 1065), box 14, code A . . .	1a	
b	If you received social security retirement or disability benefits, enter the amount of Conservation Reserve Program payments included on Schedule F, line 6b, or listed on Schedule K-1 (Form 1065), box 20, code X	1b	( )
2	Net profit or (loss) from Schedule C, line 31; Schedule C-EZ, line 3; Schedule K-1 (Form 1065), box 14, code A (other than farming); and Schedule K-1 (Form 1065-B), box 9, code J1. Ministers and members of religious orders, see page SE-1 for types of income to report on this line. See page SE-3 for other income to report . . .	2	19,794
3	Combine lines 1a, 1b, and 2 . . .	3	19,794
4	**Net earnings from self-employment.** Multiply line 3 by 92.35% (.9235). If less than $400, **do not** file this schedule; you do not owe self-employment tax . . . ▶	4	18,280
5	**Self-employment tax.** If the amount on line 4 is: • $102,000 or less, multiply line 4 by 15.3% (.153). Enter the result here and on **Form 1040, line 57.** • More than $102,000, multiply line 4 by 2.9% (.029). Then, add $12,648 to the result. Enter the total here and on **Form 1040, line 57** . . .	5	2,797
6	**Deduction for one-half of self-employment tax.** Multiply line 5 by 50% (.5). Enter the result here and on **Form 1040, line 27** . . . 6 | 1,399		

For Paperwork Reduction Act Notice, see Form 1040 instructions. Cat. No. 11358Z **Schedule SE (Form 1040) 2008**

Line 2 – See the schedule on page 172 for the calculation of this amount.

Line 4 – This line results in the deduction of a portion of the self-employment tax liability.

A minister may use Section A-Short Schedule unless he received nonministerial wages (subject to FICA) and the total of these wages and net ministerial self-employment earnings (W-2 and Schedule C-related) is more than $102,000.

SCHEDULE EIC
(Form 1040A or 1040)

Department of the Treasury
Internal Revenue Service (99)

Earned Income Credit

Qualifying Child Information

1040A
1040
EIC

Complete and attach to Form 1040A or 1040 only if you have a qualifying child.

OMB No. 1545-0074

2008

Attachment Sequence No. **43**

Name(s) shown on return	Your social security number
Donald L. and Julie M. Hall	482 ¦ 11 ¦ 6043

Before you begin:
- See the instructions for Form 1040A, lines 40a and 40b, or Form 1040, lines 65a and 65b, to make sure that **(a)** you can take the EIC, and **(b)** you have a qualifying child.
- Be sure the child's name on line 1 and social security number (SSN) on line 2 agree with the child's social security card. Otherwise, at the time we process your return, we may reduce or disallow your EIC. If the name or SSN on the child's social security card is not correct, call the Social Security Administration at 1-800-772-1213.

CAUTION
- If you take the EIC even though you are not eligible, you may not be allowed to take the credit for up to 10 years. See back of schedule for details.
- It will take us longer to process your return and issue your refund if you do not fill in all lines that apply for each qualifying child.

Qualifying Child Information	Child 1	Child 2
1 Child's name If you have more than two qualifying children, you only have to list two to get the maximum credit.	First name: David K. Last name: Hall	First name: Sarah E. Last name: Hall
2 Child's SSN The child must have an SSN as defined on page 41 of the Form 1040A instructions or page 47 of the Form 1040 instructions unless the child was born and died in 2008. If your child was born and died in 2008 and did not have an SSN, enter "Died" on this line and attach a copy of the child's birth certificate, death certificate, or hospital medical records.	514 ¦ 42 ¦ 7465	516 ¦ 49 ¦ 0125
3 Child's year of birth	Year 1 9 9 6 *If born after 1989, skip lines 4a and 4b; go to line 5.*	Year 2 0 0 0 *If born after 1989, skip lines 4a and 4b; go to line 5.*
4 If the child was born before 1990— **a** Was the child under age 24 at the end of 2008 and a student?	☐ **Yes.** *Go to line 5.* ☐ **No.** *Continue.*	☐ **Yes.** *Go to line 5.* ☐ **No.** *Continue.*
b Was the child permanently and totally disabled during any part of 2008?	☐ **Yes.** *Continue.* ☐ **No.** The child is not a qualifying child.	☐ **Yes.** *Continue.* ☐ **No.** The child is not a qualifying child.
5 Child's relationship to you (for example, son, daughter, grandchild, niece, nephew, foster child, etc.)	Son	Daughter
6 Number of months child lived with you in the United States during 2008 • If the child lived with you for more than half of 2008 but less than 7 months, enter "7." • If the child was born or died in 2008 and your home was the child's home for the entire time he or she was alive during 2008, enter "12."	12 months *Do not enter more than 12 months.*	12 months *Do not enter more than 12 months.*

TIP You may also be able to take the additional child tax credit if your child **(a)** was under age 17 at the end of 2008, **and (b)** is a U.S. citizen, U.S. National, or U.S. resident alien. For more details, see the instructions for line 41 of Form 1040A or line 67 of Form 1040.

If you are eligible for the Earned Income Credit, you must file page 1 of Schedule EIC if you have a qualifying child. Compute your credit on the worksheet in the IRS instruction booklet.

There could have been a much larger Earned Income Credit if Pastor Hall's business expenses had been reimbursed and a lower salary prospectively established. The expenses claimed on Form 2106-EZ do not offset earned income for the EIC calculation.

Worksheet B—Earned Income Credit (EIC)—Lines ~~65a~~ 64 and ~~65b~~ 64

Keep for Your Records

Use this worksheet if you answered "Yes" to Step 5, question 3, on page 46.

√ Complete the parts below (Parts 1 through 3) that apply to you. Then, continue to Part 4.

√ If you are married filing a joint return, include your spouse's amounts, if any, with yours to figure the amounts to enter in Parts 1 through 3.

Part 1

Self-Employed, Members of the Clergy, and People With Church Employee Income Filing Schedule SE

		Line	Amount
1a. Enter the amount from Schedule SE, Section A, line 3, or Section B, line 3, whichever applies.		1a	28,944[1]
b. Enter any amount from Schedule SE, Section B, line 4b, and line 5a.	+	1b	
c. Combine lines 1a and 1b.	=	1c	28,944
d. Enter the amount from Schedule SE, Section A, line 6, or Section B, line 13, whichever applies.	–	1d	1,399
e. Subtract line 1d from 1c.	=	1e	27,545

Part 2

Self-Employed NOT Required To File Schedule SE

For example, your net earnings from self-employment were less than $400.

2. Do not include on these lines any statutory employee income, any net profit from services performed as a notary public, or any amount exempt from self-employment tax as the result of the filing and approval of Form 4029 or Form 4361.

		Line	Amount
a. Enter any net farm profit or (loss) from Schedule F, line 36, and from farm partnerships, Schedule K-1 (Form 1065), box 14, code A*.		2a	
b. Enter any net profit or (loss) from Schedule C, line 31; Schedule C-EZ, line 3; Schedule K-1 (Form 1065), box 14, code A (other than farming); and Schedule K-1 (Form 1065-B), box 9, code J1*.	+	2b	
c. Combine lines 2a and 2b.	=	2c	

*Reduce any Schedule K-1 amounts by any partnership section 179 expense deduction claimed, unreimbursed partnership expenses claimed, and depletion claimed on oil and gas properties. If you have any Schedule K-1 amounts, complete the appropriate line(s) of Schedule SE, Section A. Enter your name and social security number on Schedule SE and attach it to your return.

Part 3

Statutory Employees Filing Schedule C or C-EZ

	Line	Amount
3. Enter the amount from Schedule C, line 1, or Schedule C-EZ, line 1, that you are filing as a statutory employee.	3	

Part 4

All Filers Using Worksheet B

Note. If line 4b includes income on which you should have paid self-employment tax but did not, we may reduce your credit by the amount of self-employment tax not paid.

	Line	Amount
4a. Enter your earned income from Step 5 on page 46.	4a	
b. Combine lines 1e, 2c, 3, and 4a. **This is your total earned income.**	4b	27,545

If line 4b is zero or less, STOP You cannot take the credit. Enter "No" on the dotted line next to line ~~65a~~ 64.

5. If you have:

- 2 or more qualifying children, is line 4b less than $38,646 ($41,646 if married filing jointly)?
- 1 qualifying child, is line 4b less than $33,995 ($36,995 if married filing jointly)?
- No qualifying children, is line 4b less than $12,880 ($15,880 if married filing jointly)?

☐ **Yes.** If you want the IRS to figure your credit, see page 46. If you want to figure the credit yourself, enter the amount from line 4b on line 6 (page 50).

☐ **No.** STOP You cannot take the credit. Enter "No" on the dotted line next to line ~~65a~~ 64.

[1] Included on Line 1a:

Julie Hall's salary	$ 9,150
Schedule SE income	19,794
	$28,944

Worksheet B is found in the IRS instruction booklet. Complete this worksheet whether or not you have a qualifying child.

Worksheet B—*Continued from page 49* *Keep for Your Records*

Part 5

All Filers Using Worksheet B

6. Enter your total earned income from Part 4, line 4b, on page 49. **6** 27,545

7. Look up the amount on line 6 above in the EIC Table on pages 51–58 to find the credit. Be sure you use the correct column for your filing status and the number of children you have. Enter the credit here. **7** 2,974

If line 7 is zero, STOP You cannot take the credit. Enter "No" on the dotted line next to line ~~65a.~~ 64

8. Enter the amount from Form 1040, line 38. **8** 26,464

9. Are the amounts on lines 8 and 6 the same?

☐ **Yes.** Skip line 10; enter the amount from line 7 on line 11.

☐ **No.** Go to line 10.

Part 6

Filers Who Answered "No" on Line 9

10. If you have:

- No qualifying children, is the amount on line 8 less than $7,200 ($10,200 if married filing jointly)?
- 1 or more qualifying children, is the amount on line 8 less than $15,750 ($18,750 if married filing jointly)?

☐ **Yes.** Leave line 10 blank; enter the amount from line 7 on line 11.

☐ **No.** Look up the amount on line 8 in the EIC Table on pages 51–58 to find the credit. Be sure you use the correct column for your filing status and the number of children you have. Enter the credit here. **10** 3,142
Look at the amounts on lines 10 and 7.
Then, enter the **smaller** amount on line 11.

Part 7

Your Earned Income Credit

This is your earned income credit. **11** 2,974

Enter this amount on Form 1040, line ~~65a.~~ 64

Reminder—

√ If you have a qualifying child, complete and attach Schedule EIC.

CAUTION *If your EIC for a year after 1996 was reduced or disallowed, see page 47 to find out if you must file Form 8862 to take the credit for 2008.*

Form **8812**

Department of the Treasury
Internal Revenue Service (99)

Additional Child Tax Credit

Complete and attach to Form 1040, Form 1040A, or Form 1040NR.

OMB No. 1545-0074

2008

Attachment Sequence No. 47

Name(s) shown on return: Donald L. and Julie M. Hall

Your social security number: 482 11 6043

Part I All Filers

Line	Description	Inner box	Inner amount	Box	Amount
1	Enter the amount from line 1 of your Child Tax Credit Worksheet on page 40 of the Form 1040 instructions, page 37 of the Form 1040A instructions, or page 19 of the Form 1040NR instructions. If you used Pub. 972, enter the amount from line 8 of the worksheet on page 4 of the publication			1	2,000
2	Enter the amount from Form 1040, line 51, Form 1040A, line 32, or Form 1040NR, line 46			2	116
3	Subtract line 2 from line 1. If zero, **stop**; you cannot take this credit			3	1,884
4a	Enter your total earned income (see instructions on back) (21,950 + 963 + 1,000)	4a	23,913		
b	Nontaxable combat pay (see instructions on back) — 4b				
5	Is the amount on line 4a more than $12,050? ☐ **No.** Leave line 5 blank and enter -0- on line 6. ☒ **Yes.** Subtract $12,050 from the amount on line 4a. Enter the result	5	11,863		
6	Multiply the amount on line 5 by 15% (.15) and enter the result			6	1,779

Next. Do you have three or more qualifying children?

☐ **No.** If line 6 is zero, stop; you cannot take this credit. Otherwise, skip Part II and enter the **smaller** of line 3 or line 6 on line 13.

☐ **Yes.** If line 6 is equal to or more than line 3, skip Part II and enter the amount from line 3 on line 13. Otherwise, go to line 7.

Part II Certain Filers Who Have Three or More Qualifying Children

Line	Description	Inner box	Inner amount	Box	Amount
7	Withheld social security and Medicare taxes from Form(s) W-2, boxes 4 and 6. If married filing jointly, include your spouse's amounts with yours. If you worked for a railroad, see instructions on back	7			
8	**1040 filers:** Enter the total of the amounts from Form 1040, lines 27 and 58, plus any taxes that you identified using code "UT" and entered on the dotted line next to line 61. **1040A filers:** Enter -0-. **1040NR filers:** Enter the total of the amounts from Form 1040NR, line 53, plus any taxes that you identified using code "UT" and entered on the dotted line next to line 57.	8			
9	Add lines 7 and 8	9			
10	**1040 filers:** Enter the total of the amounts from Form 1040, lines 64a and 65. **1040A filers:** Enter the total of the amount from Form 1040A, line 40a, plus any excess social security and tier 1 RRTA taxes withheld that you entered to the left of line 43 (see instructions on back). **1040NR filers:** Enter the amount from Form 1040NR, line 60.	10			
11	Subtract line 10 from line 9. If zero or less, enter -0-			11	
12	Enter the **larger** of line 6 or line 11			12	

Next, enter the **smaller** of line 3 or line 12 on line 13.

Part III Additional Child Tax Credit

Line	Description	Box	Amount
13	**This is your additional child tax credit**	13	1,779

Enter this amount on Form 1040, line 66, Form 1040A, line 41, or Form 1040NR, line 61.

For Paperwork Reduction Act Notice, see back of form. Cat. No. 10644E Form **8812** (2008)

Line 4 – From lines 7, 12, and 21, Form 1040, page 1.

Child Tax Credit Worksheet—Line 51

Keep for Your Records

CAUTION

- To be a qualifying child for the child tax credit, the child must be **under age 17** at the end of 2008 and meet the other requirements listed on page 15.
- **Do not** use this worksheet if you answered "Yes" to question 1, 2, or 3 on page 39. Instead, use Pub. 972.

1. Number of qualifying children: 2 × $1,000. Enter the result. — **1** 2,000

2. Enter the amount from Form 1040, line 46. — **2** 116

3. Add the amounts from Form 1040:

Line 47 ______

Line 48 + ______

Line 49 + ______

Line 50 + ______

Line 52 - ______ Enter the total. — **3** ______

4. Are the amounts on lines 2 and 3 the same?

☐ **Yes.** STOP
You cannot take this credit because there is no tax to reduce. However, you may be able to take the **additional child tax credit.** See the **TIP** below.

☐ **No.** Subtract line 3 from line 2. — **4** 116

5. Is the amount on line 1 more than the amount on line 4?

☐ **Yes.** Enter the amount from line 4. Also, you may be able to take the **additional child tax credit.** See the **TIP** below.

☐ **No.** Enter the amount from line 1.

This is your child tax credit. — **5** 116

Enter this amount on Form 1040, line 51.

TIP You may be able to take the **additional child tax credit** on Form 1040, line ~~67,~~ 66 if you answered "Yes" on line 4 **or** line 5 above.

- First, complete your Form 1040 through line ~~66.~~ 65
- Then, use Form 8812 to figure any additional child tax credit.

Note: This worksheet is based on the 2007 IRS worksheets. Use the 2008 worksheet when completing your return.

Form **2106-EZ**

Department of the Treasury
Internal Revenue Service (99)

Unreimbursed Employee Business Expenses

► Attach to Form 1040 or Form 1040NR.

OMB No. 1545-0074

2008

Attachment Sequence No. **54A**

Your name	Occupation in which you incurred expenses	Social security number
Donald L. Hall	Minister	482 ¦ 11 ¦ 6043

You May Use This Form Only if All of the Following Apply.

- You are an employee deducting ordinary and necessary expenses attributable to your job. An ordinary expense is one that is common and accepted in your field of trade, business, or profession. A necessary expense is one that is helpful and appropriate for your business. An expense does not have to be required to be considered necessary.
- You **do not** get reimbursed by your employer for any expenses (amounts your employer included in box 1 of your Form W-2 are not considered reimbursements for this purpose).
- If you are claiming vehicle expense, you are using the standard mileage rate for 2008.

Caution: *You can use the standard mileage rate for 2008* ***only if:*** *(a) you owned the vehicle and used the standard mileage rate for the first year you placed the vehicle in service,* ***or (b)*** *you leased the vehicle and used the standard mileage rate for the portion of the lease period after 1997.*

Part I **Figure Your Expenses**

1	Vehicle expense using the standard mileage rate. Complete Part II and then go to line 1a below.				
a	Multiply business miles driven **before** July 1, 2008, by 50.5¢ (.505)	1a	1,622		
b	Multiply business miles driven **after** June 30, 2008, by 58.5¢ (.585)	1b	2,448		
c	Add lines 1a and 1b			1c	4,070
2	Parking fees, tolls, and transportation, including train, bus, etc., that **did not** involve overnight travel or commuting to and from work			2	
3	Travel expense while away from home overnight, including lodging, airplane, car rental, etc. **Do not** include meals and entertainment			3	800
4	Business expenses not included on lines 1c through 3. **Do not** include meals and entertainment			4	998
5	Meals and entertainment expenses: $ 1,368 × 50% (.50). (Employees subject to Department of Transportation (DOT) hours of service limits: Multiply meal expenses incurred while away from home on business by 80% (.80) instead of 50%. For details, see instructions.)			5	684
6	**Total expenses.** Add lines 1c through 5. Enter here and on **Schedule A (Form 1040), line 21** (or on **Schedule A (Form 1040NR, line 9)**). (Armed Forces reservists, fee-basis state or local government officials, qualified performing artists, and individuals with disabilities: See the instructions for special rules on where to enter this amount.)			6	6,552

Part II **Information on Your Vehicle.** Complete this part **only** if you are claiming vehicle expense on line 1.

7 When did you place your vehicle in service for business use? (month, day, year) ► 5 / 1 / 04

8 Of the total number of miles you drove your vehicle during 2008, enter the number of miles you used your vehicle for:

a Business 7,397 **b** Commuting (see instructions) 2,432 **c** Other 2,601 (Schedule C-related)

9 Was your vehicle available for personal use during off-duty hours? ☒ **Yes** ☐ **No**

10 Do you (or your spouse) have another vehicle available for personal use? ☒ **Yes** ☐ **No**

11a Do you have evidence to support your deduction?. ☒ **Yes** ☐ **No**

b If "Yes," is the evidence written?. ☒ **Yes** ☐ **No**

For Paperwork Reduction Act Notice, see page 4. Cat. No. 20604Q Form **2106-EZ** (2008)

Lines 1, 3, 4, 5 – See allocations on page 170.

Line 6 – The total expenses on this line are carried forward to Form 1040, Schedule A, line 21.

Form **3903**

Department of the Treasury
Internal Revenue Service (99)

Moving Expenses

► Attach to Form 1040 or Form 1040NR.

OMB No. 1545-0074

2008

Attachment Sequence No. **62**

Name(s) shown on return: Donald L. Hall

Your social security number: 482 | 11 | 6043

Before you begin: √ See the **Distance Test** and **Time Test** in the instructions to find out if you can deduct your moving expenses.

√ See **Members of the Armed Forces** on the back, if applicable.

1	Transportation and storage of household goods and personal effects (see instructions) . .	1	1,000
2	Travel (including lodging) from your old home to your new home (see instructions). **Do not** include the cost of meals	2	
3	Add lines 1 and 2	3	1,000
4	Enter the total amount your employer paid you for the expenses listed on lines 1 and 2 that is **not** included in box 1 of your Form W-2 (wages). This amount should be shown in box 12 of your Form W-2 with code **P**	4	
5	Is line 3 **more than** line 4? ☐ **No.** You **cannot** deduct your moving expenses. If line 3 is less than line 4, subtract line 3 from line 4 and include the result on Form 1040, line 7, or Form 1040NR, line 8. ☒ **Yes.** Subtract line 4 from line 3. Enter the result here and on Form 1040, line 26, or Form 1040NR, line 26. This is your **moving expense deduction**	5	1,000

General Instructions

What's New

For 2008, the standard mileage rate for using your vehicle to move to a new home is 19 cents a mile.

Purpose of Form

Use Form 3903 to figure your moving expense deduction for a move related to the start of work at a new principal place of work (workplace). If the new workplace is outside the United States or its possessions, you must be a U.S. citizen or resident alien to deduct your expenses.

If you qualify to deduct expenses for more than one move, use a separate Form 3903 for each move.

For more details, see Pub. 521, Moving Expenses.

Moving Expenses You Can Deduct

You can deduct the reasonable expenses of moving your household goods and personal effects and of traveling from your old home to your new home. Reasonable expenses can include the cost of lodging (but not meals) while traveling to your new home. You cannot deduct the cost of sightseeing trips.

Who Can Deduct Moving Expenses

If you move to a new home because of a new principal workplace, you may be able to deduct your moving expenses whether you are self-employed or an employee. But you must meet both the distance test and time test that follow.

TIP *Members of the Armed Forces may not have to meet the distance and time tests. See instructions on the back.*

Distance Test

Your new principal workplace must be at least 50 miles farther from your old home than your old workplace was. For example, if your old workplace was 3 miles from your old home, your new workplace must be at least 53 miles from that home. If you did not have an old workplace, your new workplace must be at least 50 miles from your old home. The distance between the two points is the shortest of the more commonly traveled routes between them.

TIP *To see if you meet the distance test, you can use the worksheet below.*

Distance Test Worksheet

Keep a Copy for Your Records

1.	Number of miles from your **old home** to your **new workplace**	1.	562 miles
2.	Number of miles from your **old home** to your **old workplace**	2.	20 miles
3.	Subtract line 2 from line 1. If zero or less, enter -0-.	3.	542 miles

Is line 3 at least 50 miles?

☒ **Yes.** You meet this test.

☐ **No.** You do not meet this test. You **cannot** deduct your moving expenses. **Do not** complete Form 3903.

For Paperwork Reduction Act Notice, see back of form. Cat. No. 12490K Form **3903** (2008)

Form **8880**

Department of the Treasury
Internal Revenue Service

Credit for Qualified Retirement Savings Contributions

▶ Attach to Form 1040, Form 1040A, or Form 1040NR.
▶ See instructions on back.

OMB No. 1545-0074
2008
Attachment Sequence No. **55**

Name(s) shown on return: Donald L. Hall
Your social security number: 482 | 11 | 6043

CAUTION

You **cannot** take this credit if **either** of the following applies.

- The amount on Form 1040, line 38; Form 1040A, line 22; or Form 1040NR, line 36 is more than $26,500 ($39,750 if head of household; $53,000 if married filing jointly).
- The person(s) who made the qualified contribution or elective deferral **(a)** was born after January 1, 1991, **(b)** is claimed as a dependent on someone else's 2008 tax return, or **(c)** was a **student** (see instructions).

Line	Description		(a) You		(b) Your spouse
1	Traditional and Roth IRA contributions for 2008. **Do not** include rollover contributions	1			
2	Elective deferrals to a 401(k) or other qualified employer plan, voluntary employee contributions, and 501(c)(18)(D) plan contributions for 2008 (see instructions)	2	500		
3	Add lines 1 and 2	3	500		
4	Certain distributions received **after** 2005 and **before** the due date (including extensions) of your 2008 tax return (see instructions). If married filing jointly, include **both** spouses' amounts in **both** columns. See instructions for an exception	4			
5	Subtract line 4 from line 3. If zero or less, enter -0-	5	500		
6	In each column, enter the **smaller** of line 5 or $2,000	6	500		
7	Add the amounts on line 6. If zero, **stop**; you cannot take this credit			7	500
8	Enter the amount from Form 1040, line 38*; Form 1040A, line 22; or Form 1040NR, line 36	8	26,464		
9	Enter the applicable decimal amount shown below:			9	X .5

If line 8 is—		And your filing status is—		
Over—	But not over—	Married filing jointly	Head of household	Single, Married filing separately, or Qualifying widow(er)
		Enter on line 9—		
---	$16,000	.5	.5	.5
$16,000	$17,250	.5	.5	.2
$17,250	$24,000	.5	.5	.1
$24,000	$25,875	.5	.2	.1
$25,875	$26,500	.5	.1	.1
$26,500	$32,000	.5	.1	.0
$32,000	$34,500	.2	.1	.0
$34,500	$39,750	.1	.1	.0
$39,750	$53,000	.1	.0	.0
$53,000	---	.0	.0	.0

Note: *If line 9 is zero, **stop**; you cannot take this credit.*

10	Multiply line 7 by line 9			10	250
11	Enter the amount from Form 1040, line 46; Form 1040A, line 28; or Form 1040NR, line 43	11	116		
12	**1040 filers:** Enter the total of your credits from lines 47 through 50, line 12 of the Line 11 Worksheet in Pub. 972 (see instructions), plus the amounts, if any, from line 13 of Form 8396, line 20 of Form 5695, and line 7 of Form 8859. **1040A filers:** Enter the total of your credits from lines 29 through 32. **1040NR filers:** Enter the total of your credits from lines 44 and 45, line 12 of the Line 11 Worksheet in Pub. 972 (see instructions), plus the amounts, if any, from line 13 of Form 8396, line 20 of Form 5695, and line 7 of Form 8859.	12	116		
13	Subtract line 12 from line 11. If zero, **stop**; you cannot take this credit			13	0
14	**Credit for qualified retirement savings contributions.** Enter the **smaller** of line 10 or line 13 here and on Form 1040, line 52; Form 1040A, line 33; or Form 1040NR, line 47			14	

*See Pub. 590 for the amount to enter if you are filing Form 2555, 2555-EZ, or 4563 or you are excluding income from Puerto Rico.

For Paperwork Reduction Act Notice, see back of form. Cat. No. 33394D Form **8880** (2008)

Computation of Unallowed Part of Business Expenses

		Taxable	Tax-Free	Total
Salary as a minister (less housing allowance designation)		$ 8,500		$ 8,500
Special occasion gifts		500		500
Reimbursement of self-employment tax		2,100		2,100
Expense allowance under nonaccountable plan		1,700		1,700
Housing allowance:				
Designated	$2,000			
Less expenses	1,000			
Excess	$ 1,000	1,000	$ 1,000	2,000
Schedule C gross income from ministry		5,200		5,200
Ministerial income		$19,000	$ 1,000	$20,000
		95%	5%	100%

Note: Each expense line on Form 2106-EZ (page 167) has been reduced by 5% because the expenses are allocable to tax-free income.

Expenses reflected on Form 2106-EZ were allocated as follows:

		95% Deductible	5% Not Deductible
Business mileage			
4,090 x 50.5 cents per mile		$ 1,962	$ 103
3,793 x 58.5 cents per mile		2,108	111
Travel expense:			
Airfare		641	34
Lodging		159	8
Business expenses:			
Subscriptions		190	10
Books and supplies		333	17
Continuing education tuition		475	25
Meals and entertainment expense:			
Meals	$ 233		
Entertainment	1,207		
	$1,440 (1)	684	36
		$ 6,552	$ 344

(1) 50% disallowed by meals and entertainment rules before allocating for taxable and tax-free income.

Housing Allowance Worksheet

Minister Living in a Parsonage
Owned by or Rented by the Church

Minister's Name: Donald L. Hall

For the period January 1, 2008 to December 31, 2008

Date designation approved December 20, 2007

Allowable Housing Expenses *(expenses paid by minister from current income)*

	Estimated Expenses	Actual	
Utilities *(gas, electricity, water)* and trash collection	$	$	
Local telephone expense *(base charge)*	250	275	
Decoration and redecoration			
Structural maintenance and repair			
Landscaping, gardening, and pest control			
Furnishings *(purchase, repair, replacement)*	1,218	460	
Personal property insurance on minister-owned contents	200	190	
Personal property taxes on contents	150	75	
Umbrella liability insurance			
Subtotal	1,818		
10% allowance for unexpected expenses	182		
TOTAL	$ 2,000	$ 1,000	(A)
Properly designated housing allowance		$ 2,000	(B)

The amount excludable from income for federal income tax purposes is the lower of A or B.

Because actual housing expenses are less than the designated allowance, the housing exclusion is limited to $1,000. The $1,000 difference between the designation ($2,000) and the exclusion ($1,000) is reported as excess housing allowance on Form 1040, line 21 (see page 157).

Self-Employment Social Security Tax Worksheet

Inclusions:

Salary paid by church as reflected on Form W-2	$ 12,800
Net profit or loss as reflected on Schedule C or C-EZ (includes speaking honoraria, offerings you receive for marriages, baptisms, funerals, and other fees)	963
Housing allowance excluded from salary on Form W-2	2,000
Fair rental value of parsonage provided (including paid utilities)	11,150
Nonaccountable business expense reimbursements (if not included on Form W-2)	
Reimbursement of self-employment taxes (if not included on Form W-2)	
Value of meals provided to you, your spouse, and your dependents whether or not provided for your employer's convenience (these amounts may have been excluded from gross income)	
Total inclusions	26,913

Deductions:

Unreimbursed ministerial business and professional expenses (included on Form W-2) or reimbursed expenses paid under a nonaccountable plan (included on Form W-2)	
A. Deductible on Schedule A before the 2% of AGI limitation whether or not you itemized[1] (see page 170), or	6,552
B. Not deductible on Form 2106/2106 EZ or Schedule C/C-EZ because expenses were allocated to taxable/nontaxable income (Schedule A $344/Schedule C $223)	567 [2]
Total deductions	7,119
Net earnings from self-employment (to Schedule SE)	$ 19,794

[1] The 50% unreimbursed meal and entertainment expense limitation applies to amounts subject to social security tax. In other words, if some of your meal and entertainment expenses were subjected to the 50% limit, the remainder cannot be deducted here.

[2] This example ignores the ruling in the Young case (see page 179).

Your net earnings from self-employment are not affected by the foreign earned income exclusion or the foreign housing exclusion or deduction if you are a U.S. citizen or resident alien who is serving abroad and living in a foreign country.

Amounts received as pension payments or annuity payments related to a church-sponsored tax-sheltered annuity by a retired minister are generally considered to be excluded from the social security calculation.

Net earnings from self-employment are entered on Schedule SE, line 2 (see page 161).

22222 Void ☐	a Employee's social security number 482-11-6043	For Official Use Only ► OMB No. 1545-0008	
b Employer identification number (EIN) 25-7921873		1 Wages, tips, other compensation 12800	2 Federal income tax withheld
c Employer's name, address, and ZIP code Lancaster Community Church 1425 Spencer Avenue Wabash, IN 46992		3 Social security wages	4 Social security tax withheld
		5 Medicare wages and tips	6 Medicare tax withheld
		7 Social security tips	8 Allocated tips
d Control number		9 Advance EIC payment	10 Dependent care benefits
e Employee's first name and initial Donald L.	Last name Hall Suff.	11 Nonqualified plans	12a See instructions for box 12
604 Linden Avenue Wabash, IN 46992		13 Statutory employee ☐ Retirement plan ☒ Third-party sick pay ☐	12b E 500
		14 Other	12c
f Employee's address and ZIP code			12d

15 State	Employer's state ID number	16 State wages, tips, etc.	17 State income tax	18 Local wages, tips, etc.	19 Local income tax	20 Locality name
IN		12800	750			

Form **W-2** Wage and Tax Statement **2008**

Department of the Treasury—Internal Revenue Service

For Privacy Act and Paperwork Reduction Act Notice, see back of Copy D.

Copy A For Social Security Administration — Send this entire page with Form W-3 to the Social Security Administration; photocopies are **not** acceptable.

Cat. No. 10134D

Do Not Cut, Fold, or Staple Forms on This Page — Do Not Cut, Fold, or Staple Forms on This Page

Explanation of compensation reported on Form W-2, Box 1:

Salary ($11,000 less $2,000 housing allowance and $500 403[b] contributions)	$ 8,500
Special occasion gifts	500
Reimbursement of self-employment tax	2,100
Expense allowance under nonaccountable plan	1,700
	$12,800

Form **1040-ES** Department of the Treasury Internal Revenue Service

2008 Estimated Tax

Payment Voucher 1 OMB No. 1545-0074

File only if you are making a payment of estimated tax by check or money order. Mail this voucher with your check or money order payable to the **"United States Treasury."** Write your social security number and "2008 Form 1040-ES" on your check or money order. Do not send cash. Enclose, but do not staple or attach, your payment with this voucher.

Calendar year—Due April 15, 2008

Amount of estimated tax you are paying by check or money order. Dollars 300 Cents

Print or type

Your first name and initial Donald L.	Your last name Hall	Your social security number 482-11-6043
If joint payment, complete for spouse		
Spouse's first name and initial Julie M.	Spouse's last name Hall	Spouse's social security number 720-94-1327
Address (number, street, and apt. no.) 604 Linden Avenue		
City, state, and ZIP code. (If a foreign address, enter city, province or state, postal code, and country.) Wabash, IN 46992		

For Privacy Act and Paperwork Reduction Act Notice, see instructions on page 5.

This is an example of one of the quarterly estimate forms. The taxpayer filed the other three estimates on a timely basis.

Citations

Chapter 1, Taxes for Ministers

- **Administrative and teaching positions**

  Treas. Reg. 31.3401(a)(9)-1(b)(3)-(5)

  Treas. Reg. 31.3121(b)(8)-1(c)(2)-(3)

  Treas. Reg. 1.1402(c)-5(b)(2)

  Ltr. Rul. 200318002

  Haimowitz v. Commissioner, T.C.M. 40 (1997)

  Ltr. Rul. 9126048

  T.A.M. 9033002

  Ltr. Rul. 9608027

  Ltr. Rul. 9144047

  Ltr. Rul. 8922077

  Ltr. Rul. 8930038

  Ltr. Rul. 8826043

  Ltr. Rul. 8646018

  Ltr. Rul. 8520043

  Flowers v. Commissioner, 82-1 USTC para. 9114 (N.D. Tex. 1981)

  Ltr. Rul. 8142076

  Ltr. Rul. 80929145

  Ltr. Rul. 8004087

  Ltr. Rul. 7907160

  Ltr. Rul. 7833017

  Boyer v. Commissioner, 69 T.C. 521 (1977)

  Rev. Rul. 70-549

  Rev. Rul. 63-90

  Rev. Rul. 57-129

- **Commissioned ministers**

  Ltr. Rul. 9221025

- **Counseling and chaplaincy positions**

  Ltr. Rul. 200002040

  Ltr. Rul. 9743037

  Ltr. Rul. 9231053

  Ltr. Rul. 9124059

  Ltr. Rul. 8825025

  Ltr. Rul. 8519004

  Ltr. Rul. 8138184

  Ltr. Rul. 8004046

  Ltr. Rul. 7809092

  Ltr. Rul. 7727019

  Rev. Rul. 71-258

- **Employees v. self-employed for income tax purposes**

  Treas. Reg. 31.3401(c)-1(b)-(c)

  Alford v. U.S., 116 F3d 334, 8th Cir. (1997)

  Radde v. Commissioner, T.C.M. 490 (1997)

  Greene v. Commissioner, T.C.M. 531 (1996)

  Weber v. Commissioner, 103 T.C. 378 (1994), Affirmed, 60 F3d 1104, 4th Cir. (1995)

  Shelley v. Commissioner, T.C.M. 432 (1994)

  Ltr. Rul. 9825002

  Ltr. Rul. 9414022

  Ltr. Rul. 8333107

  Cosby v. Commissioner, T.C.M. Sum. Op. 141 (1987)

  Rev. Rul. 87-41

  Rev. Proc. 85-18

  Rev. Rul. 80-110

- **Exempt from FICA**

  Code Sec. 3121(b)(8)(A)

- **Exempt from income tax withholding**

  Code Sec. 3121(b)(8)

  Code Sec. 3401(a)(9)

  Treas. Reg. 31.3401(a)(8)-1

- **Qualifying tests for ministerial status**

  Treas. Reg. 1.1402(c)-5

  Ltr. Rul. 199910055

  Haimowitz v. Commissioner, T.C.M. 40 (1997)

  Mosley v. Commissioner, T.C.M. 457 (1994)

  Reeder v. Commissioner, T.C.M. 287 (1993)

  Ltr. Rul. 9221025

  Eade v. U.S., Dist. Court, Western Dist., VA, Roanoke Division (1991)

  Knight v. Commissioner, 92 T.C.M. 12 (1989)

  T.A.M. 8915001

  Wingo v. Commissioner, 89 T.C.M. 922 (1987)

  Ballinger v. Commissioner, 728 F.2d 1287, 10th Cir. (1984)

  Rev. Rul. 78-301

Rev. Rul. 68-68

Lawrence v. Commissioner, 50 T.C. 494 (1968)

Kirk v. Commissioner, 51 T.C. 66 (1968)

Salkov v. Commissioner, 46 T.C. 190 (1966)

Rev. Rul. 59-270

- **Religious orders**

Ltr. Rul. 199938013

Ltr. Rul. 199937013

Ltr. Rul. 9630011

Ltr. Rul. 9418012

Ltr. Rul. 9219012

Rev. Proc. 91-20

- **Subject to income tax**

Murdock v. Pennsylvania, 319 U.S. 105 (1943)

- **Voluntary withholding of income tax for ministers**

Treas. Reg. 31.3402(p)-1

Treas. Reg. 31.4302(i)-1(a)

Rev. Rul. 68-507

- **Withholding of income tax for nonministerial employees**

Bethel Baptist Church v. U.S., 822 F.2d 1334 (3rd Cir. 1987)

Eighth Street Baptist Church, Inc. v. U. S., 295 F. Supp. 1400 (D. Kan. 1969)

Chapter 2, Compensation Planning

- **Avoiding recharacterization of income**

Ltr. Rul. 9325023

Chapter 3, The Pay Package

- **Deferred compensation**

Code Sec. 409A

Code Sec. 457

Rev. Proc. 92-64

- ***De Minimis* fringes**

Code Sec. 132(e)(1)

- **Dependent care**

Code Sec. 129

- **Disability payments**

Code Sec. 104(a)(3)

Reg. 1.104-1(d)

Ltr. Rul. 9103014

Ltr. Rul. 9103043

Ltr. Rul. 9105032

- **Educational assistance**

Code Sec. 127

- **Employer-paid vehicle fuel**

Notice 91-41

- **403(b) plans (tax-sheltered annuities)**

Code Sec. 403(b)

Code Sec. 415

Code Sec. 1402(a)

Code Sec. 3121(a)(5)(D)

Rev. Rul. 78-6

Rev. Rul. 68-395

Azad v. Commissioner, 388 F.2d 74 (8th Cir. 1968)

Rev. Rul. 66-274

- **Frequent flyer awards**

IRS Announcement 2002-18

- **Group-term life insurance**

Code Sec. 3401(a)(14)

- **Health reimbursement arrangements**

Code Sec. 105(b)

Rev. Rul. 2002-41

IRS Notice 2002-45

IRP 80,600

- **Health savings accounts**

Code Sec. 233

IRS Notice 2004-2

Rev. Proc. 2004-22

IRS Notice 2004-23

Rev. Rul. 2004-38

Rev. Rul. 2004-45

IRS Notice 2004-50

- **Healthcare flexible spending account**

Code Sec. 105(b), (e)

IRS Notice 2004-42

- **Highly compensated employees**

Code Sec. 414(q)

Treas. Reg. 1.132-8(f)(1)

- **Key employees**

Code Sec. 416(i)(1)

- **Loans to employees**

Code Sec. 7872(c)(1)(B)

Code Sec. 7872(c)(3)(A)

Code Sec. 7872(f)(10)

- **Meals and lodging**

Code Sec. 119(a)

Kalms v. Commissioner, T.C.M. 394 (1992)

Ltr. Rul. 9129037

Goldsboro Christian School, Inc. v. Commissioner, 436 F. Supp. 1314 (D.D.C. 1978), Affirmed 103 S. Ct. 2017 (1983)

Ltr. Rul. 8213005

Bob Jones University v. Commissioner, 670 F.2d 167 Ct. Cl. (1982)

Rev. Rul. 77-80

- **Medical insurance premiums paid by the employer**

Code Sec. 106(a)

Code Sec. 4980B

Treas. Reg. 1.106-1

Rev. Rul. 70-179

Rev. Rul. 58-90

- **Medical insurance premiums paid by employee/reimbursed by church**

Ltr. Rul. 9022060

Rev. Rul. 85-44

Rev. Rul. 75-241

Rev. Rul. 61-146

- **Moving expenses**

Code Sec. 132(g)

Code Sec. 217

- **Nontaxable fringe benefits**

Code Sec. 132

- **Payment of personal payments**

Whittington v. Commissioner, T.C.M. 296 (2000)

Thompson v. Commissioner, T.C.M. 2 (2004)

- **Pension plans**

Code Sec. 83

Code Sec. 401(a)

Code Sec. 414(e)

- **Property transfers**

Treas. Reg. 1.61-2(d)(2)

Potito v. Commissioner, 534 F.2d 49 (5th Cir. 1976)

- **Reasonable compensation**

Truth Tabernacle, Inc. v. Commissioner, T.C.M. (1989)-451

- **Reimbursement payments excludable from recipient's income**

Ltr. Rul. 9112022

- **Retirement gifts**

Code Sec. 102(c)

Joyce v. Commissioner, 25 T.C.M. 914 (1966)

Commissioner v. Duberstein, 363 U.S. 278 (1960)

Perkins v. Commissioner, 34 T.C. 117 (1960)

Stanton v. U.S., 163 F.2d 727 (2nd Cir. 1959)

Rev. Rul. 55-422

Abernathy v. Commissioner, 211 F.2d 651 (D.C. Cir. 1954)

Kavanagh v. Hershman, 210 F.2d 654 (6th Cir. 1954)

Mutch v. Commissioner, 209 F.2d 390 (3rd Cir. 1954)

Schall v. Commissioner, 174 F.2d 893 (5th Cir. 1949)

Rev. Rul. 55-422

- **Sabbatical pay**

Kant v. Commissioner, T.C.M. 217 (1997)

- **Social security reimbursements**

Rev. Rul. 68-507

- **Special occasion gifts**

Goodwin v. U.S., 67 F.3d 149, 8th Cir. (1995)

Banks v. Commissioner, 62 T.C.M. 1611 (1991)

- **Tuition and fee reductions**

Code Sec. 117(d)

Ltr. Rul. 200149030

Rasmussen v. Commissioner, T.C. 7264-92 (1994)

Chapter 4, Housing Allowance

- **Allowed without documentation**

Kizer v. Commissioner, T.C.M. 582 (1992)

- **Designation of housing allowance**

Treas. Reg. 1.107-1(b)

Whittington v. Commissioner, T.C.M. 296 (2000)

Logie v. Commissioner, T.C.M. 387 (1998)

Mosley v. Commissioner, T.C.M. 457 (1994)

Ltr. Rul. 9052001

Kizer v. Commissioner, T.C.M. 584 (1992)

Ltr. Rul. 8511075

Holland v. Commissioner, 47 T.C.M. 494 (1983)

Libman v. Commissioner,
44 T.C.M. 370 (1982)

Hoelz v. Commissioner,
42 T.C.M. 1037 (1981)

Boyd v. Commissioner,
42 T.C.M. 1136 (1981)

T.A.M. 8120007

Rev. Rul. 75-22

Rev. Rul. 62-117

Ling v. Commissioner,
200 F. Supp. 282 D.D.C. (1962)

Eden v. Commissioner,
41 T.C. 605 (1961)

- **Determination of housing exclusion amount**

Clergy Housing Allowance Clarification Act of 2002, Public Law 107-181

Warren v. Commissioner,
114 T.C. No. 23 (1998)
Appealed by IRS to 9th Cir. Court of Appeals (2000)
Case dismissed by 9th Cir. Court of Appeals (2002)

Radde v. Commissioner,
T.C.M. 490 (1997)

Rasmussen v. Commissioner,
T.C.M. 311 (1994)

Ltr. Rul. 8937025

Swaggart v. Commissioner,
48 T.C.M. 759 (1984)

Ltr. Rul. 8350005

Hoelz v. Commissioner,
42 T.C.M. 1037 (1981)

Rev. Rul. 78-448

Rev. Rul. 59-350

- **Double deduction of interest and taxes**

Code Sec. 265(6)

Rev. Rul. 87-32

- **Exclusion of the housing allowance**

Code Sec. 107

- **Fair rental value test**

Warren v. Commissioner,
114 T.C. No. 23 (2000)

Rucker v. David,
203 F. 3d 627, 638 9th Cir. (2000)

Ltr. Rul. 200435022

Ltr. Rul. 200435021

Ltr. Rul. 200435020

Ltr. Rul. 200435019

Ltr. Rul. 8825025

Reed v. Commissioner,
82 T.C. 208, 214 (1984)

Rev. Rul. 71-280

Rev. Rul. 63-156

- **Housing expenses only applicable to years in which paid**

Ltr. Rul. 8348018

T.A.M. 8039007

- **Including interest on home equity loan**

Ltr. Rul. 9115051

- **Minister performing routine services**

Rev. Rul. 57-129

- **Minister who owns home outright cannot exclude parsonage allowance**

Ltr. Rul. 9115051

Chapter 5, Business Expenses

- **Accountable expense reimbursement plans**

Treas. Reg. 1.62-2

Treas. Reg. 1.274-5T(f)

Ltr. Rul. 9317003

Ltr. Rul. 9325023

- **Accounting for business and professional expenses by independent contractors**

Treas. Reg. 1.274-5(g)

- **Allocation of unreimbursed business expenses**

Young v. Commissioner,
T.C.M. 440 (1992)

McFarland v. Commissioner,
T.C.M. 440 (1992)

Dalan v. Commissioner,
T.C.M. 106 (1988)

Deason v. Commissioner,
41 T.C.M. 465 (1964)

- **Auto depreciation**

Rev. Proc. 2003-75

Rev. Proc. 2004-20

- **Auto expense substantiation**

Parker v. Commissioner,
T.C.M. 15 (1993)

- **Cellular phones**

INFO 2007-0025

Ltr. Rul. 200435022

Ltr. Rul. 200435020

- **Club dues**

T.D. 8601

- **Computer expenses**

Bryant v. Commissioner,
T.C.M. 597 (1993)

- **Contributions treated as business expenses**

  Forbes v. Commissioner, T.C. Sum. Op. 167 (1992)

- **Deductibility of spouse's travel**

  Code Sec. 1.162-2(c)

  Stockton v. Commissioner, 36 T.C.M. 114 (1977)

  U.S. v. Disney, 413 F.2d 783 9th Cir. (1969)

- **Educational expenses**

  Ltr. Rul. 9431024

  Burt v. Commissioner, 40 T.C.M. 1164 (1980)

  Glasgow v. Commissioner, 31 T.C.M. 310 (1972)

- **Holy Land trips**

  Rev. Rul. 64-154

- **Home-office expenses**

  Code Sec. 280A

  Rev. Rul. 94-24

  Rev. Rul. 94-47

- **Other business and professional expense deductions**

  Treas. Reg. 1.1402(a)-11(a)

  T.A.M. 200435018-22

  Bass v. Commissioner, T.C.M. 536 (1983)

  Rev. Rul. 80-110

  Rev. Rul. 79-78

- **Per diem allowance**

  IRS Publication 1542

- **Personal computer expenses**

  Code Sec. 280F

  Rev. Rul. 86-129

- **Substantiation of business expenses**

  Temp. Rev. 1.274-5T

  Code Sec. 274(d)

  Rev. Proc. 92-71

- **Temporary workplace**

  Rev. Rul. 99-7

- **Travel/Away from home**

  Rev. Rul. 83-82

  Rev. Rul. 75-432

- **Travel/Commuting**

  Treas. Reg. 1.262-1(b)(5)

  Rev. Rul. 94-47

  Rev. Rul. 90-23

  Walker v. Commissioner, 101 T.C.M. 537 (1993)

  Soliman v. Commissioner, 94 T.C.M. 20 (1990), Supreme Court (1993)

  Hamblen v. Commissioner, 78 T.C.M. 53 (1981)

- **Travel/Mileage rates**

  Rev. Proc. 2003-76

- **Unreimbursed business expenses**

  Gravett v. Commissioner, T.C.M. 156 (1994)

Chapter 6, Retirement and Social Security

- **General**

  IRS Publication 517

  IRS Publication 1828

  Social Security Protection Act of 2004

- **Age not a limitation**

  Levine v. Commissioner, T.C.M. 469 (1992)

- **Exemption for certain religious faiths**

  U.S. v. Lee, 455 U.S. 252 (1982)

  Varga v. U.S., 467 F. Supp. 1113 (D. Md. 1979)

- **Nullifying the exemption**

  Rev. Rul. 70-197

- **Opting out of social security**

  Code Sec. 1402(e)

  Treas. Reg. 1.1402(e)-3A

  Brannon v. Commissioner, T.C.M. 370 (1999)

  McGaffin v. Commissioner, T.C.M. 290 (1996)

  Hairston v. Commissioner, T.C.M. (1995)

  Hall v. Commissioner, (10th Cir. 1994)

  Ltr. Rul. 9431024

  Reeder v. Commissioner, T.C.M. 287 (1993)

  Keaton v. Commissioner, T.C.M. 365 (1993)

  Ltr. Rul. 9221025

  Eade v. U.S., Dist. Court, Western Dist. VA, Roanoke Div. (1991)

  T.A.M. 8741002

  Balinger v. Commissioner, 728 F.2d 1287 10th Cir. (1984)

  Treadway v. Commissioner, 47 T.C.M. 1375 (1984)

Olsen v. Commissioner,
709 F.2d 278 (4th Cir. 1983)

Holland v. Commissioner,
47 T.C.M. 494 (1983)

Paschall v. Commissioner,
46 T.C.M. 1197 (1983)

Hess v. Commissioner,
40 T.C.M. 415 (1980)

Rev. Rul. 80-59

Rev. Rul. 82-185

Rev. Rul. 75-189

- **Private insurance program participation**

T.A.M. 8741002

Rev. Rul. 77-78

- **Second ordination/social security exemption**

Hall v. Commissioner,
T.C.M. 360 (1993),
10th Cir. (1994)

- **Social security coverage for ministers**

Code Sec. 1402(c)(2) and (4)

Code Sec. 3121(b)(8)(A)

Code Sec. 3401(a)(9)

Rev. Rul. 80-110

Rev. Rul. 79-78

Silvey v. Commissioner,
35 T.C.M. 1812 (1976)

- **Social security deductions for unreimbursed business expenses**

Young v. Commissioner,
T.C. Summary Opinion 76 (2005)

- **Social security recipients must still pay social security taxes**

Foster v. Commissioner,
T.C.M. 552 (1996)

- **Taxability of fair rental value of church-owned parsonage for social security purposes**

Treas. Reg. 1.1402(a)-11(a)

Flowers v. Commissioner,
T.C.M. 542 (1991)

Bass v. Commissioner,
T.C.M. 536 (1983)

Federal Tax Regulation (Reg.)

Treasury Decision (T.D.)

Private Letter Ruling (Ltr. Rul.)

Field Service Advice (F.S.A.)

Revenue Ruling (Rev. Rul.)

Revenue Procedure (Rev. Proc.)

Tax Court Memorandum (T.C.M.)

Technical Advice Memorandum (T.A.M.)

Index

10 Biggest Tax Mistakes Made by Ministers

1. Filing as self-employed for income tax purposes on your church salary, using tax benefits only available to employees, and leaving yourself vulnerable to reclassification by the IRS to employee status. Chapter 1.

2. Failure to have unreimbursed medical expenses covered under a properly documented plan. Chapter 3.

3. Failing to have at least a modest housing allowance designated when living in a church-provided parsonage. Chapter 4.

4. Failure to understand the implications of the fair rental test for the housing allowance. Chapter 4.

5. Confusing the fair rental value of a church-provided parsonage (only includible for social security purposes) with the designation of a portion of your salary as housing allowance (providing an exclusion for income tax purposes). Chapter 4.

6. Claiming office-in-the-home treatment — rarely justified under present law. Chapter 5.

7. Failure of minister-employees to use an accountable reimbursement plan. Chapter 5.

8. Not documenting business expenses to reflect business purpose, business relationship, cost, time, and place. Chapter 5.

9. Failing to keep a log of miles driven for personal use vs. church purposes. Chapter 5.

10. Improperly opting out of social security because you don't believe it is a good investment. Chapter 6.

10 Tax and Finance Questions Most Frequently Asked by Ministers

1. **Social security filing status.** Should I have FICA-type social security tax withheld from my pay or pay self-employment social security tax calculated on Schedule SE and pay it with my income tax return? Chapter 1.

2. **Income tax filing status.** Should I file as an employee (receiving a Form W-2 from my employer) or as an independent contractor (receiving a Form 1099-MISC) for income tax purposes? Chapter 1.

3. **Unreimbursed medical expenses.** Which of the three approved plans should I use to get tax-free treatment for my unreimbursed medical expenses: health savings account (HSA), health reimbursement arrangement (HRA), or healthcare flexible spending account (FSA)? Chapter 3.

4. **Structuring the pay package.** How should my pay package be structured to achieve the best tax benefit for me? Chapter 3.

5. **Fringe benefit planning.** How do I determine which fringe benefits I receive are tax-free, tax-deferred, or taxable? Chapter 3.

6. **Housing allowance exclusion.** How much can I exclude as a housing allowance for income tax purposes? Chapter 4.

7. **Accountable expense reimbursements.** Do the payments I am receiving from the church or parachurch ministry for expenses qualify as tax-free reimbursements? Chapter 5.

8. **Cell phone expense.** How do ministers cope with the tough IRS regulations on the documentation of the business use of cell phones? Chapter 5.

9. **Opting out of social security.** Under what conditions is it appropriate for me to opt out of social security? Chapter 6.

10. **Paying income and social security taxes.** Should I have enough income tax withheld from my salary to cover my income and social security tax obligation or should I pay quarterly estimated taxes? Chapter 6.

Bible Reference Discoverer's Pack

Life is full of questions. The Bible is full of answers. However, in order to find them, sometimes a little help is needed. Now, Zondervan has made it easier than ever to get that help. The *Bible Reference Discoverer's Pack* includes three proven resources, now packaged into one convenient starter kit.

Organized according to Zondervan's intuitive Bible reference system—Overview, Find, Understand—it provides the three key Bible reference tools Christians need to grow in their understanding of the Bible. The bestselling *Zondervan Handbook to the Bible* (over 3 million copies sold) provides an Overview of the Bible. The *Zondervan NIV Bible Verse Finder* helps your congregation Find a verse in the Bible. The *Zondervan Bible Dictionary* arranges topics alphabetically and will help your church members Understand more about the people, places, events and teachings of the Bible.

The *Bible Reference Discoverer's Pack* serves as a great entry point for both families and new Christians to begin using reference tools. As your congregation experiences the value of these resources they will be more confident in their knowledge of the Bible: its context, meaning, and how to locate key verses. This will deepen their understanding of the faith and grow in their relationship with the Lord.

Inspire Discovery. Recommend the *Bible Reference Discoverer's Pack*.

Hardcover Set: 978-0-310-29305-7

Pick up a copy today at your favorite bookstore!

ZONDERVAN®
.com